UNESCO AND SOCIAL SCIENCES

Concepts in Communication Informatics & Librarianship–3

General Editor :
S. P. Agrawal

UNESCO AND SOCIAL SCIENCES
Retrospect & Prospect

S. P. Agrawal
J. C. Aggarwal

CONCEPT PUBLISHING COMPANY, NEW DELHI-110059

ISBN 81-7022-201-X

First Published 1988

Published by
Ashok Kumar
Concept Publishing Company
A/15-16, Commercial Block, Mohan Garden
New Delhi-110059 (India)

Photo-composing by
Microtech Advance Printing Systems (P) Ltd.
New Delhi-110015

Printed by
Taj Press
A-35/4, Maya Puri
New Delhi

PREFACE

Not failure, but low ambition is a crime, it is said. Unesco was started with the noblest of aims, and despite some set-backs and occasional controversies about issues and policies, has kept its flag flying high.

Unesco's five-digit functions, besides the natural sciences, are in the fields of culture, education, communication, and the social sciences which are also naturally connected with the preceding four.

The results which this international organisation can produce depend on the functional efficiency of various national commissions.

In the case of India, a member since its inception, it is no different. While enumerating its achievements, one must not forget the documentation and research projects Unesco has supported.

The present compilers document in this compendium Unesco's work in general and relating to social sciences in the hope of providing researchers a handy reference tool.

We have no words to express our deep sense of gratitute to Professor Yogesh Atal, without whose inspiring guidance, the work would never have been completed.

We also owe much to Professor Iqbal Narain, Member Secretary, ICSSR, who guided and encouraged us at every stage of our work.

Our thanks are due to Mrs. T. Sondhi, of the Unesco office in New Delhi who took great interest in locating and placing at our disposal the required Unesco publications for our use.

To all those institutions, too numerous to mention here fully, which readily granted permission to use material in this volume, our heartfelt thanks.

S.P. AGRAWAL
J.C.AGGARWAL

CONTENTS

PART I

UNESCO AND ITS FUNCTIONS

ONE

WHAT IS UNESCO ?

November 4, 1946, is a landmark in the history of the world as the United Nations Educational, Scientific and Cultural Organization (UNESCO), popularly known as Unesco, came into being on this day when 20 States ratified the Constitution which had been drawn up at the London Conference a year earlier.

The striking phrase, "Since wars begin in the minds of men, it is in the minds of men that the defences of peace must be constructed", based on the words of a man of State and of a poet stands at the forefront of Unesco's Constitution and contains the key to all its activities.

The man of State was Clement Attlee, the Prime Minister of the United Kingdom who inaugurated the Conference in November 1945, which led to the creation of Unesco. The poet was Archibald Macleish, the famous American, who was on the Committee which drafted the Constitution. For them and the representatives of 54 nations who met in war-scarred London, the quest for peace was the evident and overriding priority.

The immediate ancestor of Unesco was a war-time Conference of Allied Ministers of Education which had the limited aim of planning ahead for the reconstruction needed after the war. This conference was held in London in November 1942. Within one year the Conference moved towards setting up a truly international organization. The United States of America and the USSR sent observers to the meetings of the Allied Ministers of Education. Australia, Canada, China, India, Luxembourg, New Zealand and South Africa became members.

The Conference examined a proposal by a committee headed by the British scholar Gilbert Murray calling for a permanent organization for education and better understanding and agreed that all members of the United Nations should be asked to join. It also set up an executive Bureau to consider the long-term project of a United Nations Bureau of Education. The British and French Governments invited all United Nations Member States to a conference in London in November 1945, which decided on the creation of an educational and cultural organization of the United Nations. Science which had lately produced the atom bomb was also to be a major concern along with education and culture.

The Constitution adopted at the 1945 Conference took effect a year later when Greece, as the 20th State to do so, deposited the instrument of ratification in London. The organization thus began its official life on November 4, 1946. A Preparatory Commission with which the Secretariat had moved into Hotel Majestic on the Avenue Kleber in Paris became Unesco, with the British biologist Julian Huxley as its first Director General.

Of all the agencies in the United Nations system, Unesco alone is devoted to the idea of humanism, to man in his entirety. French philosopher Etienne Gibson ventured to call it "the soul" of the United Nations body.

Unesco is a specialized agency of the United Nations but both constitutionally and financially is independent though its work is coordinated with the United Nations and other specialized agencies through the United Nations Economic and Social Council.

The organization's headquarters are in Paris where the General Conference and Executive Board meet periodically, and where its general directorate and the Directors of various Departments, Bureaus and Services have their offices. Yet a significant proportion of the Secretariat is not stationed in Paris. It is scattered all over the world.

Today Unesco is a group of 158 member States with two Associate Member States, ranging round the world from the vastness of China to the tiny San Marine. All the sovereign States together, voting with equal rights in Unesco's General Conference, decide the organization's Programme and pay for its implementation. Many of these are young nations that cast off the colonial yoke only recently and are set to determine their own destinies. The past three decades have seen the birth of many new nations, principally in Africa, the Middle East and Asia. These nations want a higher standard of living for themselves and their children. This "revolution of rising expectations", as it has been called, has had a profound effect on the evolution of the work of Unesco and the whole United Family in recent years.

General Conference

The General Conference of Member States, which is the supreme authority of the organization, consists of representatives of all Member States. It meets every two years to adopt the programme and vote the budget for the operating period. The General Conference also elects members of the Executive Board, and, on the recommendation of the Board, appoints the Director General who has a six-year tenure.

The first session was held in Paris in November 1946. Until 1952, it met every year; since then sessions have been held every two years. For 12 years it met either in Paris or in other cities upon the invitation of Member States. With the completion of permanent buildings at Place de Fontenoy at Paris (1958), this practice was discontinued and ever since sessions of the General Conference have been held at Unesco's headquarters at Paris.

Executive Board

The Executive Board, which supervises activities on behalf on the General Conference, is composed of 45 persons who have distinguished themselves in the fields of education, science, culture and communications. It originally consisted of 18 members who were elected by the General Conference for four years and who served in a personal capacity. Now members are elected for six years, and in accordance with an amendment of the Constitution in the seventh General Conference held in 1954, the Board members, though elected individually, represent their governments.

Besides supervising the execution of the programme and the administration of the budget between sessions of the General Conference, the Executive Board examines the Draft Programme and Budget for the following two-year period and submits its report to the Conference along with recommendations, if any. It also nominates the Director General prior to his appointment by the General Conference. The Board generally meets twice a year for sessions of three to four days.

Secretariat

The Secretariat is organized and directed by the Director General and is the executive body responsible for Unesco's formal functioning and for the application of decisions taken by the General Conference and the Executive Board, particularly in carrying out the programme. Responsible for an international task the Secretariat itself is international in its composition and status. Its members are recruited on as wide a geographical basis as possible, subject to the paramount consideration of securing of highest standards of integrity, efficiency and technical competence. Their status, similar to that of all secretariats in the United Nations system, gives these officials certain privileges and immunities similar to those granted to diplomats. But it carries with it strict obligations of objectivity and impartiality along with the discretion and tact indispensable for international service. In particular, they are expected neither to seek nor accept instructions from any authority - governmental or otherwise - outside the organization.

Permanent Delegations

Many Member States have set up permanent delegations to Unesco. They have their offices in Paris. These offices act as direct liaison agencies between Unesco and the representative governments and are responsible for maintaining day-to-day contact. There are at present 124 permanent delegations, six Liaison Officers and six Observers.

Working Languages

Working languages in the Secretariat are English and French; the languages of the General Conference and the Executive Board are English, French, Russian and Spanish. The General Conference has, since its 15th session, provided interpretation into and from Arabic for its plenary sessions and the meetings of its two Principal Commissions and also the translation into Arabic of its more important documents. Arabic was used for the first time during the 16th General Conference in 1970

Relations with other Organizations

Unesco has been called "the latest specialized of the specialized agencies". As a specialized agency of the United Nations, however, Unesco collaborates closely with other agencies. Agreements have been concluded with the Food and Agriculture Organization (FAO), International Atomic Energy Agency Development (IAEAD), International Development Association (IDA), International Labour Organization (ILO), United Nations High Commissioner for Refugees (UNHCR), United Nations Industrial Organization (UNIDO), World Health Organization (WHO), etc. Unesco also works closely with the United Nations Regional Economic Commissions.

Unicef and Unesco

The United Nations Children Fund (UNICEF) previously limited to food and health problems extended its interests in 1963 to education, and this has led to active collaboration with Unesco. Joint Unicef/Unesco projects - mostly for training primary teachers - are carried out in several countries, and Unicef contribution to education is considerable.

Similar collaboration has been initiated between Unesco and the World Food Programme (WFP) which devotes most of its resources to aiding governments in the execution of certain development projects. WFP assistance takes the form of funds and provisions supplied to primary, secondary teacher training, technical and vocational higher educational establishments as well as to literacy or youth activities projects.

Non-Governmental Organizations

From the beginning Unesco has worked closely with various non-governmental organizations known as NGOs, each one bringing together on an international level specialists from disciplines within its competence or endeavouring to give direction to the interests and loyalties evoked by certain aspects or goals of Unesco's work, within specific social groups or sectors of public opinion. Unesco maintains official relations with these organizations and some of them have consultative status. No other agency in the United Nations has built up so extensive a network of international cooperation on a non-governmental level. There are at present more then 400 non-governmental organizations around the globe with whom Unesco is working.

Why Unesco Cooperates

Unesco's reasons for cooperating with NGOs stem directly from its constitution. This document's preamble affirms "That a peace based exclusively on the political and economic arrangements of governments would not be a peace which could secure the unanimous, lasting and sincere support of the peoples of the world,and that the peace must therefore by founded, if it is not to fail, upon the intellectual and moral solidarity of mankind."

Four complementary conclusions may be drawn from this affirmation. First, that the "support of the peoples of the world" must be secured without which peace is not possible. Second, that to create conditions in which peace is possible, Unesco must work to forge "intellectual and moral solidarity" among "the peoples of the world". Third, both these things must be done outside as well as through governments. Fourth, as the foregoing preconditions, an extra-governmental channel of communication and action must be opened between Unesco and "the peoples of the world".

So vital are NGOs to Unesco's activities that it has helped to create several non-governmental partners. Broadly interpreting its constitutional mandate to "invite them to undertake specific tasks", Unesco has played an instrumental part in founding certain NGOs in fields where no representative international body existed before. Unesco also has encouraged union or federation of similar NGOs and strengthened those already in existence. Among these are the International Association of Universities, International Music Council, International Council of Museums and International Council for Philosophy and Humanistic Studies.

Generally "the specific tasks" that Unesco helps an NGO to undertake are rather more specific than its own creation. In some cases, substantial aid is provided on a long-term basis to subsidize an NGO fulfilling some basic function in its field of competence such as running a documentation centre or sponsoring a series of meetings. In other instances, limited help is provided under contract on a short-term basis to enable an NGO to carry out a single project, e.g. execution of a study or organization of a symposium.

Unesco Fellowships

The Unesco Training Abroad Programme, which originated initially in the exchange of personnel service in 1947, offers fellowships and travel grants to mature persons already engaged in careers to improve their academic and professional competence. In many development-oriented projects, fellowships equip persons already intimately connected with the project to take over as counterparts of outside experts upon return. In some cases, fellowships go to promising young candidates to provide career training in vital areas for which study abroad is required, for example, in documentation, librarianship and the use of visual aids in education.

These Unesco fellowships are available to nationals of all Member States, Associate Member States and Trusts and Non-Self-governing territories. Prospective fellows may apply to their own Governments which forward lists of most promising candidates to Unesco for consideration and choice. Unesco fellowships are available for study in fields falling within the domain of Unesco's overall programme; education, natural sciences, social sciences, human sciences, culture and mass communication.

The different categories of fellowships offered by Unesco are financed out of the funds provided or made available to Unesco under a regular programme, a Participation Programme, Technical Assistance and Special Fund (the last two were amalgamated in 1960 under the United Nations Development Programme), Funds-in-Trust, Voluntary Contributions and assistance from the International Bank for Reconstruction and Development (IBRD). In addition, the sponsored fellowships are paid for by the donating countries or organizations.

Generally speaking, all Unesco fellowships provide for study outside the holder's own country; the rare exception is a fellowship given for study at an institute established to serve an entire region (for example, in Latin America) which happens to be located in the fellow's own country.

Fellowships under the Regular Programme are created by the General Conference when it decides on the Organization's biennial programme; these are offered either to specific nations or in open competition. Fellowships under the Participation Programme first awarded in 1955, are initiated by Member States in agreement with the Director General in fields of study selected by the General Conference. Education Assistance Fellowships, first awarded in 1951, were created at the request of Member States with a view to promoting their economic and social development and often as an integral part of the Education Assistance Project. Fellowships financed from the Special Fund, first awarded in 1960, are always an integral part of a project initiated by a Member State; they are included in the Plan of Operation for the project which usually covers a period of several years. Sponsored fellowships are negotiated between the donor and Unesco.

Study and travel programmes for fellowship holders are worked out in the Unesco Secretariat with the advice of specialists in the relevant programme departments as well as of the administering agency in the host country. It is concerned with the implementation of the fellow's study programme. An academic Supervisor is appointed when considered essential.

Extension of the duration of a fellowship is granted only at the request of the fellow's Government and the United Nations Agency concerned, on the basis of recommendations made by the academic Supervisor and the administering agency.

Unesco fellows are required to submit a report of their work upon completion of their fellowship.

Unesco Travel Grants

Unesco travel grants are awarded to groups and individuals.

Travel grants were first awarded to European workers for study tours lasting from 10 to 15 days in European countries, not their own. In 1955, a similar inter-regional programme was begun in Latin America, Asia and Africa.

Individual Grants

Individual grants were first awarded to youth and student leaders in 1952 and are given every year since. The first individual grants for workers were awarded between 1955 and 1958, under a long-term workers' exchange programme.

National Commissions

Article VII of the Constitution of Unesco requires that "Each Member State shall make such arrangements as suit its particular conditions for the purpose of associating its principal bodies interested in educational, scientific and cultural matters with the work of the organization, preferably by the formation of National Commission broadly representative of the Government and such bodies", and that "National Commissions or National Cooperating Bodies, where they exist, shall act in an advisory capacity to their representative delegations to the General Conferences and to their governments in matters relating to the organization and shall function as agencies of liaison in all matters of interest to it."

In fulfilment of the requirements of the Constitution of Unesco and with a view to ensuring active participation of the people, Member States have set up National Commissions. These para-governmental National Commissions which are a distinctive feature of Unesco's constitutional structure have become valuable liaison agents with the international secretariat. In this role, the National Commissions tend increasingly to fill an executive as well as an advisory function both for their governments and for Unesco, and within countries, they serve as a link between the organized State and free culture and they prepare the material which is given purpose and legal form by the session of the General Conference.

Regional Conferences are held at regular intervals to stimulate cooperation among National Commissions.

United Nations System and Unesco

Unesco's relationship with the United Nations is stated in "the agreement between the United Nations and the United Nations Educational, Scientific and Cultural Organization", which became effective on December 14, 1946. The Agreement, inter alia, states:

1. Both the United Nations and Unesco will send representatives and propose subjects for discussion at a range of conferences including each other's General Assembly.

2. In response to recommendations from the UN, Unesco will present these recommendations to the appropriate body as soon as possible and will report to the UN on the progress made in implementing such recommendations.

3. A full and speedy exchange of reports and written material shall take place between the UN and Unesco.

4. Unesco will discuss the drawing up of its budget with the UN.

Eight Principal Sectors of Unesco

The Unesco Secretariat at the Headquarters is divided into following eight principal sectors:

1. *Education Sector*

(a) Division of Educational Policy and Planning.
(b) Division of Financing of Education.
(c) Division of Equality of Educational Opportunity and Special Pr
(d) Division of Educational Sciences, Contents and Methods of Edu
(e) Division of Science, Technical and Environmental Education.
(f) Division of Higher Education and of Training of Educational Pe
(g) Division of Primary Education, Literacy and Adult Education ar Rural Areas.

Activities of the Education Sector are supplemented by the following institutions:

i. International Bureau of Education (IBE) , Geneva.
ii. European Centre for Higher Education (CEPES), Bucharest.
iii. International Institute of Educational Planning (IEP), Paris.

2. *Natural Science Sector*

(a) Division of Ecological Sciences.
(b) Division of Science and Technology Policies.
(c) Division of Scientific Research and Higher Education.
(d) Division of Water Sciences.
(e) Division of Earth Sciences.
(f) Division of Technological Research and Higher Education.
(g) Division of Marine Sciences.
(h) Secretariat of the International Oceanographic Commission.

3. *Social and Human Sciences Sector*

(a) Economic and Social Science Division.
(b) Division of Philosophy and Human Sciences.
(c) Division of Human Rights and Peace.
(d) Population Division.
(e) Youth Division.

4. *Culture Sector*

(a) Division of Cultural Heritage.
(b) Division of Studies and Dissemination of Cultures.
(c) Division of Cultural Development and Artistic Creation.

Liaison Office is at Venic, Italy.

5. *Communication Sector*

(a) Division of Free Flow of Information and Communication Policies.
(b) Division of Development of Means of Communication.
(c) International Programme for the Development of Communication.
(d) Division of Book Promotion, Audio-Visual and Inter-national Exchanges.

6. *External Relations and Information Sector*

(a) Office for External Relations:

i. Africa Division.
ii. Asia and Pacific Division.
iii. Arab States Division.

iv. Europe Division.
v. Latin America and Caribbean Division.
vi. National Commissions and Unesco Clubs Division.
vii. International Organizations and Foundation Division.
viii. Public Relations Division.

(b) Office of Public Information:

i. Press Division.
ii. Division of Audio-Visual Information.
iii. Division of Production, Distribution and Pooling of Basic Information and Documentation Material.

Liaison Offices are at Geneva and New York and Information Services at Washington and Vienna.

7. *General Programmes and Programme Support Sector*

(a) Division of Copyright.
(b) Office of Statistics.
(c) Unesco Courier and Periodical Division.
(d) Division of the General Information Programme.
(e) Unesco Library Archives and Documentation Services Division.
(f) Office of the Unesco Press.
(g) Office of Conferences, Languages and Documents.

8. *General Administration Sector*

(a) Bureau of the Comptroller.
(b) Bureau of Personnel.
(c) Bureau of Data Processing Services.
(d) Bureau of General Services.

In addition there are the secretariat of the General Conference, Secretariat of the Executive Board, Office of International Standards and Legal Affairs, four Regional Coordinators (Africa, Arab States, Asia and the Pacific, Latin America and the Caribbean), Inspectorate General, Office of Mediator, Bureau of Studies and Programming, Bureau of the Budget and Central Evaluation Unit.

TWO

UNESCO CONSTITUTION

"Since wars begin in the minds of men, it is in the minds of men that the defences of peace must be constructed"

The Governments of the States parties to this Constitution on behalf of their peoples declare:

That since wars begin in the minds of men, it is in the minds of men that the defences of peace must be constructed;

That ignorance of each other's ways and lives has been a common cause, throughout the history of mankind, of that suspicion and mistrust between the peoples of the world through which their differences have all too often broken into war;

That the great and terrible war which has now ended was a war made possible by the denial of the democratic principles of the dignity, equality and mutual respect of men, and by the propagation, in their place, through ignorance and prejudice, of the doctrine of the inequality of men and races;

That the wide diffusion of culture, and the education of humanity for justice and liberty and peace are indispensable to the dignity of man and constitute a sacred duty which all the nations must fulfil in a spirit of mutual assistance and concern;

That a peace based exclusively upon the political and economic arrangements of governments would not be a peace which could secure the unanimous, lasting and sincere support of the peoples of the world, and that the peace must therefore be founded, if it is not to fail, upon the intellectual and moral solidarity of mankind.

For these reasons, the States parties to this Constitution, believing in full and equal opportunities for education for all, in the unrestricted pursuit of the objective truth, and in the free exchange of ideas and knowledge, are agreed and determined to develop and to increase the means of communication between their peoples and to employ these means for the purposes of mutual understanding and a truer and more perfect knowledge of each other's lives;

In consequence whereof they do hereby create the United Nations Educational, Scientific and Cultural Organization for the purpose of advancing, through the educational and scientific and cultural relations of the peoples of the world, the objectives of international peace and of the common welfare of mankind for which the United Nations Organization was established and which its Charter proclaims.

ARTICIE I. Purposes and Functions

1. The purpose of the Organization is to contribute to peace and security by promoting collaboration among the nations through education, science and culture in order to further universal respect for justice, for the rule of law and for the human rights and fundamental freedoms which are affirmed for the peoples of the world, without distinction of race, sex, language or religion, by the Charter of the United Nations.

2. To realize this purpose the Organization will:

(a) Collaborate in the work of advancing the mutual knowledge and understanding of peoples, through all means of mass communication and to that end recommend such international agreements as may be necessarv to promote the free flow of ideas by word and image;

(b) Give fresh impulse to popular education and to the spread of culture; by collaborating with Members, at their request, in the development of educational activities;

By instituting collaboration among the nations to advance the ideal of equality of educational opportunity without regard to race, sex or any distinctions, economic or social;

By suggesting educational methods best suited to prepare the children of the world for the responsibilities of freedom;

(c) Maintain, increase and diffuse knowledge:

By assuring the conservation and protection of the world's inheritance of books, works of art and monuments of history and science, and recommending to the nations concerned the necessary international conventions; N.P. By encouraging cooperation among the nations in all branches of intellectual activity, including the international exchange of persons active in the fields of education, science and culture and the exchange of publications, objects of artistic and scientific interest and other materials of information;

By initiating methods of international cooperation calculated to give the people of all countries access to the printed and published materials produced by any of them.

3. With a view to preserving the integrity and fruitful diversity of the cultures and educational systems of the State Members of the Organization, the Organization is prohibited from intervening in matters which are essentially within their domestic jurisdiction.

ARTICIE II. Membership

1. Membership of the United Nations Organization shall carry with it the right to membership of the United Nations Educational, Scientific and Cultural Organization.

2. Subject to the conditions of the Agreement between this Organization and the United Nations Organization, approved pursuant to Article X of this Constitution, States not Members of the United Nations Organization may be admitted to membership of the Organization, upon recommendation of the Executive Board, by a two-thirds majority vote of the General Conference.

3. Territories or groups of territories which are not responsible for the conduct of their international relations may be admitted as Associate Members by the General Conference by a two-thirds majority of Members present and voting, upon application made on behalf of such territory or group of territories by the Member or other authority having responsibility for their international relations. The nature and extent of the rights and obligations of Associate Members shall be determined by the General Conference.

4. Members of the Organization which are suspended from the exercise of the rights and privileges of membership of the United Nations Organization shall, upon the request of the latter, be suspended from the rights and privileges of the organization.

5. Members of the Organization which are expelled from the United Nations Organization shall automatically cease to be Members of this Organization.

6. Any Member State or Associate Member of the Organization may withdraw from the Organization by notice addressed to the Director General, such notice shall take effect on 31 December of the year following that during which the notice was given, no such withdrawal shall affect the financial obligations owed to the Organization on the date the withdrawal takes effect. Notice of withdrawal by an Associate Member shall be given on its behalf by the Member State or other authority having responsibility for its international relations.

ARTICLE III. Organs

The Organization shall include a General Conference, an Executive Board and a Secretariat.

ARTICLE IV. The General Conference

A. Composition

1. The General Conference shall consist of the representatives

of the State Members of the Organization. The Government of each Member State shall appoint not more than five delegates, who shall be selected after consultation with the National Commission, if established, or with educational, scientific and cultural bodies.

B. Functions

2. The General Conference shall determine the policies and the main lines of work of the Organization. It shall take decisions on programmes submitted to it by the Executive Board.

3. The General Conference shall, when it deems desirable and in accordance with the regulations to be made by it, summon international conferences of States on education, the sciences and humanities or the dissemination of knowledge; non-governmental conferences on the same subjects may be summoned by the General Conference or by the Executive Board in accordance with such regulations.

4. The General Conference shall, in adopting proposals for submission to the Member States, distinguish between recommendations and international conventions submitted for their approval. In the former case a majority vote shall suffice; in the latter case a two-thirds majority shall be required. Each of the Member States shall submit recommendations or conventions to its competent authorities within a period of one year from the close of the session of the General Conference at which they were adopted.

5. Subject to the provisions of Article V, paragraph 5(c). the General Conference shall advise the United Nations Organization on the educational, scientific and cultural aspects of matters of concern to the latter; in accordance with the terms and procedure agreed upon between the appropriate authorities of the two Organizations.

6. The General Conference shall receive and consider the reports sent to the Organization by Member States on the action taken upon the recommendations and conventions

referred to in paragraph 4 above or, if it so decides, analytical summaries of these reports.

7. The General Conference shall elect the members of the Executive Board and, on the recommendation of the Board, shall appoint the Director-General.

C. Voting

8. (a) Each Member State shall have one vote in the General Conference. Decisions shall be made by a simple majority except in cases in which a two-thirds majority is required by the provisions of this Constitution, or the Rules of Procedure of the General Conference. A majority shall be a majority of the members present and voting.

(b) A Member State shall have no vote in the General Conference if the total amount of contributions due from it exceeds the total amount of contributions payable by it for the current year and the immediately preceding calendar year.

(c) The General Conference may nevertheless permit such a Member State to vote, if it is satisfied that failure to pay is due to conditions beyond the control of the Member Nations.

D. Procedure

9. (a) The General Conference shall meet in ordinary session every two years. It may meet in extraordinary session if it decides to do so itself or if summoned by the Executive Board, or on the demand of at least one-third of the Member States.

(b) At each session the location of its next ordinary session shall be designated by the General Conference. The location of an extraordinary session shall be decided by the General Conference if the session is summoned by it, or otherwise by the Executive Board.

10. The General Conference shall adopt its own rules of procedure. It shall at each session elect a President and other officers.

11. The General Conference shall set up special and technical committees and such other subordinate bodies as may be necessary for its purposes.

12. The General Conference shall cause arrangements to be made for public access to meetings, subject to such regulations as it shall prescribe.

E. Observers

13. The General Conference, on the recommendation of the Executive Board and by a two-thirds majority, may, subject to its rules of procedure, invite as observers at specified sessions of the Conference or of its Commissions representatives of international organizations, such as those referred to in Article XI, Paragraph 4.

14. When consultative arrangements have been approved by the Executive Board for such international non-governmental or semi-governmental organizations in the manner provided in Article XI, Paragraph 4, those organizations shall be invited to send observers to sessions of the General Conference and its Commissions.

F. Transitional Provision

15. Notwithstanding the provisions of Paragraph 9(a) of this Article, the General Conference shall hold its twentysecond session in the third year following its twentyfirst session.

ARTICLE V. Executive Board

A. Composition

1. The Executive Board shall be elected by the General Conference from among the delegates appointed by the Member States and consist of fiftyone members each of whom shall

represent the Government of the State of which he is a national. The President of the General Conference shall sit ex-officio in an advisory capacity on the Executive Board.

2. In electing the members of the Executive Board the General Conference shall endeavour to include persons competent in the arts, the humanities, the sciences, the education and the diffusion of ideas, and qualified by their experience and capacity to fulfil the administrative and executive duties of the Board. It shall also have regard to the diversity of cultures and a balanced geographical distribution. Not more than one national of any Member State shall serve on the Board at any one time, the President of the Conference excepted.

3. Members of the Board shall serve from the close of the session of the General Conference which elected them until the close of the second ordinary session of the General Conference following that election. They shall not be immediately eligible for a second term. The General Conference shall, at each of its ordinary sessions, elect the number of members required to fill vacancies occurring at the end of the session.

4. (a) In the event of the death or resignation of a member of the Executive Board, his replacement for the remainder of his term shall be appointed by the Executive Board on the nomination of the Government of the State the former member represented.

   (b) The Government making the nomination and the Executive Board shall have regard to the factors set forth in Paragraph 2 of this Article.

   (c) When exceptional circumstances arise, which, in the considered opinion of the represented State, make it indispensable for its representative to be replaced, even if he does not tender his resignation, measures shall be taken in accordance with the provisions of sub-paragraph (a) above.

B. Functions

5. (a) The Executive Board shall prepare the agenda for the General Conference. It shall examine the programme of work for the Organization and corresponding budget estimates submitted to it by the Director-General in accordance with Paragraph 3 of Article VI and shall submit them with such recommendations as it considers desirable to the General Conference.

(b) The Executive Board, acting under the authority of the General Conference, shall be responsible for the execution of the programme adopted by the Conference. In accordance with the decisions of the General Conference and having regard to circumstances arising between two ordinary sessions, the Executive Board shall take all necessary measures to ensure the effective and rational execution of the programme by the Director General.

(c) Between ordinary sessions of the General Conference, the Board may discharge the functions of adviser to the United Nations, set forth in Article IV, Paragraph 5, whenever the problem upon which advice is sought has already been dealt with in principle by the Conference, or when the solution is implicit in decisions of the Conference.

6. The Executive Board shall recommend to the General Conference the admission of new Members to the Organization.

7. Subject to decisions of the General Conference, the Executive Board shall adopt its own rules of procedure. It shall elect its officers from among its members.

8. The Executive Board shall meet in regular session at least twice a year and may meet in special session if convoked by the Chairman on his own initiative or upon the request of six members of the Board.

9. The Chairman of the Executive Board shall present, on behalf of the Board, to each ordinary session of the General Conference, with or without comments, the reports on the activities of the Organization which the Director General is required to prepare in accordance with the provisions of Article VI 3(b).

10. The Executive Board shall make all necessary arrangements to consult the representatives of international organizations or qualified persons concerned with questions within its competence.

11. Between sessions of the General Conference, the Executive Board may request advisory opinions from the International Court of Justice on legal questions arising within the field of the organization's activities.

12. Although the members of the Executive Board are representatives of their respective Governments they shall exercise the powers delegated to them by the General Conference on behalf of the Conference as a whole.

C. Transitional Provisions

13. Notwithstanding the provisions of Paragraph 3 of this Article.
    (a) Members of the Executive Board elected prior to the seventeenth session of the General Conference shall serve until the end of the term for which they were elected.

    (b) Members of the Executive Board appointed, prior to the seventeenth session of the General Conference, by the Board in accordance with the provisions of Paragraph 4 of this Article to replace members with a four-year term shall be eligible for a second term of four years.

ARTICLE VI. Secretariat

1. The Secretariat shall consist of a Director General and such staff as may be required.

2. The Director General shall be nominated by the Executive Board and appointed by the General Conference for a period of six years, under such conditions as the Conference may approve, and shall be eligible for reappointment. He shall be the chief administrative officer of the Organization.

3. (a) The Director General, or a deputy designated by him, shall participate, without the right to vote, in all meetings of the General Conference, of the Executive Board, and-or the committees of the Organization. He shall formulate proposals for appropriate action by the Conference and the Board, and shall prepare for submission to the Board a draft programme of work for the Organization with corresponding budget estimates.

   (b) The Director General shall prepare and communicate to Member States and to the Executive Board periodical reports on the activities of the Organization. The General Conference shall determine the periods to be covered by these reports.

4. The Director General shall appoint the staff of the Secretariat in accordance with staff regulations to be approved by the General Conference. Subject to the paramount consideration of securing the highest standards of integrity, efficiency and technical competence, appointment to the staff shall be on as wide a geographical basis as possible.

5. The responsibilities of the Director General and of the staff shall be exclusively international in character. In the discharge of their duties they shall not seek or receive instructions from any Government or from any authority external to the Organization. They shall refrain from any action which might prejudice their positions as international officials. Each State Member of the Organization undertakes to respect the international character of the responsibilities of the Director General and the staff, and not to seek to influence them in the discharge of their duties.

6. Nothing in this Article shall preclude the Organization from

entering into special arrangements within the United Nations Organization for common services and staff and for the interchange of personnel.

Transitional Provision

7. Notwithstanding the provisions of Paragraph 2 of this Article, the Director General nominated by the Executive Board and appointed by the General Conference in 1980 shall serve for a term of seven years.

ARTICLE VII. National Cooperating Bodies

1. Each Member State shall make such arrangements as suit its particular conditions for the purpose of associating its principal bodies interested in educational, scientific and cultural matters with the work of the Organization, preferably by the formation of a National Commission broadly representative of the Government and such bodies.

2. National Commissions or National Cooperating Bodies, where they exist, shall act in an advisory capacity to their respective delegations to the General Conference and to their Governments in matters relating to the Organization and shall function as agencies of liaison in all matters of interest to it.

3. The Organization may, on the request of a Member State, delegate, either temporarily or permanently, a member of its Secretariat to serve on the National Commission of that State, in order to assist in the development of its work.

ARTICLE VIII. Reports by Member States

Each Member State shall submit to the Organization, at such times and in such manner as shall be determined by the General Conference, reports on the laws, regulations and statistics relating to its educational, scientific and cultural institutions and activities, and on the action taken upon the recommendations and conventions referred to in Article IV, Paragraph 4.

ARTICLE IX. Budget

1. The Budget shall be administered by the Organization.

2. The General Conference shall approve and give final effect to the budget and to the apportionment of financial responsibility among the State Members of the Organization subject to such arrangement with the United Nations as may be provided in the agreement to be entered into pursuant to Article X.

3. The Director General, with the approval of the Executive Board, may receive gifts, bequests, and subventions directly from Governments, public and private institutions, associations and private persons.

ARTICLE X. Relations with the United Nations Organization

This Organization shall be brought into relation with the United Nations Organization, as soon as practicable, as one of the Specialized Agencies referred to in Article 57 of the Charter of the United Nations. This relationship shall be effected through an agreement with the United Nations Organization under Article 63 of the Charter, which agreement shall be subject to the approval of the General Conference of this Organization. The agreement shall provide for effective cooperation between the two Organizations in the pursuit of their common purposes, and at the same time shall recognize the autonomy of this Organization, within the fields of its competence as defined in this Constitution. Such agreement may, among other matters, provide for the approval and financing of the budget of the Organization by the General Assembly of the United Nations.

ARTICLE XI. Relations with other Specialized International Organizations and Agencies

1. This Organization may cooperate with other specialized inter-governmental organizations and agencies whose interests and activities are related to its purposes. To this end the Director General, acting under the general authority of the

Executive Board, may establish effective working relationships with such organizations and agencies and establish such joint committees as may be necessary to assure effective cooperation. Any formal arrangements entered into with such organizations or agencies shall be subject to the approval of the Executive Board.

2. Whenever the General Conference of this Organization and the competent authorities of any other specialized inter-governmental organizations or agencies whose purpose and functions lie within the competence of this Organization deem it desirable to effect a transfer of their resources and activities to this Organization, the Director General, subject to the approval of the Conference, may enter into mutually acceptable arrangements for this purpose.

3. This Organization may make appropriate arrangements with other inter-governmental organizations for reciprocal representation at meetings.

4. The United Nations Educational, Scientific and Cultural Organization may make suitable arrangements for consultation and cooperation with non-governmental international organizations concerned with matters within its competence, and may invite them to undertake specific tasks. Such cooperation may also include appropriate participation by representatives of such organizations on advisory committees set up by the General Conference.

ARTICLE XII. Legal Status of the Organization

The provisions of Articles 104 and 105 of the Charter of the United Nations Organization concerning the legal status of that Organization, its privileges and immunities, shall apply in the same way to this Organization.

ARTICLE XIII. Amendments

1. Proposals for amendments to this Constitution shall become effective upon receiving the approval of the General Con-

ference by a two-thirds majority; provided, however, that those amendments which involve fundamental alterations in aims of the Organization or new obligations for the Member States shall require subsequent acceptance on the part of two-thirds of the Member States before they come into force. The draft texts of proposed amendments shall be communicated by the Director General to the Member States at least six months in advance of their consideration by the General Conference.

ARTICLE XIV. Interpretation

1. The English and French texts of this Constitution shall be regarded as equally authoritative.

2. Any question or dispute concerning the interpretation of this Constitution shall be referred for determination to the International Court of Justice or to an arbitral tribunal, as the General Conference may determine under its rules of procedure.

ARTICLE XV. Entry into Force

1. This Constitution shall be subject to acceptance. The instrument of acceptance shall be deposited with the Government of the United Kingdom.

2. This Constitution shall remain open for signature in the archives of the Government of the United Kingdom. Signature may take place either before or after the deposit of the instrument of acceptance.

3. This Constitution shall come into force when it has been accepted by twenty of its signatories. Subsequent acceptances shall take effect immediately.

4. The Government of the United Kingdom will inform all Members of the United Nations of the receipt of all instruments of acceptance and of the date on which the Constitution comes into force in accordance with the preceding paragraph.

In faith whereof, the undersigned, duly authorized to that effect, have signed this Constitution in the English and French Languages, both texts being equally authentic.

Done in London the sixteenth day of November, one thousand nine hundred and forty-five, in a single copy, in the English and French languages, of which certified copies will be communicated by the Government of the United Kingdom to the Governments of all the Members of the United Nations.

THREE

OBJECTIVES OF UNESCO IN THE 1980'S

A Unesco publication entitled UNESCO on the Threshold of the 80's lists the following problems and objectives:

I. Assurance of Human Rights

1. Promotion of research on measures aimed at assuring human rights, on the manifestation, causes and effects of the violation of human rights, with particular reference to racialism, colonialism, neocolonialism and apartheid, as well as on the application of the rights to education, science, culture and information and the development of normative measures to further these rights.

2. Promotion of the appreciation and respect for cultural identity of individuals, groups, nations or regions.

3. Improvement of the status of women.

4. Development of activities to aid refugees and national liberation movements in the fields of Unesco's competence.

5. Promotion of education and wider information concerning human rights.

II. Reinforcement of Peace

1. Promotion of peace research, in particular on manifestations of violation of peace, causes preventing its realization, ways and means to eliminate them and proper measures to be taken in order to maintain and reinforce just, lasting and con-

structive peace at the level of groups, societies and the world.

2. Promotion of the study of the role of international law and of international organizations in the establishment of a peaceful world order.

3. Development of school and out-of-school programmes as well as of information aimed at furthering peace and international understanding.

III. Making Man as the Centre of Development

1. Promotion of the formulation of a global, multidisciplinary interpretation of development, having regard to the interrelations between the various factors contributing to this and which are in turn affected by it.

2. Studies of socio-cultural conditions, systems of values, motivations and procedures for participation by the population likely to foster endogenous, diversified development processes in keeping with the practical conditions and needs of the different societies.

3. Contribution to the development of infrastructures and programmes in the social sciences with a view to increasing the different societies' ability to find ways of solving social and human problems.

4. Development and application of tools and methods of socio-economic analysis and development planning.

5. Promotion of wider participation in cultural life and encouragement of endogenous cultural activities.

6. Stimulation of artistic and intellectual creativity.

IV. The Application of Science and Technology for Man and Society

1. Investigation of interactions between science, technology and society, as well as of the implication of scientific and tech-

nological change for man, within the context of the long-term development of science and technology in line with social progress and changing ways of life.

2. Promotion of the formulation and application of policies and improvement of planning and financing in the field of science and technology.

3. Development of scientific and technological research and training and promotion of international and regional cooperation in the field of science and technology with a view to increasing the endogenous capabilities for scientific and technological creation making it possible, in particular, to work out appropriate technologies or to adapt existing technologies.

4. Development of a better understanding of the nature of science and technology and of their role in a changing society, by improving and extending their teaching in school and out-of-school education, and by promoting public information in these fields.

V. Educational Action Response to Individual and Social Requirements in the Context of Life-long Education and within the Framework of Economic, Social and Cultural Development.

1. Promotion of the formulation and application of policies and improvement of planning in the field of education.

2. Improvement of educational administration and management.

3. Contribution to the establishment of Comprehensive, diversified and flexible educational structures.

4. Improvement of educational content, methods and techniques.

5. Promotion of the training of educational personnel.

6. Promotion and intensification of adult education.

7. Promotion of the role of higher education in society.

VI. Quantitative and Qualitative Improvement in the Opportunities for Certain Groups to Achieve Their Individual and Social Potential.

1. Intensification of the struggle against illiteracy.

2. Extension of Unesco's contribution to integrated rural development.

3. Promotion of participation by women in economic, social and cultural development.

4. Development of the role of youth in educational, social and cultural activity.

5. Contribution to the working out of concerted approaches to the problems of social disharmony.

VII. Harmony between Man and His Environment

1. Development of understanding of the processes governing the evolution of the earth's crust, particularly with regard to the origin, extent and rational use of the earth's mineral and energy resources.

2. Improvement of knowledge of terrestrial biological resources and interrelationships between human activities and terrestrial ecosystems.

3. Improvement of knowledge concerning water resources and development of the scientific basis for understanding interrelationships between human activities and the hydrological system and for developing the rational management of water resources.

4. Development of the scientific basis for understanding and improving interrelationships between man and natural marine systems, oceanic and coastal.

5. Improvement of knowledge concerning the ecological, social, moral and cultural implications of the interrelationships between man and his environment and quest for a "better design for living" in human settlements.

6. Promotion of the preservation and presentation of the cultural and natural heritage of mankind.

7. Contribution through general education and through public information to the improvement of individual and collective behaviour towards the human environment and to the perception of its quality.

VIII. Population Control

Development of knowledge relating to population phenomena and of a greater awareness of the issues involved.

IX. Better Communication between Persons and between Peoples

1. Promotion of a free and balanced flow of information and of international exchanges.

2. Promotion of copyright and of access to copyrighted works.

3. Promotion of a better understanding and appreciation of the process and role of communication in society, and of high professional standards.

4. Promotion of policies, infrastructures and training in the field of communication, and encouragement of a better use of the media for social ends.

X. Improvement in Transfer and Exchange of Information

1. Development and promotion of information systems and services at the national, regional and international levels.

2. Improvement in the collection and analysis of statistical data, and of methods, techniques and international comparability of statistics for use in planning, research, administration and evaluation.

FOUR

UNESCO'S MEDIUM TERM PLAN – 1984-1989

Analysis of World Problems

A Worldwide Context

The first observation concerns what might be called "globalization" of human activities, henceforth placed in worldwide context. As predicted by the French poet Paul Valery more than half a century agó, "Nothing will be done any more without the whole world being involved." Yet despite this clear awareness of the worldwide nature of problems we generally have only incomplete analytic and predictive tools with which to tackle them.

Interdependence

The second observation is that interdependence co-exists, paradoxically, with fault lines criss-crossing the world, and the disparities between individuals and populations are widening and hardening and threatening to reduce vast numbers of human beings to despair.

The Arms Race

The arms race has reached such proportions that it now dominates the international scene. But peace too has its dynamic reflected in the growing movements which exist in all countries. However, disparities and the arms race must be seen in their context: on the one hand, what might be called "maldevelopment" which affects all societies and an international economic system whose dysfunctions are having painful effects; on the other, tensions and conflicts which emerge on a worldwide scale and in the various regions.

A New International Economic Order

It is in this perspective that we must place the efforts being made to introduce a more equitable system of inter-national economic relations and to adopt approaches based on the idea that "genuine development has to be elicited from within, willed and conducted by all the vital forces of a nation".

Human Rights

The analysis of human rights brings out the paradoxical nature of the present situation. The concept of human right has increased in scope and substance, it applies to civil and political rights and economic, social and cultural rights. Not only individuals but also peoples should enjoy their own specific rights. On the other hand there are massive violations, particularly under the apartheid regime, infringements of the rights of peoples to self-determination, millions of refugees, the challenge to individual freedoms, mainly in the context of the repression of opposition movements, the use of torture.

The Environment

The threats overhanging the environment bear witness to the links that now bind individual and collective destinies: hence the search for common ground and the forging of bonds of solidarity in the quest for solutions.

Universality and Diversification

A further line of reflection concerns the dialectical tensions that are appearing between a trend towards the universalization of certain ways of life, thought and action and a claim to uniqueness, to diversification.

New Forms of Communication

The development of new forms of communication is of

fundamental importance. It may be a source of enrichment and progress provided, however, that it does not lead to the pre-eminence of certain poles of production and dissemination of knowledge, know-how and life-styles. However, there are already signs of a trend towards uniformity in the patterns of behaviour and ways of life that may prove to be an impoverishment for mankind.

A New Configuration of Knowledge

A new configuration of knowledge is being established and the new relations being formed between the natural and the social sciences should make it possible better to apprehend the complexity of reality. From this may result changes not only in modes of production and consumption but also in social relations themselves. The fact remains that the uneven development of the world scientific and technological potential is such that a small number of countries alone hold the key to the great advances of the future.

Culture the Driving Force Behind Development

Science and technology, communication and information, like education, are an integral part of culture, and the main conclusion to emerge from this reflection on world problems is that culture is the driving force behind development. Similarly, environmental problems refer back to fundamental value choices, which means, once again, a cultural viewpoint. Threats to peace, flagrant violations of human rights, intolerance and racism also have cultural roots.

PLAN AT A GLANCE

The Five Main Tasks

In keeping with its fundamental constitutional mission, the main tasks of Unesco over the years to come may be defined as follows :

1. To contribute to a continuing study of present world problems to create a greater awareness of the common destiny which now unites individuals and peoples alike.

2. To help pave the way for the widest participation by individuals and groups in the life of the societies to which they belong and in that of the world community.

3. To assist in strengthening problem-solving capability by fostering the development and democratization of education and the advancement of science, by increasing and developing the creative potential, both scientific and technological, of all peoples by reinforcing aptitudes and abilities, by developing research and training infrastructures and by promoting the free flow of knowledge and know-how.

4. To help facilitate the changes and transitions that are now recognized as necessary by the international community, as a whole, in fields where the convergence of aspirations gives rise to broad consensus.

5. To arouse and encourage a renewal of values within a context of genuine understanding among peoples, thereby advancing the cause of peace and human rights.

Each of these five tasks corresponds to an essential measure that the Organization must take, given the state of the world as it emerges from an analysis of world problems.

The Major Programmes

I. Reflection on world problems and future-oriented studies.
II. Education for all.
III. Communication in the service of man.
IV. The formulation and application of education policies.
V. Education, training and society.
VI. The sciences and their application to development.
VII. Information systems and access to knowledge.
VIII. Principles, methods and strategies of action for development.
IX. Science, technology and society.
X. The human environment and terrestrial and marine resources.
XI. Culture and the future.

XII. The elimination of prejudice, intolerance, racism and apartheid.

XIII. Peace, international understanding, human rights and the rights of peoples.

XIV. The status of women.

This major programme seeks to define a new vision of the roles of men and women in all fields of human activity. But the feminine dimension of the problems with which Unesco is concerned appears in all parts of the plan.

FIVE

UNESCO - IN RETROSPECT AND PROSPECT

In order to examine the extent to which Unesco has fulfilled the goals set out in its Constitution, to analyse whether and, if so, why it has fallen short of their attainment, and what are the possible remedies, an International Seminar on "UNESCO - In Retrospect and Prospect" was organized by the India International Centre at New Delhi from January 1 to 3, 1986. The Seminar was attended by the distinguished representatives from India and abroad with an intimate knowledge of the functioning of Unesco. They included past and present Members of Unesco's Executive Board, educationists, academicians, journalists and Unesco as well as UNDP officials.

The importance of Education within Unesco's programmes was evident from the budgetary allocation. It was also evident that education has a crucial role to play in the coming decades in the creation of a new world order and in ensuring social and economic progress on an equitable basis. The participants noted the significant efforts already made by Unesco in regard to the Universal right to education and emphasized that there was need to focus sharply in the coming years, particularly during the Third Medium-Term Plan 1989-1994, on universalization of elementary education and on the elimination of illiteracy. While the main responsibility of achieving these goals rested with the Member States, the participants stressed that Unesco should assist national efforts particularly through new ideas. It was noted that the General Conference held at Sofia (Bulgaria) had recommended that in the Third Medium-Term Plan, Unesco should work towards elimination of illiteracy by 2000.

The session on Unesco's Role in Science focussed attention on the number of scientists from the developing countries, trained in various areas of science, and the initiatives Unesco had taken in advancing the frontiers of science, promoting and organizing large-scale, inter-governmental projects, such as those on oceanography, meteorology, etc. There was a consensus on the positive results achieved through these programmes. Prof. M. G. K. Menon from India, in his keynote paper at the Session, focussed the attention of the Seminar on the three major dimensions of the work of Unesco in the areas of science :

Firstly, the change which had taken place in science, from that of its being a contribution of gifted individuals to a more organized activity. Further, the euphoria generated that the application of science and technology would automatically lead to social benefits had evaporated, as also the feeling that technology transfer would change the developing countries. It was realized that science and technology would develop primarily through endogenous effort and social benefits could accrue through meaningful management.

Secondly, peace, it was felt, was born out of justice and was individually linked up with social justice. The development of science and technology since World War II had increased the disparities, and they had operated for the benefit of the better-off.

Lastly, the gap which existed in Unesco's activities in evolving and applying a holistic approach to its areas of activities, particularly in integrating science, education and culture.

During the Session on Culture, Dr. Kapila Vatsyayan from India, in her Keynote Paper, commended Unesco's efforts in the preservation of world heritage in different parts of the world and in creating an awareness of it. Discussing the issues relating to cultural identity and universalism, the participants emphasized that communication was the key to the spread of culture which is a moving and dynamic force as well as a powerful component of development. Unesco should, therefore, play its role by providing adequate means of communication to increase mutual appreciation of literary, artistic, architectural and traditional work of the peoples of the world.

The Session on Communication focussed on the New World Information and Communication Order (NWICO) and the emerging trends in the communication sector. Participants in the Seminar felt that this was perhaps one of the most crucial issues facing Unesco in its current difficulties.

The Keynote Paper by Mr. P. Unnikrishnan from India referred to the conflicting views on the implications of the NWICO, sensitivities of some of the developed countries, expansion of communication technology and its implications, and cooperation among developing and non-aligned countries.

The points highlighted during the discussion related to the misunderstandings over the relevance, significance and meeting of NWICO, the need for individual countries to evolve a national information and communication order, a better appreciation of the recommendations of the McBride Commission's report, and the need for improved cooperation between countries of the regions. Participants stressed the importance of projecting a correct image of women in the media consistent with the principles of equality and dignity.

The Seminar reviewed Unesco's work over the past 40 years, examined the nature and ramifications of its present situation and made several recommendations for the future orientation of its programme.

The Seminar noted that there was a crisis in the U.N. system as a whole. The world situation had for some time been unfavourable to the evolution and maintenance of world peace : there was continued international tension and a proliferation of regional conflicts. The arms race was unabated while the proliferation of nuclear weapons, particularly vertical proliferation, continued unchecked, and might spread even to outer space. While the international economic situation adversely affected the entire world, the Third World countries suffered most. Though there had been some positive developments recently, a long term and viable solution to these problems had still not been found. There was an unfortunate tendency to ignore the United Nations and its peace-making and peace-keeping role and a movement away from multilateralism.

While noting that the U.N. system was not perfect and had many shortcomings, the participants regretted that Unesco in particular had become the prime target of criticism. The seminar reaffirmed its faith in Unesco's goals and objectives which call upon it to build a sound basis for a lasting peace. It took stock of the significant changes witnessed in the organization, especially since the advent of new nations on the international scene. Unesco had responded in some measure to the urges and aspirations of all the Member States, within its fields of competence.

Unesco has endorsed the need for an equitable world order, particularly in such vital areas as information and communication, viewed as a continuous and evolving process, so as to reduce the disparities between the developed and the developing nations. The concept of development itself had been enlarged to encompass ideas of social justice, participatory democracy and self-reliance. Unesco had, moreover, fully recognized the intrinsic ties that link education, science, culture and communication. The most significant issues in these fields had been viewed in terms of their interdependence. Unesco's standard-setting activities, its role as a forum for dialogue between differing political systems and cultures and its operational projects, all taken together, have demonstrated its capacity to carry out the mandate it has received from the international community.

But Unesco suffers from the ills bred by any large bureaucracy. Also, with its large variety of tasks, its limited resources are too thinly spread out. While politics is unavoidable in any intergovernmental organization, in Unesco extraneous political issues have sometimes detracted attention from matters that fall within its orbit. At the same time many of its achievements have not been made widely known by the Member States.

However, the participants in the Seminar felt that these shortcomings could not explain, much less justify, the decisions of the United States of America, Britain and Singapore to withdraw from the Organization. These withdrawals appeared to be politically motivated. They constituted a regrettable withdrawal from multilateral cooperation and democratic functioning within the framework of international organizations. The decisions were all the more regrettable as they were taken at a time when Unesco had embarked on a far-reaching plan of reform and when the General Conference, at its 23rd Session held in Sofia in October-November 1985, had approved all its programmes by consensus. The participants were gratified to note the very considerable opposition to Unesco's leaving the intellectual, scientific and cultural communities in those Member States which had decided to withdraw, and agreed that channels of communication especially with these communities should be kept open.

The Seminar reiterated the hope that those Member States which had left would soon return to the organization. Despite these withdrawals, and the many constraints resulting from this, the Seminar urged that Unesco's remaining Member States should ensure that the organization continue to fulfil its mandate. They also stressed the importance of the role of National Commissions which needed to be reactivated wherever necessary. They also stressed the necessity for improved interaction between the Secretariat and the governing bodies, particularly the Executive Board of Unesco.

The Seminar made the following recommendations:

1. The relevance of Unesco's goals and objectives and its many achievements deserve to be more widely known in all Member States as well as in those countries which have left the Organization. Efforts should be intensified by Unesco and its Member States to improve the image of Unesco and to mobilize public opinion in support of its programmes. The National Commissions, non-governmental organizations and intellectual, scientific and cultural communities should be more actively associated by the Member States with these efforts. Not only officials and government nominees but also independent personalities from disciplines related to Unesco's work should be members of National Commissions.

2. Unesco's programmes ought to be articulated more forcefully within an integrated framework. For this purpose Unesco should launch pilot projects that link education, science, culture and communication.

3. Unesco should take urgent measures to involve the intellectual, scientific and artistic communities as well as universities

and other institutions of higher learning in each country more closely in the elaboration, implementation and evaluation of its programmes. Unesco's role not only as a catalyst but also as a promoter of intellectual cooperation among the peoples needs to be fully emphasized.

4. In order to check further bureaucratization and to ensure the optimization of available funds for human resource development programmes in which Unesco's functions overlap with those of other specialized agencies, efforts should be made at coordinating their activities.

5. Unesco needs to devote much greater attention to issues facing women. It should associate women at every stage with the elaboration and implementation of its programmes for them. All programmes concerning women should be given enhanced budget funding.

6. Unesco should also devote much greater attention to the problems of youth.

7. The duration of the term in office of the elected heads of the United Nations and its specialized agencies should be re-examined. A few participants felt that the tenure should be limited to one or two terms and, in the case of the office of the Director General of Unesco, it should be rotated so as to ensure representation of the different regions and cultures. This has no reference to personalities and the Seminar deplored the personal attacks on the Director General of Unesco in certain sections of the media.

8. Unesco should take steps to ensure the free flow of scientific and technical information, the latter through free access to conferences, meetings of scientists and publication of the results of research. Efforts should also be made to reduce the cost of the transfer of information through international computer networks.

9. The implications of a New World Information and Communication Order, seen as a continuous and evolving process,

need to be widely disseminated in order to remove the doubts and misunderstandings created by the media in some countries and sustained efforts should be madc to mobilize public opinion in favour of a freer and more balanced flow of information.

10. For the successful implementation of a New World Information and Communication Order, there is need for evolving national communication policies based on the sovereign rights of nations, the rights of individuals and the rights and responsibilities of journalists.

11. The seminar recorded its appreciation of the useful work done under the International Programme for the Development of Communication and urged its expansion and strengthening specially in the context of the phenomenal technological advances which need to be harnessed and channelized through efforts at indigenization.

12. Cooperation among the countries of a region should be pursued through action-based programmes in the communication sector because such a process would form, in the long run, a vital component in the success of the North-South dialogue.

13. Unesco has tried to create consciousness, within its fields of competence, about the need for nuclear disarmament. However, as disarmament is closely connected with issues relating to the removal of poverty, Unesco should associate social scientists with the discussion of these issues.

(Adapted from ROSTSCA BULLETIN, Number 23, July 1986.)

PART II

UNESCO AND SOCIAL SCIENCES

SIX

UNESCO AND SOCIAL SCIENCES AN OVERVIEW

Social Sciences have figured in Unesco's first programmes from the very beginning. Its range of activities is wider than suggested by its title. Its responsibilities include communication and social sciences also.

Unesco's main task of building up the defences of peace in the minds of men makes it clear that the Organization's main concern is with people and their relationships with each other - the field of social sciences.

Building the defences of peace is the task of the social scientist. If the origins of war lie in social attitudes, then modification of these attitudes could work towards peace. It is here that the social scientist plays his most important role.

Its constitution has given Unesco an active role in the struggle against intolerance and racial discrimination - factors that aggravate international tensions. Beginning in 1949, the organization launched a campaign of scientific study into the basis of racism.

Anthropologists, psychologists, sociologists and biologists participated in this work and their conclusion was categoric;there is no basis in science for the claims of so-called "Pure" races.

Ever since Unesco was founded in 1946. It has participated in the growth of social sciences. It was realized early that the social sciences suffered from a lack of organization. To remedy this, Unesco began to build "bridges" between nations by encouraging the establishment of professional associations on the international level in comparative law, political science, sociology, economics and documentation. At the same time it supported the Inter-national Institute of Administrative Sciences and the International Statistical Institute. An international and an interdisciplinary body was set up which began to function in 1952 in Paris:the International Social Science Council (ISSC), subsidized by Unesco. This unifying trend was helped by a shift in the thinking of social scientists themselves. No longer was the mere specialist sought, it was the "all-round" man who could contribute to a consensus of pooled knowledge who was in great demand.

Beginning in 1960's a number of young nations, particularly the newly independent developing countries of Africa,joined the organization. Not only did the total number of Member States rise from about 40 in 1946 to about 130 in the 1970's but also Unesco's programme underwent a shift towards increasingly concrete and technical activities aimed at helping these countries in their efforts to develop.

Starting in 1950, social science experts held posts in cooperative offices set up by Unesco in 1947 and 1948 at Cairo, New Delhi and Havana. At the same time, experts were sent on missions and symposia were organized to deal with specific regional problems.

In the 1950's certain permanent regional centres were also established. The Unesco Institute for Social Sciences was set up at Cologne in 1952, originally to deal mainly with serious social problems that emerged from the war. In 1953, the Research Office on Social Implications of Technological Change came into being in Paris with Unesco's assistance. This office was integrated into ISSC in 1961.

Centres were also being set up elsewhere. Originally located in Calcutta, the Research Centre on Social and Economic Development in Southern Asia later moved to New Delhi. In Latin America an entire structure was brought into being with the aid of Unesco in 1957 at Rio de Janeiro, the Latin American Centre for Social Sciences Research (CENTRO) was established; at Santiago, Chile, the Latin American Social Science Faculty (FLACSO) was set up the following year. To Santiago's original School of Sociology, a school of Public Administration and Political Science was added.

National centres, schools or institutes were opened in Greece, Iran, Colombia and Pakistan and International centres in Tangier and Vienna.

The European Coordination Centre for Social Science Research and Documentation, set up in Vienna in 1964, originated with a resolution introduced by Austria and Yugoslavia at the 12th session of the Unesco General Conference two years earlier. Its activities covered three major areas: research on peace; aid for developing countries and the study of changing societies in modern Europe. Its fields run from disarmament to juvenile delinquency.

Parallel with the establishment of these centres, Unesco works in and for the social sciences by means of surveys, seminars and publications.

A meeting held in 1950 on University Social Science teaching resulted in 15 studies which were published later on.

Annual seminars have been held since 1962 on the use of mathematical methods in the social sciences.

Seminars and training courses for university teachers and researchers have been organized in Africa and Asia under the United Nations Expanded Programme for Technical Assistance (EPTA) which was later incorporated into the United Nations Development Programme (UNDP). Within its programme Unesco sends consultants and professors to Member States on request, as well as grants scholarships.

All these activities have resulted in numerous specialized publications. The *Dictionary of Social Sciences* appeared in English in 1964. Its editions were prepared in other languages. Standardized terminology is one of the major aims of this work.

In cooperation with the International Committee for Social Science Documentation, Unesco publishes international bilingual bibliographies, lists, periodical catalogues and other reference works for scholars and researchers. Equally useful is the series on "Social Science Reports and Documents".

A division of Unesco's Social Science Department is specially charged with one of the newest disciplines : Statistics. Its *Statistical Yearbook*, brought out every two years is widely quoted by the Press throughout the world.

The quarterly *International Social Science Journal*, successor since 1959 to a "bulletin" with the same purpose, devotes each of its issues to a thorough study of a major scientific theme.

In 1963, Unesco launched a project of an international study of the main trends in research in the social and human sciences. Coming under both the Department of Social Sciences and the Department of Culture, it covers the entire spectrum of disciplines, from economics to history and from demography to literary criticism. Prominent experts from all over the world participate in this project begun under the direction of the late Julian Hochfeld of Warsaw University, Assistant Director of Unesco's Department of Social Sciences.

A main line of the current programme is the study and planning of development particularly what is called endogenous development arising from a country's own dynamics and meeting its particular needs. Training of specialists is thus a feature and projects aim at reducing inequalities and involving local populations.

Other special areas of study are the socio-cultural factors of development particularly in rural areas, analysis of the social implications of the new conditions of growth and the influence of transnational corporations in Unesco's fields of competence.

Under its medium-term plan of action the Organization shapes its programmes so as to tackle selected world problems. Among these is the relationship of man with his environment. The Social Science Sector is undertaking an important series of publications and studies helping efforts to improve the knowledge of the general public and training of specialists who, as engineers, architects and town planners, shape the places where we live.

Unesco is also promoting studies on problems such as migration and the effect of education on marriage rates and fertility as well as promoting POPCOM communication to inform the general public about population problems.

Unesco was created to promote human rights and the current programme gives this No.1 priority; it is following up the Declaration on Race adopted by its General Conference in 1978, studying how to combat violations of existing human rights and how far it is possible to take account of new ones (the rights of solidarity), investigating the exercise of human rights in urban areas and promoting teaching about them.

Women as a group are frequently deprived of their human rights and the current programme includes studies on why this is so as well as efforts to promote women's participation in development.

An important effort is devoted to developing the role of youth in educational, social and cultural activity and ensuring their commitment to the cause of human rights and peace.

The aim of building peace which is common to all Unesco undertakings finds a special place in the current social sciences programme which covers development of national and regional peace research centres, promotion of studies and training seminars for specialists in disarmament education in Latin America and the Caribbean, Asia and Africa.

Role of Unesco in social sciences may be described under the following broad heads:

1. Development of the Social Sciences
2. Study and Planning of Development
3. Environment and Human Settlements
4. Population
5. Human Rights and Peace
6. Status of women and their participation in Development
7. Youth
8. Technical Cooperation Programmes
9. Publications
10. Exhibitions

SEVEN

UNESCO AND DEVELOPMENT OF SOCIAL SCIENCES

Objectives

Elucidating contemporary social problems and examining the capacity of social sciences towards their solutions.

Encouraging research on the subject of "work relations and social relations".

Conducting studies on the conditions in which knowledge in the social and human sciences can be exchanged so as not to impede endogenous development.

Granting subvention to the International Social Science Council (ISSC). Encouraging professional non-governmental organizations to undertake studies on contemporary social problems.

Organizing international meetings of experts for inter-regional cooperation. Developing and promoting philosophical studies and the teaching of philosophy.

Recent Programmes and Activities Relating to the Development of Social Sciences:

1. *Elucidating contemporary social problems and examining the capacity of social sciences towards their solutions*

Two international meetings organized by Unesco in 1981 in Mexico city on social science tasks and priorities in the Third War and at the Headquarters on the tasks of the social sciences with regard to their scientific development as well as their contributions to the solutions of the world problems have helped considerably in arousing interest among social science communities around the world and encouraged them to further efforts to identify future tasks in the social sciences.

Many meetings with assistance from Unesco have also been organized on this topic by international and regional non-governmental bodies such as the International Federation of Social Science Organizations (IFSSO), the Asian Association of Social Science Research Councils (AASSRES), the Association international des sociologues de langue francaise, and the Vienna Centre.

2. *Encouraging research on the subject of "work relations and "social relations"*

In some countries of different regions, research on this topic has been encouraged and systematic field work done.

3. *Conducting studies on the conditions in which knowledge in the social and human sciences can be exchanged so as not to impede endogenous development.*

The book, *Domination or Sharing*, which is a collection of reports on international research carried out by anthropologists, ethnologists, sociologists, jurists and economists on this subject was published in 1981 in French, English and Spanish in the Unesco series *Insights*.

The network of researchers working on Economics has been enlarged and the results of their studies have been collected in a work entitled *Economic and Endogenous Development*. Three teams of researchers, linguists, anthropologists and psychologists have been set up - the first to study the question of African languages and the exchange of knowledge reflecting Member States' desire to develop their national languages for this purpose, rather than use internationally established languages; the second to study the conditions for the exchange of knowledge between Andean migrants and coastal populations, taking into account the linguistic problems and the varying cognitive systems involved; the third to work on the impact of psychology on Third War development.

4. *Granting subvention to the International Social Science Council (ISSC)*

A subvention of US $ 841,000 has been granted to the ISSC for the activities of its member organizations. Cooperation has also been strengthened through regular consultations similar to the arrangements for cooperation with the International Council of Scientific Unions (ICSU).

5. *Encouraging professional non-governmental organizations to undertake studies on contemporary social problems*

A number of professional non-governmental organizations have been encouraged to undertake studies on contemporary social problems, for example a comparative study by the International Association for Mass Communication, a study by the International Social Science Council on questions of social transition, covering the process of industrialization in certain countries of Europe and Latin America, research by the International Sociological Association on development in Brazil and the non-achievement of certain classes, including field work in Brazil and a study of the relationship between the selection process in education, marginalization and social mobility.

The first training seminar was held by the African Council on Communication Education in Cotonou (Benin) in February, 1983, with the help of Unesco. The contents of textbooks in the training of mass media researchers were discussed.

6. *Organizing international meetings of experts for interregional cooperation*

An international meeting of experts was held in Nairobi (Kenya) in 1983 to discuss theories on rural urban interactions, social transformations among the peasantry, types of political mobilization in rural areas, and the relationship between the villages and the towns and the role of petty traders as intermediaries.

7. *Developing and promoting philosophical studies and the teaching of philosophy*

A series of researches have been carried out reviewing the epistemological and axiological approaches used in the social sciences and their applicability to the understanding of human phenomena.

A meeting on the teaching of philosophy in Africa - the first of a series of regional studies on this theme - was held in Nairobi (Kenya) in 1980 and its report has been published under the title *Teaching and research in philosophy : Africa*. It covers pre-colonial, Islamic, European and post-colonial philosophical contents in this region.

This collection is most illuminating on such subjects as traditional wisdom; the role of the sage, past and present; the oral tradition; the problems, linguistic and otherwise, of recovering pre-colonial systems of thought and thinking. It is a provocative work not only on the meaning and uses of philosophy in Africa today, but in post-colonial societies in general.

A meeting of experts on teaching and research in philosophy in Asia and the Pacific held in Bangkok (Thailand) in 1983 resulted in a scheme for the establishment of a research and documentation centre in the field. Both meetings stressed that teachers should receive more training in theory and teaching methods; the need to develop continuing training, to readjust and at the same time strengthen the teaching of philosophy and to support and promote interdisciplinary exchanges.

Islam, Philosophy and Science was published in 1981. It contains lectures by eminent persons on Tolerance in the Prophet's deeds at Medina; the development of philosophical thought in its relationship with Islam up to Avicenna, Islam and innovation; Modern Muslim thinkers of the Indian Subcontinent, Islam and the flowering of the exact sciences.

Unesco associated itself with the celebrations on October 21, 1981, under the auspices of the Permanent Delegation of Chile and the Latin American and Caribbean group of Member States, to mark the bicentenary of the birth of Andres Bello. It assisted the International Commission for the Arabic edition of the works of Averroes in April, 1982. It also helped the "Centre interdisciplinaire de researchers sur la paix et d'etudes strategigues" in the organization of an international debate on the theme, "The Philosophy of Peace in a Time of Exterminism" in November, 1983. Cooperation was also extended to Greek authorities in organizing a symposium in 1983 on the theme, "Democritus, the fate of atomism"

To mark the birth centenary of philosopher Jacques Maritain a commemorative booklet containing a selection of his writings was published. Unesco also assisted the International 'Jacques Maritain' Study Institute, Rome (Italy), and the Association des Amis de Jacques Maritain, Paris (France), in organizing two symposia at Headquarters.

Similarly, Unesco cooperated with the Universities of Basel and Heidelberg in organizing the symposia held on June 13-14 and 15-16, 1983, in connection with the centenary of the birth of the philosopher Karl Jaspers. Unesco also organized a round-table on June 17, 1983, on "Karl Jaspers and the idea of Universal Philosophy "Ethics and the Future of Humanity" and mounted an exhibition of his works. A booklet entitled *Jalons Jaspersiens* containing a selection of Karl Jasper's writings was published in French.

An international round-table on "Karl Marx To-day" was held from December 14 to 16, 1983. In this connection an exhibition of original works and documents, manuscripts and photographs was organized with the assistance of several institutions. A booklet was also published containing selected writings of Karl Marx.

Unesco associated itself with the Academy of the Asiatic Languages in paying tribute to Louis Massignou in October, 1983. An exhibition on his life and work, to mark the centenary of his birth, was organized in December, 1983. A booklet containing a selection of his writings was also published.

Unesco convened a round-table on "Philosophy in International Life" on the occasion of the World Congress of Philosophy organized by the International Federation of Philosophical Societies in August,

1983, in Montreal (Canada).

An international symposium on "Transcultural Universals" was held in (Canada) in 1983 with the assistance of the Canadian National Commission for Unesco and with financial support from the Humanities Research Council of Canada and the Ambassador International Cultural Foundation, Pasadena (California). A booklet entitled *Histoire et diversite des cultures* appeared in French in February, 1984.

An international symposium entitled "Moral and Political Vision of Islam" was organized at the Headquarters in December, 1982. The debate centred on the function of the State in Islamic theory, the experiences of Islam and their significance from the point of view of the conception of the State and the contribution of the Islamic view to the improvement of moral and political conditions. Assistance in organizing the symposium was made available from the Islamic Call Society (Socialist People's Libyan Arab Republic).

Recent Activities Concerning Development of the Social Science in Each Region:

Africa

The activities, functioning and future prospects of the Centre for the Coordination of Social Science Research and Documentation in Africa south of the Sahara (CERDAS) at Kinshara (Zaire) were evaluated and a fresh impetus was given to the Centre's activities.

A training seminar on methodologies in the social sciences was held in November, 1983, at Kinshasa with participants from Zaire, Rwanda, Burundi and Gabon.

A meeting to study the coordination of post-university social science education in Southern Africa was organized at Maputo (Mozambique) in 1982.

The University of Dar es Salaam (Tanzania) undertook a study on the possible establishment of a sub-regional network for research and training in the social and human sciences in East Africa.

Support was given to the following for organizing various programmes :

Conference of Universities of Southern Africa on the Social Sciences (SAUSSC) for its sixth conference on the theme, "Development and Regional Cooperation in Southern Africa", held at Lusaka (Zambia) in 1982.

African Association of Political Science (AAPS) for its fifth Biennial Conference on the theme, "The State in Africa: Problems and Challenges for the 1980's", held at Dakar (Senegal) in 1983.

African Council of Sociologists and Anthropologists (CASA) for meeting at Dakar in 1983 on the theme, "Social Sciences and African Societies".

Social Sciences Council of Nigeria for its first General Assembly in 1983.

African Council for Communication Education for the organization of a workshop for the teaching of sociology of communication in Africa, held at Cotonou (Benin) in 1983.

African Council for Communication Education for a post-graduate teaching seminar on theories and methodologies in the sociology of communication held at Lagos (Nigeria) in 1983.

Asia and the Pacific

Unesco cooperated with the Association of Asian Social Science Research Councils (AASSRC) in the publication of the proceedings of its third Conference and the Organization of its fourth and fifth Conferences. (Bangkok, 1981 and Sydney, 1983).

Training courses were organized on social science research methodology for the Association of South-East Asian Nations (ASEAN) in collaboration with the Regional Institute of Higher Education and Development (RIHED) and on the changing paradigms of development held in 1982 in Delhi.

Unesco cooperated with both the Social Science Research Centre of Sri Lanka and the Association of South East Asian Institutes of Higher Learning (ASAIHL) to send officials to India to study the working of the Indian Council of Social Science Research.

Unesco prepared reports on the status of sociology and social anthropology in 12 countries of the region.

At an Asian symposium the relevance of current concepts and theories in social sciences was critically examined in the context of differing local situations in Asia, and of the problems concerning transcultural research among these countries.

A training seminar on comparative socio-economic development was held in Beijing (China) in 1983, in collaboration with the Chinese Academy of Social Sciences.

Arab States

A seminar was organized in Tunis in November 1981 in collaboration with the Social Science Research and Documentation Centre for the Arab Region (ARCSS) on the role of information and documentation systems in the development policy of local communities. Experts from 10 countries of the region took part.

A post-graduate training course for social science teachers and specialists was organized in Abu Dhabi (United Arab Emirates) in April 1983. It was attended by teachers and specialists from Algeria, the United Arab Emirates, Egypt, Jordan, Somalia, Sudan and Tunisa. The theme of the course was "The endogenous approach and its significance in social sciences in the Arab States Region".

Unesco assisted in conducting detailed surveys in the urban area of Giza in Cairo (Egypt) and two villages in Upper Egypt. The experience acquired in Egypt helped in making it possible to apply the methodology and survey techniques and to adapt the systems of analysis to the social structures and cultural values of the countries of the region.

Latin America and the Caribbean

An expert meeting was held in February 1982, in Panama on the exchange of lectures, students and documentation between social science institutions in Latin America and the Caribbean. The meeting outlined areas of collaboration between Latin America and the Caribbean, including the English-speaking Caribbean and it suggested lectureship exchanges, joint research and joint accreditation in order to ensure real interchange of students and lectures.

Unesco encouraged a research project in Bolivia to study, within the mining industry, the relationship between levels of occupation and ethnic groups with particular reference to Indians in Bolivia.

At the request of the Bolivian Government a FLASSCO project was set up in La Paz in July, 1983.

Europe

Unesco provided support for two international training seminars on Crossnational Comparative Research in 1981 and 1982 in the Federal Republic of Germany and Yugoslavia.

Support was provided for a regional conference on the tasks and challenges for European social sciences in 1980's (Brussels, 1982).

Cooperation was strengthened with the Social Science Research Centre in Athens in order to promote the regional role of the Centre and to enable it to launch sub-regional social science research activities.

The information and documentation activities in the region were supported through the Vienna Centre's International Committee for Social Science Documentation (ICSSID) programme.

In North America, a regional meeting was held in Quebec (May 1983) to discuss problems and priorities in the social sciences in North America.

SELECT UNESCO PUBLICATIONS

Data-based teaching in the social sciences

International Federation of Data Organizations, Unesco Invitational Seminar, Waterloo, Ontario, November, 1979. In memory of Stein Rokkan (1921-79) (Reports and papers in the social sciences. 50) 1983, 46pp, tables, ISBN 92-3-102113-3.

Examines standard national, local and individually developed social sciences data-based teaching resources, studies them from the point of view of social science disciplines in different geographic areas of the world, as well as the influence of computer-assisted instruction.

The impact of microelectronics and information technology

Case studies in Latin America by Juan F. Rada, 1982, 108 pp., tables. ISBN 92-3-102004-8.

The far-reaching consequences of new developments in microelectronics have been much debated in industrialized nations but little is known about their impact on the economics of developing countries. This report aims to fill a gap in our knowledge by examining the social and economic impact of microelectronics in three countries in Latin America - Argentina, Brazil and Bolivia.

Social sciences in Asia and the Pacific

1984, 621 pp., tables. ISBN 92-3-102148-6.

A collection of reports from 23 countries of Asia and the Pacific covers both classical traditions and modern scientific developments, exploring conceptual, theoretical and methodological issues; problems of infrastructure; professionalization of the social sciences, their relevance and utility; cooperation and exchange among social science communities in the region.

Sociology and social anthropology in Asia and the Pacific

1984,720pp., ISBN 92-3-102172-9. Co-published with Wiley Eastern

Ltd., New Delhi, who have exclusive sales rights in India.

Reports from 12 countries - Australia, Bangladesh, China, India, Indonesia, Japan, Republic of Korea, New Zealand, Pakistan, the Philippines, Singapore and Thailand - covering the history of each of these disciplines in the country, research trends, problems of the profession and future plans and prospects.

Teaching and research in philosophy : Africa

(Studies on teaching and research in philosophy throughout the world), 1984, 287 pp., ISBN 92-3-102124-9.

EIGHT

UNESCO : STUDY AND PLANNING OF DEVELOPMENT

Objectives

Undertaking activities relating to the philosophical investigation of the basic problems of endogenous development.

Carrying out original experiments in different socio-political, socio-economic and cultural contexts for finding out the role and interactions of factors conducive to endogenous, self-reliant development, particularly for the least developed countries.

Conducting experiments for identifying national development prospects with a view to encouraging the investigation of innovatory methods and exploring new ways of development that may be adapted to the needs and possibilities of societies.

Conducting experiments to identify the practical conditions required for establishing "participative management for endogenous development".

Carrying out studies in the various regions of the world to identify measures to reduce economic inequalities and socio-cultural disparities within States.

Implementing development strategies specifically designed to reduce economic and socio-cultural inequalities.

Commissioning research studies to examine the social and cultural conditions affecting the production and marketing of the food crops of small farmers in some countries.

Providing support to non-governmental organizations for the production and distribution of documentation on the creation of a climate of public opinion favouring the establishment of a new economic order.

Identifying principles and methods for devising indicators for socio-economic analysis and progress on several levels.

Supporting research on the quality of life through the informal network of research institutions.

Improving studies analysing the imbalances between available and needed planning methods.

Taking up national studies to review evaluation experience in different parts of the world, to identify methodological shortcomings and suggest improvement of evaluation methods.

Planning regional symposiums on evaluation techniques in social action projects.

Recent Activities Relating to the Study and Planning of Social Science Development

A regional Training Seminar on "Problems and Methods after Implementing Endogenous Development through participation in Administration" was organized in cooperation with the Tunisian National Commission and the Tunisian Ministry of Social Affairs, at Hammamet (Tunisia) in 1983. It was attended by some 20 participants from Arab States.

A national seminar was held at Doha (Qatar) in 1981 with a considerable financial contribution from the Government of Qatar, on the reduction of inequalities in different socio-cultural contexts. Nineteen psychologists, sociologists, educators and pediatricians from 16 countries in all regions took part. The processings of the symposium were published with the assistance from the University of Qatar, under the title "Childhood Inequalities and Development".

As part of Unesco's contribution to the follow-up to the

Programme of Action adopted by the World Conference on Agrarian Reform and Rural Development in Rome in 1979, a number of research studies were commissioned to examine the social and cultural conditions affecting the production and marketing of the food crops of small farmers in nine countries of Latin America and the Caribbean, seven African countries and one Asian country.

The research conducted at the Caribbean was analysed at a meeting of governmental experts, social scientists and representatives of small farmers and agricultural workers, held at Barbados in August 1981. In the meeting, proposals were made inter alia to set up a network of Caribbean Social Scientists and Institutions concerned with Rural Development (CANSIRD) and to establish an institutional framework at the sub-regional level so that peasants and agricultural workers' associations could participate in the formulation and implementation of rural development programmes. The framework for the implementation of these recommendations was defined at meetings in Barbados and Saint Lucia in 1982.

In Africa, a consultation meeting for researchers was held at Dakar (Senegal) in 1983 to propose priority areas for further research on the structural and cultural factors in food dependency and alimentary behaviour and the possibility of establishing sub-regional networks with the assistance of the National Commissions.

Eight status reports on the role of the social sciences in agricultural education in Asia and the Pacific were summarized and distributed under the title "Social Sciences in Agricultural Education".

Studies were carried out on the interactions between development, environment and population and their impact on policy making in Bangladesh, Botswana, Dominican Republic, France, Ghana, Grenada, Italy, Romania and the United Kingdom.

Two studies dealing with West Africa and South East Asia showed the scant attention that is paid to socio-cultural factors in regional integration and cooperation policies and the role devolving on Unesco in promoting the integration of the cultural dimension in sub-regional and regional development strategies.

A consultation of experts was held with 12 participants who identified the main elements of the socio-economic strategies and policies of the transnational companies.

Activities concerning research on socio-economic indicators included the preparation of 12 studies and the convening of three meetings, attended by 95 participants. Training materials on indicators of children and of women have been prepared and training courses held.

Three international meetings were held on (i) Indicators of socio-economic change for development planning (Seoul), Republic of Korea 1981, attended by 32 participants from 15 countries, (ii) Elaboration and use of social indicators of the handicapped (Brussels, 1981) attended by 28 participants from 14 countries and (iii) Social minorities (Ottawa, Canada, 1981) attended by 35 participants from 15 countries.

Six comparative studies on the quality of life have been carried out in different cultural contexts, covering Africa, Asia and the Pacific and Europe. No. 5 of "Socio-economic studies", "Quality of life-problems of assessment and measurements" included some of these studies.

With financial assistance from Unicef, an informal consultation to identify social concerns and indicators of changing conditions of children in society was held at Paris in 1983.

Training materials have been prepared on the use of quantitative instruments for measuring and evaluating the role of women in development and on the use of socio-economic indicators in decision-making and planning projects relating to children.

An international symposium on planning methods and the elaboration of such methods was held in Paris in 1983.

Two inter-disciplinary research studies on quantification in social sciences and the use of such methods in policy making have been followed by three national case studies (Tanzania, Peru, Republic of Korea).

A regional workshop for the Arab States on the use of modelling techniques in national planning has been held at Rabat (Morocco) in 1982, with 35 participants from nine Arab countries.

At the request of Member States, workshops on the Unesco Educational Simulation Model (ESM) were held at Nairobi (Kenya) in 1981; Lusaka (Zambia) in 1981; Baghdad (Iraq) in 1982; and Dhaka (Bangladesh) in 1984.

A series of national studies to review evaluation experience, identify methodological shortcomings and suggest improvement of evaluation methods were carried out in Ecuador, India, Malawi, Nigeria and the United Kingdom.

A regional symposium on evaluation techniques in social projects in Latin America and the Caribbean took place in Caracas (Venezuela) in 1982 with participants from 10 Latin American and Caribbean Member States.

Three national training courses for increasing the capacity to make use of techniques for evaluating social action projects have been organized at Jakarta (Indonesia) in 1982; Lima (Peru) in 1983 and Harare (Zimbabwe) in 1983.

SELECTED UNESCO PUBLICATIONS

Community development

Comparative case studies in India, Republic of Korea, Mexico and United Republic of Tanzania. Editors Ronald Dore and Zoe Mars. 1981, 446pp., ISBN 92-3-101877-9. Co-published with Crom Helm Ltd. who have exclusive sales rights in the United Kingdom.

Presents four different cases of community development experience. Working to a common research plan, the authors chose to compare pairs of villages, one of which was counted as a successful example of development and the other as unsuccessful.

Indicators of social and economic change and their implications: (Reports and papers in social sciences), 1977, 95pp., ISBN, 92-3-

101493-5

A new concept of development

Basic tenets by Francois Perroux, 1983, 224pp., ISBN 92-3-102057-9, Co-published with Crom Helm Ltd., London, who have exclusive sales rights in the United Kingdom.

The concept of development brings out the major paradox of our era : the desire for progress and the mistrust of its consequences. Francois Perroux, a leading political economist whose innovative thinking has made a major contribution to development studies, aims in this work to analyse the ideas and theories propounded by an economic approach to development and to clarify the meaning and direction of current research.

Project evaluation : Problems of methodology

1984, 141pp., ISBN 92-3-102132-X

Three case studies of evaluation procedure in three developing countries - India, Malawi and Nigeria - critically review designs, methods and techniques with respect to projects ranging from nutrition and health through education, housing and family planning, giving concrete suggestions for improvements.

Quality of Life : Problems of assessment and measurement

(Socio-economic studies, 5)
1983, 177pp., ISBN 92-3-10209

Towards a new international economic order

'By Mohammed Bedjaoui (New challenges to international law), 1979, 287pp., ISBN 92-3-101670-9. Co-published with Holmes & Meier, New York and London, who have exclusive sales rights in the United States and share rights throughout the rest of the world.

The study examines some of the most pressing current problems : What do we mean by "new international economic order?" What realizations and hopes brought the concept into being? What is the extent and significance of the current crisis? What obstacles are there to the establishment of the new international economic order? What facts or invariables and their dependent parameters reveal the forces at work and the power balances, changing and renewed, on which progress to new stages in the history of mankind depends? What ways and means are there for establishing this new order? Is the adaptation of the United Nations necessary and sufficient to this end?

Transnational corporations and endogenous development

By Jean-Louis Reiffers with Andre Cartapanis, William Experton and Jean-Luc Fuguet, 1982, 280pp., ISBN 92-3-101853-1.

Considers the effects of the activities of transnational corporations on the development process in the fields of culture, communication, education and science and technology. Of particular interest to researchers, specialists and officers responsible for national and international development policies.

NINE

UNESCO : ENVIRONMENT AND HUMAN SETTLEMENTS

Objectives

Carrying out research on improving the management of physical and socio-economic resources at the international level.

Undertaking studies on the interaction between man and his environment.

Organizing meetings and seminars on the use of audio-visual aids material in perception of the environment and landuse planning.

Mounting exhibitions on the traditional rural habitat for increasing awareness among professionals - architects, town planners, decision makers - of the merits of the traditional conceptions and techniques of this habitat.

Organizing inter-disciplinary training courses and seminars for educators, managers and officials in the public sector with direct responsibility for the planning and administration of human settlements and environment in rural and urban areas.

Cooperating with United Nations Environmental Programme (UNEP), the United Nations Centre for Human Settlements (UNCHS-Habitat), International Association of City and Regional Planners (IACRP) and the International Union of Architects (IUA).

Recent Activities Relating to Environment and Human Settlements:

1. A series of inter-disciplinary studies on the interaction be-

tween man and his environment on the minor islands of the Mediterranian have been undertaken and completed in cooperation with the MAB programme and the National Committees involved (Tunisia, Greece, Malta and Italy) and with the assistance of national scientific institutions.

2. An international seminar on the use of audio-visual materials in perception of the environment and land-use planning and in the training of specialists in these matters was held at Palermo (Italy) in November, 1981.

3. A training course organized on the island of Kerkennah (Tunisia) in 1983 led to the formation of proposals for an integrated land-use programme of the island.

4. A dynamic intersectoral model of the operation of the island of Gozo (Malta) has been studied and programmed on a microcomputer.

5. Synopses of national studies on the minor islands of Mediterranian environment disseminated in the "Human Settlement" series.

6. An exhibition was mounted on the traditional rural habitat and a brochure issued which was intended to increase awareness among professionals - architects, town planners, decision-makers - of the merits of the traditional conceptions and techniques of this habitat.

7. A project for the rehabilitation of a district of the historic centre of Evora (Portugal) was started in 1981.

8. A large number of inter-disciplinary courses for the training of educators and managers and officials in the public sector with direct responsibility for the planning and administration of human settlements and the environment in rural and urban areas have been organized in these countries : Argentina, Brazil, France, Guinea-Bissau, Sudan, Thailand, Tunisia, United Republic of Cameroon and Zaire.

9. A course was held at Mopti (Mali) in 1981 on the subject of "Environmental Planning Tools and Methods for Medium-sized Towns in Africa".

10. Three meetings have been organized in conjunction with the International Association of City and Regional Planners : the first in Tunis in 1981 on the subject of the training of town planners in developing countries; the second in Istanbul in 1982 on the theme "Habitat for all : what is the solution?"; and the third in Amsterdam in 1983 on the theme, "Implementation of town planning : the partners".

11. The first seminar on the training of "barefoot" architects was held in "Kampung" in Jakarta in 1981 in collaboration with the International Union of Architects (IUA) and the Jakarta municipal authorities. The seminar aimed at setting up a training programme for specialists wishing to help the inhabitants of precarious human settlements to improve their physical living conditions. Subsequently seminars were held on this subject at Bangkok in June, 1983, and at New Delhi in December, 1983.

Unesco Clubs in Malian Village Afforestation

An original model for cooperation between Unesco Clubs in Europe and Africa has been set up between Belgium and Mali to help counter desertification and drought. The project, deliberately small, is based in a village called Faira (200 inhabitants), about 340 kms (150 miles) from Bamako, in a region straddling the Sahelian Sudanic zones, which is gradualy but inexorably succumbing to the encroaching desert. In the first phase, financed by the Belgian Federation of Unesco Centres and carried out in 1983 by the Malian Federation of Unesco Clubs in close collaboration with Water and Forestry authorities, young villagers cleared two hectares of land and planted 1,500 seedlings of a variety of species (Gmelina, Neem, Eucalyptus, Balanzan....) selected for their low water needs, usefulness as animal feed, for their healing properties or rapid growth rate. Today, over 82 per cent of the saplings have taken root and the two Federations are pursuing a second socio-cultural phase, involving upkeep of the plantation, and development of an awareness among the villagers of their responsibilities in regard to the causes of desertification. This includes promotion of "improved stoves" which reduce by 60% the consumption of firewood - one of the causes, along with over-grazing and clearing of bush for hunting, of deforestation. Since the Mali Federation proposes to assist and advise other countries in the region wishing to undertake similar projects, its President, Abdoulaye Djire, was invited to Europe by the Belgian Federation in October, 1984. Unesco paid travel expenses for the trip which included an information and lecture tour of Belgian Clubs (12 among the 2.800 Unesco Clubs in 80 countries) and a visit to the Federal Republic of Germany where the Federation of Unesco Clubs is supporting research on a plant strain which is particularly well suited to conditions in the Sahel countries.

Latin American Youth Seminar on Development and Protection of the Environment

In the context of the International Youth Year 1985, about 30 young university students from 15 countries in the Latin American and Caribbean region took part in a symposium on "Economic Development and the Protection of the Environment" held in Caracas from November 12 to 16, 1984. Working sessions during the meeting, organized by the Eugenio Mendoza Foundation with support from Unesco, the Polar Foundation and the World Federation of Unesco Clubs and Associations, centred on means for reconciling population growth, industrial development, agricultural production and technologies with urgent necessity of protecting the environment. Participants also discussed ways of promoting rational environmental policies through Unesco Clubs in their respective countries. At one of the sessions, Milena Sardi de Selle, Venezuelan Minister of Youth, said that the solutions which America found for these critical and very complex problems could have vital repercussions for the rest of humanity. She also stressed the responsibility of youth in the light of the fact that a majority of the population in the region is under 25 years old.

More than 1,000 MAB Research Projects carried out

More than 1,000 field research projects in 100 countries have been undertaken under Unesco's interdisciplinary Man and the Biosphere

Programme (MAB) since it was set up in 1971. Opening the 8th session of the MAB International Cordinating Council, held at Unesco's Paris headquarters from December 3 to 8, 1984, Director General Amadou-Mahtar M'Bow stressed the originality an innovative character of the programme as a means for developing international scientific cooperation on the management of land, water and coastal ecosystems. Some pilot projects, he said, such as those undertaken in Kenya, Tunisia, Ivory Coast and Chile, have led to setting up, or strengthening, of ecological research stations of regional or international value. He pointed out that the MAB programme has led to the mobilization of many thousands of researchers working on a wide variety of projects which, in turn, has generated several hundred publications yearly through MAB national committees. In addition, more than 1,000 specialists and young researchers now benefit each year from training activities under the programme,he said. During the session, representatives of the 30 Member States which make up the Council discussed continuing action under MAB's 14 major project areas, and laid down plans for further development of the international network of biosphere reserves, or protected zones, which now (1985) number 225 sites in 62 countries.

2200 Geographers from 86 Countries

Two thousand and two hundred geographers met in Paris from August 27 to 31, 1984, at the 25th International Geographical Congress, organized every four years by the International Geographical Union (IGU). As in the past, the Congress was co-sponsored by Unesco which has long-standing links with the IGU, notably in areas connected with the Organization's four main scientific programmes : International Geological Correlation Programme (IGCP), Intenational Hydrological Programme (IHP), Programme on Man and the Biosphere (MAB) and the programmes of the Intergovernmental Oceanographic Commission (IOC). These links have been particularly reinforced over recent years between Unesco-MAB and a series of IGU Commissions and Working Groups concerned with MAB-related issues such as mountain geoecology, resource management of drylands, perception of the environment, coastal ecosystems and cartography of a dynamic environment. Another IGU Commission maintains close contact with Unesco-IHP. Nine of the 38 pre-Congress symposia received direct support from the Organization in line with its regular programme activities, and $22,400 in financial aid as a contribution towards travel and per diem expenses for participants from developing countries.

Environmental Training for Economists

The urgent need for training economists in environmental concerns, particularly in developing countries, was the subject of an international conference, organized by the European Coordination Centre for Research and Documentation in the Social Sciences (Vienna Centre), under contract with Unesco, in Budapest (Hungary) from September 6 to 10,1985. At the meeting,15 high-level economists and environmentalists compared the widely varying conditions between their countries and regions with regard to the gravity and nature of environmental problems, protective legislation and public awareness. They pointed out that while industrial disasters such as that in Bhopal (India, December,1984) may serve as dramatic reminders, economists and other planners must also be capable of gauging the less obvious long-term consequences of improper landuse, deterioration, even depletion,living and non-living resources, etc., in order to achieve and maintain the delicate, and vital, balance between development needs and environmental realities. The Vienna Centre, created in 1963 following a resolution of Unesco's General Conference, is an autonomous body of the International Social Science Council.

Barrio Rio Salado - A Pilot Project for Rehabilitation of Shanty Towns

By the year 2000, over half the world's population will be living in urban areas, many in the shanty towns burgeoning around Third World cities. In 1986, Unesco completed a feasibility study for a pilot project in just such a community - Barrio (quarter) Rio Salado on the outskirts of La Romana (108,300 inhabitants) in the Dominican Republic. Sprawled over 1.5 kms along the Rio Romana, ramshackle dwellings house a population of 3,427, most of whom came from rural areas to find work in La Romana's sugar refineries. Sanitary conditions are deplorable. Garbage and sewerage go directly into the already polluted river and drinking water is scarce. There are no schools, health or recreational facilities. The Unesco study team, led by architect Altagracia Reyes, spent 45 days collecting data in the settlement. Together with the townspeople who set up their own Association during that period, they met with local authorities, representatives of the Central Romana Corp. and the Regional Development Agency. At the conclusion of her comprehensive 107-page study, Mrs. Reyes outlined a plan for sanitary and social installations and for increasing the town's productive capacity (traditional crafts, small trades...). By doing much of the work themselves, the townspeople are convinced that, with a minimum of outside help, they can, during Phase II of the Unesco project, transform Rio Salado into a comfortable, healthy and attractive community to serve as an inspiration for the billions of urban dwellers living in precarious conditions around the world.

SELECTED UNESCO PUBLICATIONS

Approaches to the study of environmental implications of Contemporary Urbanisation

By R.White and I.Burton (MAB technical notes, 14), 1983, 142pp., ISBN 92-3-102170-2.

An integrative ecological approach to the study of human settlements

By Stephen Boyden (MAB technical notes 12), 1979, 87 pp., figs, tables, ISBN 92-3-101689-x

Landuse in semi-arid Mediterranean Climates

Iraklion Symposium, 1962, (Arid zone research xxvi), 1984, 177 pp., ISBN 92-93-3-000561-4

Man in arid lands : Momads in transition

(MAB audio-visual series, 4), slide-tape package - 55 slides and 15-minute cassette, ISBN 92-3-001952-6

Man and the humid tropics

(MAB audio-visual series) slide-tape package - 74 slides and 23-

minute cassette, 1979, ISBN 92-3-101768-3

Man and the Mountains

(MAB audio-visual series, 2), slide-tape package - 55 slides and 15 - minute cassette, ISBN 92-3-001953-4

Man : The prey to conservation

(MAB audio-visual series, 3), slide tape package - 55 slides and 15-minute cassette, ISBN 92-3-001952-6

Planning methods and human environment

By Giberte C. Gallopin (socio-economic studies, 41), 1981, 68pp., ISBN 92-3-102132-x

Population-environment relations in tropical islands : The case of eastern Fiji

Unesco/UNFPA pilot project studies on Population-Environment Relationships in the Eastern Islands of Fiji, edited by H.C. Brookfield (MAB Technical notes, 13), 1980, 228pp., figs, ISBN 92-3-101821-3

TEN

UNESCO AND POPULATION EDUCATION

Objectives

Taking up research networks in three key areas - internal and international migration; effects of demographic trends and development on the status of women.

Developing a methodology for quantifying the relationship between population, resources and human welfare.

Preparing and publishing technical documents giving an analysis of the pilot experiments integrating human rights factors in population communication programmes.

Recent Activities in the Field of Population

1. Research has been undertaken on the dynamics of internal migration.

2. Four country studies on the dynamics, pattern and consequences of migration in France, India, Mexico and Nigeria have been undertaken.

3. Comparative research projects have been undertaken in India, Pakistan, Sri Lanka and Thailand on the impact of migration in the Middle East (West Asia) on rural communities and families.

4. Studies have been conducted in Africa, Asia and the Pacific, Latin America and the Caribbean, the Middle East (West

Asia), Western Europe and North America which aimed at identifying the main trends in international migration.

5. An international symposium was held in October, 1983, to investigate migration problems.

6. With the financial assistance of the United Nations Fund for Population Activities (UNFPA) attention has been focussed on the development of knowledge about population issues in the overall development context.

Youngest African States Hold Population Training Seminar

For the first time since many of them became independent less than 10 years ago, representatives of five African countries whose official language is Portuguese (Angola, Mozambique, Guinea-Bissau, Cape Verde, Sao Tome and Principe) and Spanish-speaking Equatorian Guinea met to discuss their mutual concerns in matters of population and development, with emphasis on the role of communication. The meeting, organized by Unesco with financing from the United Nations Fund for Population Activities (UNFPA) from November 12 to December 6,1984, in Maputo, People's Republic of Mozambique, was attended by high-ranking officials from Ministries of Health, National Planning and Education, and by representatives of women's organizations. UNDP, ILO and Unicef also sent observers as did the Lisbon-based Commission of Portuguese Women. Work sessions were devoted to the relation of population and natural resources with regard to the satisfaction of basic needs, elimination of hunger, disease, ignorance and unemployment. Particular stress was placed on the development of programmes for maternal and child care, and on the training of specialized personnel responsible for furthering the participation of women in the life of the country.

Co-action Programme Highlights Youth and Women

Youth and women occupied a special place in 1985 in Unesco's Cooperative Action (Co-Action) Programme, through which individuals or associations could participate directly in development. In 1984, over $586,000 was made available to about 75 projects which range from "Mothers' Clubs" (UCA/73) in Bolivia, carried out with the Confederation de Clubes de Madres de Bolivia, to "Vocational

Courses for Young Blind People" (UCA/614) supported in collaboration with the World Blind Union. In the 1985 Co-Action catalogue, contributors could choose from a long list of projects, corresponding to a wide, but always urgent, variety of needs. "Water for All" (UCA/71), a project in which Unesco is collaborating with the Associated Country Women of the World (ACWW), is, for instance, improving the provision of drinking water and sanitation in many countries.

Harmonizing Population Growth and Development Goals in Cape Verde

After Independence (in 1975), Cape Verde, an archipelago of nine inhabited islands off the coast of Senegal, is suffering from growing pains. The annual population growth rate of 1.6 per cent is low when compared to that of over 4 per cent in Kenya or over 3 per cent for Africa as a whole. Yet, according to data collected during Phase I of the Unesco/UNFPA (UN Fund for Population Activities) project for "Family and Sex Education", an estimated population increase from 300,000 to over 380,000 by the year 2000, or over 400,000 by 2025, could seriously jeopardize development goals in the small, densely populated country. Massive emigration, once a safety valve, has slowed due to the world recession, and, in any case, planners aim at providing living conditions which would make emigration unnecessary. To take stock of the situation, and formulate an Action Plan in line with Phase II of the Unesco/UNFPA project, 60 representatives of government bodies, women's, youth and religious organizations...met from April 22 to 26, 1985, in Praia, the capital. The plan called for urgent measures, including both in-school and out-of-school courses in family and sex education, counselling centres, and greater participation of women in the development process. Of the 74 projects in population education or communication which Unesco is currently executing in collaboration with UNFPA on the global, regional, or national - in 43 Member States - level, 23 are in Africa.

Unesco and WHO Collaborate to Increase Media Involvement in Health Education

Recognizing the mass media as a major determining factor in shaping public attitudes and awareness about health and nutrition, Unesco and the World Health Organization (WHO) have, since 1984, pooled their expertise in a vast project to increase involvement of the media in this sector. Two initial phases, carried out in 11 Asian countries, resulted in innovative and successful country-level health and nutrition education projects employing a variety of designs and approaches ranging from radio listening groups to promotion campaigns through rural Press to the training of media professionals in health education. A third phase (1986-1988) has been launched with two round-tables for decision-makers in education, health and information services in 17 French-speaking countries - in Yaounde, Cameroon (November 25-28, 1986) for eight Central African countries, end in Dakar, Senegal (December 1-5, 1986) for nine countries in West Africa. At the meetings, financed by the French Foreign Ministry, the Canadian International Development Agency (CIDA) and a $25,000 contribution from Unesco's International Programme for the Development of Communication (IPDC), participants laid plans for national level mass media/public health pilot projects.

Intensive Seminar on Population Education

An Intensive Seminar on Population Education was held in Dakar (Senegal) from July 7 to August 1, 1986, and was attended by 31 specialists from 10 West African countries, Morocco, Tunisia and Haiti. The Seminar, which preceded a similar meeting for East African Member States (September 8-30) in Nairobi (Kenya), was largely devoted to the training of teachers, methods and the inclusion in materials used in general education, literacy and post-literacy programmes of subject-matter related to population problems. At both meetings, emphasis was placed on the close interrelationship of these problems with the quality of life, the environment, nutrition and health, ethical and human rights concerns and the role of women in development. While Africa is still sparsely populated when compared to Asia, the continent's population growth rate of 3 per cent (against 1.8 per cent for Asia, 2.3 per cent for Latin America) is the world's highest. About one-third (28) of the 90 national, regional or global projects in population education or communication being executed by Unesco in collaboration with the UN Fund for Population Activities (UNFPA) are in Africa. Since close cooperation with the UNFPA began in 1970, Unesco has assisted in formulation and implementation of $60 million of UNFPA-funded projects. With world population now over the five billion mark, this collaboration is being intensified, both in terms of activities and expenditure - from $11,300,000 in UNFPA-funding for Unesco's 1984-85 biennium to $ 14 million for 1986-87 period.

RECENT UNESCO PUBLICATIONS

Human rights aspects of population programmes with special reference to human right law

1977,154pp.,figs., ISBN 92-3-101487-0.

Immigrant Workers in Europe : Their legal status

A comparative study by Eric-Jean Thomas, Study Director, 1982, 245pp., tables, ISBN 92-3-101867-1.

Shows how the status of immigrant workers is determined with reference to the economic, political and social conditions peculiar to each host country and particularly, how the legal machinery controlling immigration affects the future of migrants. Chapters discuss the specific situation in Belgium, France, the Netherlands, the Federal Republic of Germany, Sweden and Turkey.

Living in two cultures

The socio-cultural situation of migrant workers and their families.

1982,325pp., tables, ISBN 92-3-101869-8. Co-published with Gower Publishing Co. Ltd., who have exclusive sales rights in the United Kingdom.

A collection of studies on the social and cultural situation of immigrants in Europe and the United States. Part One is concerned with conditions, nature and their families in the United States and Europe. Part Two addresses the particular problems faced by female migrants and how the characteristics of the old culture affect their adaptation to the requirements of the new.

A manual on evaluation on population communication programmes

(Population Communication Manuals, 2), 1981,129pp., ISBN 92-3-101559-1.

A manual on mass media in population and development (Population Communication manuals, 1), 1977, 105pp. ISBM 92-3-101512-5.

Why people move

Comparative perspectives on the dynamics of internal migration. Edited by Jorge Balan, 1981, 342pp., figs, tables, ISBN 92-3-101909-0.

An examination of the relationships between migratory movements and development which assesses the policy implications of these movements and identifies needs for future research. Contents include a discussion of the ways in which the causes and consequences of migration are studied; specific country studies on the relationship between migration and development at a societal, family and community level; case studies that focus on rural-urban interactions; specific discussions of policies and alternatives.

ELEVEN

UNESCO AND HUMAN RIGHTS AND PEACE

Objectives

Preparing reports on the world situation in the fields covered by the Unesco Declaration on Race and Racial Prejudice.

Formulating methods for combating violations of Human Rights.

Strengthening collaboration with United Nations bodies and with universities, research centres and non-governmental organizations for the promotion of Human Rights.

Promoting teaching of Human Rights.

Promoting disarmament education.

Conducting studies on military research and development.

Collaborating with the International Peach Research Association, the Latin American Peace Research Council and the Asian Peace Research Association.

Awarding the Unesco Prize for Peace Education.

Publication of books on Peace and Conflict Studies.

In 1978 the first International Congress on the Teaching of Human Rights was held in Vienna at the invitation of Austrian Government. At this major event nearly 300 participants from more than 60 countries adopted by consensus a final document setting out

10 principles which should guide human rights teaching at all levels, a series of suggestions regarding teaching programmes and methods, and three major recommendations:

1. The preparation by a committee of experts of a six-year plan for developing human rights teaching:

2. A study of the desirability of drawing up an international convention in this field;

3. The establishment within Unesco, and with the support of the General Assembly of the United Nations, of a voluntary fund for the development of knowledge of human rights through education and information.

The Vienna Congress was followed up by resolutions of the Twentieth Session of the General Conference, one of which invited the Director General to give high priority to the teaching of human rights in the Organization's programme and to explore the possibility of setting up a voluntary fund which would serve the entire United Nations system, Member States and all institutions concerned.

In order to develop the study and teaching of human rights at university level, Unesco issued in French a publication on the Internation Dimensions of Human Rights, which is intended for faculties of law and political science. For the same purpose a Unesco Prize for the Teaching of Human Rights was established by the Executive Board on the occasion of the 30th anniversary of the Universal Declaration of Human Rights. It is awarded to educational institutions, organizations or individuals that have made a particularly deserving and effective contribution to the development of human rights teaching, and will make it possible to encourage new initiatives in this field.

In June,1978, a meeting of experts on human rights, human needs and the establishment of a new international economic order was held at Unesco. A part of the programme of research into the reasons for violations of human rights and the socio-economic phenomena which affect the exercise of such rights, it was convened in order to establish criteria for determining the human rights which it would seem necessary to recognize within the context of a new international economic order. The participants recommended that Unesco consider the establishment of an advisory group, the composition of which would reflect the different approaches to the interdependent issues connected with human rights, human needs and a new international economic order.

In July, 1978, a committee of experts on the concept of race in history met in Montreal to study the origins of racist attitudes and practices, so that they could be denounced and eradicated.

The meeting specifically called for recognition of the right to be different - a right involving not only the equality in dignity and rights of all human beings and all peoples, but also asserting the rights of such minority groups as migrant workers.

At the culmination of a long effort of research and analysis a Declaration on Race and Racial Prejudice was adopted by the General Conference at its twentieth session by acclamation.

Article II of the Declaration lays down that any theory claiming superiority or inferiority for any racial or ethnic group "has no scientific foundation and is contrary to the moral and ethical principles of humanity". *Article IV specifically condemns apartheid as a crime against humanity which gravely disturbs international peace and security.*

The text of the Declaration which was adopted by consensus at an intergovernmental conference in March,1978, attended by 99 Member States raises to the status of an international legal definition a number of principles which Unesco has been promoting ever since its foundation. For, by its Constitution Unesco is bound to work for all peoples "without distinction of race, sex, language or religion".

Since it was on account of this doctrine that South Africa left the Organization in 1956, it was only natural that Unesco should play an active part in the Anti-Apartheid Year, which began on March 21,1978. Speaking to some 1,500 people at the inaugural ceremony at Unesco's headquarters, the Director General denounced apartheid as "the vilest form of modern slavery" which was turning South Africa into a huge concentration camp, and he called for "a peaceful mobilization of public opinion to end this shame to the whole of humanity".

In addition Unesco prepared publications on the situation of women and of the Press in South Africa, as well as a revised edition of *Apartheid : its effects on education, science and communication*. It also launched three studies on South African methods of organizing pro-apartheid pressure groups abroad, on the inculcation of the racist ideology through school textbooks, and violations of human rights in South Africa.

Finally, as part of its drive to make the evils of apartheid known,the Organization staged an exhibition, distributed photographs and posters, and produced and distributed one million copies of a pamphlet for the general public entitled *Apartheid in Black and While.*

Also in 1978 a working group set up by the Executive Board to "study the procedures which should be followed in the examination of cases and questions which might be submitted to Unesco concerning the exercise of human rights in the spheres of its competence, in order to make its action more effective", drew up a draft decision setting forth such procedures, which was adopted by the Board by consensus.

Finally, the studies made by social science specialists from the region on ethnic group relations in Bolivia, Chile, Mexico and the English-speaking Caribbean Countries and originally published in 1977 in English under the title *Race and Class in Post-Colonial Society* were published in Spanish in 1978. They examine the extent to which the relationship between race or ethnicity and social stratification has been affected by the colonial structure during the post-colonial period and the extent to which changes in the economy have facilitated the social mobility of certain groups.

Racism, however, is only one of the major problems which it is Unesco's task to help resolve. The social science encompasses many different disciplines and a large part of the Organization's programme is aimed at applying the methods and knowledge of those disciplines to such questions as development, population, environment, involvement of youth and overriding aim of *building a peaceful world.*

At its 17th session the Unesco General Conference recommended that the Director General encourage research on "the dangers to man and his environment inherent in modern armaments and techniques of warfare". As an aid to researchers, students and administrators of the developing countries, Unesco prepared two annotated bibliographies illustrating current trends of research in this area. The first, on the social and economic consequences of the arms race and of disarmament, was published, in English, French and Spanish, in the series *Reports and papers in the social sciences.* The second, concerning the dangers to man and his environment inherent in modern armaments and techniques of warfare, was published under the auspices of the International Peace Research Association in Oslo.

Recent Activities in the Field of Human Rights

A symposium to examine pseudo-scientific theories to justify Racism and Racial Discrimination was held at Athens in 1981. The experts reviewed the principal findings of recent studies in such disciplines as anthropology, ethnology, biology and psychology and drafted the Athens Appeal. The proceedings of the symposium were published.

2. A meeting of experts on the Analysis of the Basis and Forms of Individual and Collective Action by which Violations of Human Rights can be combated was held at Freetown (Sierra Leone) in 1981. In addition to the analysis, participants considered sanctions that might be applied at both domestic and international levels against such violations, especially those connected with apartheid and colonialism.

3. Unesco gave financial assistance to Artists of the World against Apartheid for the organization of an exhibition in Paris in December, 1983.

4. A meeting held in Algiers in 1982, attended by experts and 16 representatives or observers from intergovernmental and non-governmental organizations, studied the potential influence of certain private authorities, in particular transnational corporations, as factors limiting human rights and the rights of people at both national and international levels.

5. Assistance has been given to the international commission of jurists for the preparation and publication of a study comparing the principles proclaimed in the Universal Declaration of Human Rights with the real situation in South Africa.

6. Regional meetings have been held on the subject of ethnodevelopment and ethnocide. The first, concerning Latin America, was held at San Jose (Costa Rica) in 1981. The second concerning Africa was held at Quagadaugou (Upper Volta) in 1983. The third concerning Europe was held in Karasjok (Norway) in 1983. These meetings were attended by anthropologists, educationists, historians, linguists and sociologists.

7. Financial support was given for the International Symposium on the theme "Rights of Solidarity and the Rights of People" held at San Marino in 1982.

8. A meeting of experts on improving the exercise of human rights in urban areas was held at Cairo (Arab Republic of Egypt) in 1983 with the support of the Arab Regional Centre for Social Sciences (ARCSS)

9. A meeting of experts was held in Strasbourg (France) in 1982 regarding teaching of human rights.

10. Cooperation with the International Institute of Human Rights, Strasbourg (France), has enabled many university human rights teachers from developing countries to participate in the Institute's re-training session.

11. To promote the establishment of institutions capable of engaging in teaching and research activities in the field of

human rights, Unesco has organized three regional training seminars in Asia and the Pacific, Latin America and the Caribbean and Africa.

12. A symposium on the rights of refugees was organized in Tokyo in 1981 in cooperation with the United Nations Commission for Refugees and the United Nations University.

13. In the field of disarmament education, a phased action plan was drawn up at an international consultation of experts at the Headquarters in August 1981.

14. Three regional seminars on disarmament have taken place; the first in 1981 in Caracas (Venezuela), the second in 1982 in Jakarta (Indonesia) and the third in 1983 in Dakar (Senegal).

15. A Seminar on Scientists, the Arms Race and Disarmament was organized in Ajaccio (France) in 1982, in collaboration with the Pugwash Movement.

16. Besides experts, representatives of the United Nations Centre for Disarmament, the United Nations Institute for Disarmament Research and the United Nations University as well as observers from Member States and non-governmental organizations also took part in a meeting held at the Headquarters in November, 1982, on different perceptions of the threat of war and different conceptions of security.

17. An international symposium on the role of the media concerning disarmament was organized in 1981 in Nairobi (Kenya).

18. A study on the axiological content of images of war and peace was carried out by the "Institute detudes et de researchers interethniques et interculturelles" of the University of Nice (France).

19. Collaboration with the International Peace Research Association, the Latin American Peace Research Council and the Asian Peace Research Association has been strengthened.

The activities of the Chilean Peace Research Association and the Brazilian Peace Research Association have been supported and a contribution made towards the creation of a Peruvian Peace Research Association.

20. The Unesco Prize for Peace Education was awarded for the first time in 1981.

SELECT UNESCO PUBLICATIONS ON HUMAN RIGHTS AND PEACE

Apartheid: A teacher's guide

By Godfrey N. Brown, 1981, 104pp., illus., tables, ISBN 92-3-101896-5.

A handbook for teachers presenting essential facts concerning apartheid and its effects, and international and national efforts to eleminate it. Seventeen accompanying "Apartheid Exercises" aim at stimulating students' individual awareness of the problem.

Apartheid and social research

Edited by John Rex, 1981, 199pp., tables, ISBN 92-3-101898-1.

A series of articles written by social scientists within the Republic of South Africa which seek to analyse the effects of apartheid on social science training and research.

Apartheid : Power and historical falsification

By Marianne Cornevin (Insights, 3), 1980, 144pp., ISBN 92-3-101769-1.

Armaments, arms control and disarmament

A Unesco reader for disarmament education edited by Marek Thee, 1981 446pp., fig., tables, ISBN 92-3-101920-1.

A comprehensive reader aiming to further the cause of disarmaments education with contributions from eminent individuals and organizations around the world. Contents include : basic data and information about armament build-up and efforts at arms control and disarmament; a historical perspective; and analysis of the nature and dynamics of the arms race; a view of the relationship between disarmament and development efforts; an outline of alternative strategies; a balanced view from East, West, North and South.

Becoming aware : human rights and the family

By Margaret Gallagher, 1984, 102 pp., ISBN 92-3-102178-8.

Consensus and Peace

Amadou-Mahtar M'Bow, Mario Amadeo, Gerald Antoine Rachid Daker, Asbjorn Eide, Mihajlo Javorski, Joaquin Ruiz-Gimenez and Abdoulaye Wade; edited by Eseart Kiffle Selassie, 1980, 231pp., ISBN 92-3-101851-5.

Human rights, questions and answers by Leah

Bv Levin, 1981, 86pp., illus, ISBN 92-3-101957-0.

A booklet containing answers to basic questions on the meaning of internationally recognized human rights and the procedures which exist for their implementation. Describes the scope and meaning of international human rights and explains the meaning of each article of the Universal Declaration of Human Rights. Illustrated by the famous French political cartoonist, Plantu

Human Rights, aspects of population programmes with special reference to human rights law

1977, 154pp., ISBN 92-3-1487-0.

Human rights in urban areas

1983, 169pp., tables. ISBN 92-3-101983-X

An analysis of the obstacles encountered in the implementation of human rights in urban areas. Part One investigates the factors responsible for the marginalization of such groups as the elderly poor, vagrant children, ethnic minorities, immigrants and nomads. Part Two discusses the projects that local authorities might implement to rectify the structural injustices which victimize these people.

The International Dimensions of Human Rights

General editor : Karel Vasak; Revised and edited by Philip Alston, 1982, 755pp., ISBN 92-3-101477-3 (2 Volumes, not sold separately) hardbound. Co-published with Greenwood Press, Inc., Westport, Conn., which has exclusive sales rights in the United States.

This collective work presents a diversity of views and is intended for use in the teaching of human rights in faculties of law and political sciences. It is the result of Unesco's efforts to further the systematic study and development of an independent scientific discipline of human rights at university level, taking into account the principal legal systems of the world.

The book is structured around the two principal international dimensions of human rights : standard-setting and enforcement. Part One deals with the principles of self-determination, equality and non-discrimination and explains the meaning of economic, social and cultural as well as civil and political rights. Part Two deals with the enforcement of these norms through universal institutions (essentially the United Nations system) and regional institutions in Europe, the Americas, Arab States, Africa, socialist countries and Asia.

Obstacles to disarmament and ways of overcoming them

Edited by Swadesh Rana (Insights, 7), 1981, 233pp., ISBN 92-3-101879-5.

A contribution to Unesco's campaign to launch disarmament education during the second Disarmament Decade proclaimed for the 1980s.

The essays contained in this publication were prepared for an expert meeting that Unesco convened in April 1978. They aim at providing educators amd the general public with materials that may be used in the classroom or in more informal discussion environments.

Race and class in post-colonial society

1977, 458pp., figs., tables, ISBN 92-3-101445-5.

Race relations and mental health

By Marie Jahoda, 1960, 2nd impr., 1961). 48pp., ISBN 92-3-100444-1.

Racism and apartheid in Southern Africa and Namibia

1974, 156pp., ISBN, 92-93-10199-5.

Racism, science and pseudoscience

1983, 158 pp., figs., tables, ISBN 92-3-101993-7.

Scientists, the arms race and disarmament

A Unesco/Pugwash symposium. General editor : Joseph Rotblat, 1982, 323pp., figs., tables, ISBN 92-3-102021-8. Co-published with Taylor & Francis Ltd, who have exclusive sales rights in the United Kingdom.

A group of eminent scientists and scholars consider the involvement of scientists in military undertakings, particularly with reference to nuclear weapons. Chapters discuss: the role of science and technology in the arms race; social responsibility of scientists; measures to encourage scientists to be actively concerned with disarmament.

Social implications of the peaceful uses of nuclear energy

Edited by Otto Klineberg, 1964, 169pp., ISBN 92-3-100583-7

Suicide or survival? The challenge of the year 2000

1978, 287pp., ISBN 92-3-102124-9

Threats of modern warfare to man and his environment

An annotated bibliography, 1979, 25pp., ISBN 929-3-101608-3

Unesco yearbook on peace and conflict studies 1982

1983, 269pp., ISBN 92-3-102119-2

Unesco yearbook on peace and conflict studies 1983

1985, 285pp., ISBN 92-3-102282-2. Co-published with Greenwood Press Inc., who have exclusive sales rights in the United States and Canada.

A new annual series investigating a wide range of topics relevant to the study of conflict and conflict prevention by groups, societies, and the world at large.

The 1981 Yearbook contains four sections: trends and approaches in peace and conflict studies; a bibliographical essay providing background documentation on non-violent action and civilian-based defence; the peace-related activities of Unesco highlighting the World Congress on Disarmament Educations institutional developments at the international, regional and national levels.

The 1982 Yearbook is designed to stimulate reflection on the approaches to teaching and research. The section on "Applications of Peace Research" includes an essay on "Peace and the Apartheid System : Militarization and Conflict Formation in South Africa".

The 1983 volume concentrates on perception of threat and definitions of security. It also contains a unique theoretical and bibliographical survey.

Violation of human rights : possible rights of resource and forms of resistance

1984, 236pp., ISBN 92-3-102114-1

Based on a 1981 Unesco symposium, this collection brings together the views of eight international experts who deal with the legal, political, philosophical, sociological and historical aspects of the age-old concept of the right to resistance in an attempt to define its limits and to suggest peaceful means of action against the abuse of power. Among the topics explored are: the ways in which this right is likely to develop and compel recognition in both general and international law, notably with respect to racism, apartheid and genocide; the role of non-governmental organizations and liberation movements; political, legal and economic sanctions, both national and international.

Violence and its causes : Methodological and theoretical aspects of recent research on violence

1980, 269., ISBN 92-3-101809-4

Women and racial discrimination in Rhodesia

By A.K.H. Weinrich, 1979, 143pp., figs., tables, ISBN 92-3-101621-0

TWELVE

UNESCO : STATUS OF WOMEN AND THEIR PARTICIPATION IN DEVELOPMENT

Objectives

Undertaking research to throw light on factors contributing to the perpetuation of discrimination against women in various societies.

Analysing the social practices which promote the application of the Convention on the Elimination of all Forms of Discrimination against women in various cultural contexts.

Conducting studies to get information on action by national institutions and women's groups for formulation and application of innovatory legislation based on the principles and concepts of the Convention.

Examining the forms of women's participation in political life; economic, cultural and political variables that inhibit or strengthen women's participation in political life; and the relationship of women's movements to political parties and institutions.

Organizing seminars on the women's participation in political and public life.

Taking up research to find out the interrelations between the status of women and certain socio-economic phenomena on the situation of women, remaining as de facto heads of households in the communities of origin in situations of male migrations.

Encouraging research on the role of women in peace. Analysing the role of women in national liberation-struggles.

Undertaking research on the role of women in national reconstruction.

Organizing meetings of women researchers and university professors of sociology, anthropology, law, psychology, economics and history.

Recent Unesco Activities Relating to Status of Women and their Participation in Development

1. Studies have been conducted in 15 countries in different regions to analyse the social practices which impede or promote the application of the Convention on the Elimination of All Forms of Discrimination against Women in various cultural contexts.

2. An international meeting of experts on "The participation of women in political life and the means of increasing this participation was held at Lisbon in 1983.

3. Studies on the forms of women's participation in political variables that inhibit or strengthen women's participation in political life have been undertaken and results of some of these studies published in a special issue of the *International Social Science Journal* (No. 98, 1983) on the theme "Women in Power Spheres", as well as in the issue of *Cultures* on the theme "Women on the Move - Towards What" (Vol.VIII, No. 4, 1982).

4. The theme of women's participation in political and public life has also been the subject of three meetings organized in Europe through the National Commissions an international seminar on "The participation of women in decision-making " (Belgrade, 1982); a European seminar on "Women's participation in social and political life" (Bonn, 1982), and a European workshop on "Strategies for Power : Methods and measures by which women can become participants in making public policies" (Ottawa, 1983).

5. Multidisciplinary research in sociology, anthropology, economics and law have been carried out in Algeria, Italy, Spain and Turkey to identify the different historical, economic, legal and cultural variables which affect the position and role of women in those societies.

6. Many studies on the interrelationships between the status of women and certain socio-economic phenomena on the situation of women remaining as de facto heads of households have been carried out in Greece, Italy, Portugal, Turkey, Bangladesh, India, the Philippines, Republic of Korea and Thailand.

7. Studies have been undertaken by women specialists on the experience of newly independent countries in Africa and of national liberation movements recognized by OAU. The results of these studies were discussed at a regional meeting of experts held in 1983 in Bissau (Guinea-Bissaau).

8. A seminar on "Women's studies programme in Latin America and the Caribbean" was held in 1981 in Rio de Janeiro (Brazil).

9. A meeting of experts was organized on "Multidisciplinary research on women in the Arab World" in 1981 in Tunis. This meeting brought together for the first time researchers from 12 countries of the Arab State Region.

10. A Unesco regional meeting on "Women's studies and social sciences" in Asia was organized in New Delhi in October, 1982.

11. Financial contribution was made for the organization of a seminar by the Association of African Women for Research and Development on "Research on African Women: What types of methodology"? in Dakar in 1983.

Women in Decision-making roles

Are women gradually playing a greater role in deciding how to run a country or a corporation? or are they still confined to subordinate positions, making decisions only when it comes to running a household or raising a child? To answer these questions and act accordingly, 18 experts from 17 countries took part in an international seminar, organized by Unesco in Dubrovnik, Yugoslavia, from December 10 to 14, 1984. Before planning for the future, the participants, leading professional women from all regions, heard reports on factors influencing women's access to decision-making roles in widely different situations. Openings and barriers to women's participation in political life were examined in such far-flung countries as Denmark, Sri Lanka, Canada, Kuwait and the Gulf States, or viewed in the light of the transition from traditional to modern society in Nigeria or Samoa. Other speakers assessed women's position with regard to the trade and commerce sector in West Africa, the labour force in Brazil, the workers self-management system in Yugoslavia or in scientific fields in Bulgaria, India and Argentina. Finally, the discussion focused on measures and strategies for increasing women's level and range of responsibilities - the relative weight which might be placed on the educational process or on State intervention, or the role which might be played by women's movements, political parties, trade unions.

UN Women's Decade

Unesco's diary-desk calendar for 1986 marked the end of the UN Decade for Women (1976-1985) and highlighted Unesco's Major Programme XIV - the Status of Women. Genevieve Claisse, a prominent member of the school of geometric abstraction, designed the cover for the diary which, in English or French, sells for 50 FF and, along with lots of space for appointments and notes, contains photos and useful information, including addresses of women's groups worldwide. All proceeds will go, through Unesco's Co-Action Programme, to national or international women's organizations for self-help projects in the least developed countries. Among these, the World Young Women's Christian Association (WYWCA), for instance, is teaching young women on the chronically drought-stricken Fijian island of Vanua to build reinforced concrete water tanks, and creating jobs for them as teachers of the method (UCA-15). Another project (UCA-14), for an innovative rural training centre for women, is sponsored by the Guinea-Bissau

Democratic Union of Women.

SELECT UNESCO PUBLICATIONS ON THE STATUS OF WOMEN AND THEIR PARTICIPATION IN DEVELOPMENT

Bibliographic guide to studies on the Status of Women Development and Population Trends

(Women in a world perspective), 1983, 292p., ISBN 92-3-102122-2.

Co-published with Bowker Publishing Company, Epping and Unipub, New York.

An annotated bibliography of recent research and world literature on the status of women in every geocultural region. Apart from published material, covers unpublished untranslated works written in local languages, theses, unpublished documents and up-to-date information on institutions undertaking research and major events related to the field of women's studies, each regional section compiled by women social scientists of the area itself.

Women and racial discrimination in Rhodesia

By A.K.H. Weinrich, 1979.

Women as heads of households in the Caribbean : Family structure and feminine status

By Joycelin Massiah (Women in a world perspective), 1983, 69pp., ISBN 92-3-102047-1.

A surprising one-third of households in the Caribbean are headed by women. This study gives valuable insights into the composition of such households, the reasons for their existence, their problems and the multiple survival strategies employed by women in such a position.

Social Science Research and Women in the Arab World

1984, 250 pp., ISBN 92-3-102140-0.

Co-published with Frances Pinter (Publishers) Ltd., who have exclusive sales rights in the United Kingdom (and from whom a hardbound edition is available). Eight studies carried out by Arab women social scientists focus on the state of research on women in the Arab world and ways in which future research could be made more relevant to the concerns and needs of women in the region.

Women and work in Uruguay

By Graciela Taglioretti (Women in a world perspective), 1984, 80pp., ISBN 92-3-102110-9.

This case study of Uruguay indicates a significant correlation between international migration and a substantial increase in female participation in the labour force, implying that women operate as a replacement labour force and achieve mobility only under such conditions.

Women in the villages, men in the towns

(Women in a world perspective), 1984, 526pp., illus., ISBN 92-3-102039-0.

A pioneering, cross-cultural study of the women whose men have left them behind in rural areas to supplement the family income in the cities of five Asian countries : Bangladesh, India, the Republic of Korea, the Philippines and Thailand. Women social scientists of each nation analyse the vast range of changes in the social organization of the family, both nuclear and extended : its authority structures, its economy, the participation of its women in the social and political life of the community, the vitality of the village itself.

Women on the move: contemporary changes in family and society

(Women in a world perspective), 1984, 324pp., ISBN 92-3-102157-5.

The fruit of a 1980 Unesco meeting on women, development and population trends, this collection of 17 studies by women social scientists covering a broad range of societies demonstrates how, too often, the benefits of modernization lead to a deterioration of women's status. Divided into five sections, the book deals first with the consequences of rural transformations for women's productive and reproductive roles, next with women in internal and international migration, then turns to patterns of women's employment and the adjustments necessary to reconcile their jobs with their domestic lives. The final section illustrates how women's issues tend to be defined in terms of the society's broader priorities, these priorities being in turn a reflection of the country's particular level and chosen path of development.

THIRTEEN

UNESCO AND YOUTH

Objectives

Conducting studies on the main trends in youth problems and aspirations, at regional and international levels.

Cooperating with Member States in the promotion of research on topics such as role of young researchers.

Holding Regional Workshops on the elaboration and promotion of indicators in the analysis and planning of programmes for youth.

Organizing symposiums on children and the family.

Holding consultations with non-governmental youth organizations.

Cooperating with National Commissions, Youth Ministries and non-government organizations with a view to engaging in activities designed to strengthen existing and/or creating new structures and organizations for young people, particularly in the developing countries.

Cooperating with non-governmental youth organizations and National Commissions in an endeavour to strengthen young people's activities for international understanding, peace, human rights and the establishment of a new economic order and against colonialism, racism and apartheid.

Holding information courses for senior officials of youth Ministries or of youth and student organizations for giving the participants a better insight into Unesco's activities.

Promoting voluntary service by young people in projects for development and cooperation among young people throughout the world.

Undertaking consultancy missions to cooperate in the preparation or evaluation of national programmes related to disadvantaged young people.

Giving the youth and student leaders travel grants.

Unesco's Recent Activities Relating to Youth

1. The Arab regional meeting on youth was held in Tunis (Tunisia) in December 1981. Twentyseven specialists from 14 Arab countries and of the Palestine Liberation Organization participated in the meeting and discussed the socio-economic problems of urban youth and the role which young people can play in cultural development.

2. A round-table on "Youth in 1980's" was held in Costinesti (Romania) in June 1982. Its main purpose was to identify, within Unesco's fields of competence, new topics for study and new prospects for action concerning youth in the various regions of the world, particularly in relation to the International Youth Year in 1985.

3. Unesco cooperated with Member States in the promotion of research on topics such as the role of young researchers in Yugoslavia; the "Nueva Carcion" as a form of cultural expression among young people in Latin America and the Caribbean and the role and participation of youth in development in Hungary.

4. A Regional Workshop on the Elaboration and Promotion of Indicators in the Analysis and Planning of Programmes for youth was held in Colombo (Sri Lanka) in 1983, with participants from 10 countries of the region, as well as representatives from the United Nations Specialized Agencies and ob-

servers from non-governmental organizations.

5. An international symposium on children and the family, particularly in the developing countries, in an age of change was organized in Munich in 1982 by the National Commission for Unesco and the University of Munich in close cooperation with Unesco Secretariat. The meeting received financial support from the Federal Republic of Germany. The symposium contributed to expanding the international network of studies on children and family.

6. A Regional Seminar on "The Evolution of the Family in African Contexts" was organized in Maseru (Lesotho), in conjunction with the National Commission for Unesco and the National University of Lesotho.

7. A study on changes in family structures in Africa, particularly Zaire, was undertaken in cooperation with the Centre for the Coordination of Social Science Research and Documentation in Africa south of the Sahara (CERDAS).

8. Training seminars for youth leaders have been organized and meetings arranged between such leaders and between those in charge of youth exchange programmes in Unesco Clubs.

9. Technical and financial support has been provided to the European Federation for Inter-cultural Learning (EFIL) for the organization of an international seminar on the cultural dimension of the North-South dialogue in 1983 at Ouagadougo (Upper Volta).

10. The first Meso-American Congress of young environmentalists was organized in 1981 at the Honduras.

11. Many information courses have been held at the Headquarters for senior officials of youth Ministries or of youth and student organizations.

12. A meeting of senior officials from the countries of the Indian Ocean was organized in 1983 in Reunion, on Unesco's initia-

tive, with a view to promoting subregional cooperation in youth affairs.

13. Projects have been designed to develop activities for the disadvantaged young people in the Member States - Angola, Bolivia, Cape Verde, Gambia, Hungary, Liberia, Madagascar, Maldives, Maxico, Nicaragua, Rwanda, Sri Lanka, Zaire and Zimbabwe.

Attitudes of Young People in China to Family Formation

This study, commissioned by Unesco, was carried out in urban and rural areas in Beijing and Sichuan by the China Sociology Institute, Academy of Sciences of China, in collaboration with the Institute of Juvenile Studies. It brings out for the first time the attitudes of young Chinese people between the ages of 15 and 30 to family formation, notably the number of children desired and gives some remarkable insights into the varying attitude changes to traditional values and customs according to rural or urban setting, education levels, types of employment, economic status and proximity to centres of economic and social development. It also provides insights into the population policies and programmes of the People's Republic of China and the perception thereof by young men and women - particularly the latter - living in differing social and cultural conditions. Being the first of its kind, this study offers testimony of the thoroughness of Chinese researchers in developing their own methodology and their desire to examine the question of family formation from all possible angles. In English and Chinese, 127 pages, it is available free of charge on request from the Population Division, Social and Human Sciences Sector, Unesco, Paris.

World Youth Congress in International Youth Year

Some 600 participants from over 10 Member States, including many top governmental officials in charge of youth programmes, and representatives of 60 youth international non-governmental organizations, attended Unesco's "World Congress on Youth" held in Barcelona (Spain) from July 8 to 15, 1985. The Congress, one of the most important events to mark the International Youth Year, was opened by H.M. King Juan Carlos. The inaugural ceremony was also attended by Mr. Felipe Gonzalez, Prime Minister of Spain, and the Director General of Unesco. The essential part of the Congress's work was conducted in three commissions dealing with Youth in relation to : education and work, cultural development, and mutual understanding and international cooperation. In preparation for the meeting, Unesco, which places action in favour of young people at the heart of its programmes, organized five regional meetings, successively in Venice (Italy) in 1977, Kathmandu(Nepal) in 1978, Nairobi (Kenya) in 1979, Bridgetown (Barbados) in 1980, and Tunis (Tunisia) in 1981. Participants at the congress also took into account the conclusions of the round-tables on "Youth in 1980's" organized in Costinesti (Romania) in June 1982.

Unesco Consultation with Youth Movements held in Rhodes

About 50 representatives of 40 international nongovernmental youth organizations held a collective consultation with Unesco in Rhodes from September 11 to 14, 1985. At the meeting, which followed an International Youth Forum organized there and on the island of Halki by the Government of Greece (September 5-10), participants evaluated and planned follow-up to the International Youth Year 1985, using data collected, analysed and presented at the World Youth Congress in Barcelona in July 1985. On this occasion, young people aged 15 to 24, who in 1984 numbered 921 million, 734 million in developing countries, were identified as a "permanent social category particularly sensitive to changes in the contemporary world". The 71 youth NGOs having consultative status with Unesco students, workers in industry or agriculture, young disabled, religious (Catholics, Quakers, YMCA, etc.), Scouts, Youth Hostels, exchange (Experiment in International Living, etc.), volunteers (Coordinating Committee for International Voluntary Service/CCIVS, etc.) etc., collaborate closely with the Youth Division and other Sectors in the preparation and implementation of programme activities, notably through annual collective consultations set up in 1975. A working group maintains this essential contact between consultations.

Conference of Rural Youth from 31 Countries in Ghana

Young men and women from 31 countries met in Accra (Ghana) from November 6 to 12, 1986,at a conference devoted to the

"Mobilization of Rural Youth". The meeting was a follow-up to the International Youth Year when it was clearly recognized that while a vast majority of world youth live in rural areas, this segment of the population is rarely part of the mainstream of national and international life. The young participants, from all regions, shared experiences and discussed the best ways for increasing the participation of rural youth in the development process and promoting an awareness of their crucial role in alerting opinion to contemporary concerns, fostering international understanding and cooperation, and human rights as necessary components of peace and development. The conference was organized in cooperation with Unesco by the Coordinating Committee for International Voluntary Service (CCIVS) and hosted by one of its 110 Member Organizations (in 52 countries), the Voluntary Work camps Association of Ghana (VOLU).

SELECT UNESCO PUBLICATIONS

Two studies on unemployment among educated young people

Part I : Unemployment among educated young people in the developed market economy countries by Simone Morio.

Part II : Unemployment among educated young people in the French-speaking developing countries by Yarrise Zoctizoum, 1980, 133pp., tables, ISBN 92-3-101618-0.

Young People and Cultural Institutions

A Unesco survey. Eight young people give their views on the cultural institutions in their countries, 1980, 87pp., ISBN 92-3-101698-9.

Youth in the 1980's

1981, 320pp., ISBN 92-3-101885-x.

Discusses the problems and challenges confronting the world's young people in a context of economic crisis and mounting unemployment in 1980s. Comments on youth's behaviour and aspirations and contains reports on their situation in 11 countries around the world.

Youth mobilization for development in Asian settings

(Regional Youth meetings, 2), 1984, (2nd impr.). 136pp., ISBN 92-3-101696.

Youth tradition and development in Africa

Regional youth meetings. Regional Meeting on Youth in Africa. Nairobi, Kenya, December 17-22, 1979, 1981, 146pp., tables, ISBN 92-3-101918-x.

A report of the Regional Meeting of Youth in Africa, held in 1979, which was concerned with youth and culture and youth and employment in Africa. The book contains a final report of the meeting and recommendations plus background documents and a synthesis of participants' contributions.

FOURTEEN

UNESCO AND SOCIAL SCIENCES TECHNICAL COOPERATION PROGRAMMES

Objectives

Strengthening of regional and national infrastructures and programmes for the development of the social sciences.

Training of national development planning specialists.

Planning and execution of research programmes on population problems and population communication programmes.

Promoting participation of young people in national development.

Recent Programmes in Technical Cooperation

1. *Strengthening of regional and national infrastructures and programmes for the development of the social sciences*

The United Nations Development Programme has made it possible for Unesco to expand its collaboration with the Latin American Social Science Faculty (FLASCO) and the Latin American Social Science Council (CLACSO) and to assist in the establishment of the "Consortium Graduate School in Applied Social Sciences - University of the West Indies; University of Guyana and University of Surinam.

Unesco has been instrumental in developing the training and research activities carried out in FLACSO institutions, particularly in

Mexico City, Quito and San Jose.

At the request of the Bolivian Government, Unesco assisted in the launching of activities in La Paz.

An effort has been made to expand CLACSO activities in Brazil and in the Caribbean.

Unesco has supported the training programme for young researchers organized by CLACSO.

Fellowships have been awarded for the training of young Latin American researchers in economics, anthropology and political science.

Unesco has also supported the CLACSO guest-teacher programmes which have made it possible for Latin American teachers to take part in seminars organized by Universities in the region.

A number of workshops have been organized in the English-speaking Caribbean countries in order to establish, with the help of UNDP, a consortium Graduate School in Applied Social Sciences uniting Universities and Research Establishments within the region.

At the request of the governments concerned, projects to train government officials in the use of socio-economic indicators and other social science planning techniques have been jointly prepared for China, Jamaica, Trinidad and Tobago, Barbados, the countries of the Association of South-East Asian Nations (ASEAN) and Central America.

2. *Training of National Development Planning Specialists*

Training facilities have been provided for the three UNDP-funded operational projects :

i. A national project in Algeria, "Assistance to the Institut des techniques de planification et deconomie appliquee";
ii. A subregional project (socio-economic planning for the Sahel

region); and

iii. A national project, "Application of socio-economic indicators in development planning and administration in Nigeria, including training therein".

3.*Planning and Execution of Research Programmes on Population Problems and Population Communication Programmes*

Unesco has carried out 27 population projects, six worldwide or interregional in scope; six regional in scope (one in Africa, one in Asia and the Pacific, two in Latin America and the Caribbean and two in the Arab States; and 16 national in scope (six in Africa, two in Latin America and the Caribbean, two in Asia and the Pacific and six in the Arab States). For these projects Unesco enlisted the services of 40 national specialists, including seven women.

Special mention may be made of the project on "Population, resources and development capacity; an approach to integrative planning", part of which being financed by UNDP, and the United Nations Trust Fund for the united interrelations between resources, environment, people and development.

National courses have been organized in Bolivia, Colombia, Dominican Republic, Ecuador, EL Salvador, Mexico, Paraguay and Peru, in the fields of education, health and family welfare. Officials in charge of national population programmes in their countries participated in these courses. The Latin American Institute of Educational Communication (ILCE, Mexico) has played an important role in the organization of these courses.

In 1982, a subregional seminar on population education and communication was organized in Tegucigalpa (Honduras) with the participation of 29 specialists (including 19 women) from five countries in the region (Costa Rica), Guatemala, Honduras, Nicaragua and the Dominican Republic).

A course organized in Colombia in 1982 aimed at the following objectives :

(a) to analyse the national education policy in order to assess the nature and extent of the progress achieved in the field of public health and, in particular, mother-and-child care;

(b) to establish the relations existing between the national health programme and the major project in the field of education in Latin America and the Caribbean; and

(c) to illustrate the significance of educational communication and the opportunities it provides for carrying out of the health programme, and to prepare relevant educational materials.

Most of the population activities in Asia and the Pacific have been carried out under a cooperation agreement with the Asian Institute for Broadcasting Development (AIBD) in Kuala Lumpur, Malaysia.

Courses for 22 different countries of Asia and the Pacific have been organized in the following fields : radio broadcasting at Kuala Lumpur (Malaysia), Seoul (Republic of Korea) and Dhaka (Bangladesh); television, film, video; low cost media at Kuala Lumpur (Malaysia) and Dhaka (Bangladesh); management of population communication programmes, Ahmedabad (India); and collection and distribution of population data at Kuala Lumpur (Malaysia).

A regional seminar on mass communication for women in charge of the population programme has been organized in Shanghai for familiarizing them with the use of mass communication techniques in support of population and development programmes.

Seminars have also been organized on the use of radio for the implementation of population programmes in Pakistan and the Socialist Republic of Vietnam.

The main feature of work in the Arab States has been technical cooperation with national population communication programmes in Bahrain, Democratic Yemen, Egypt, Jordan, Morocco, Sudan, Syrian Arab Republic and Tunisia. The cooperation consisted in the provision of experts and consultants, the organization of national training courses and contracts for development, and the testing and production of educational communication materials in support of national population programmes.

As a result of the cooperation extended by the Arab States Broadcasting Union, it has been possible to integrate population considerations in regional training programmes for mass media personnel held in Tunis, Amman, Khartoum, Rabat and Baghdad. The Communication Department of the Arab Educational Cultural and Scientific Organization (ALECSO) has cooperated in the execution of various population programmes.

4. *Promoting Participation of Women in National Reconstruction*

A project (Participation of Women in Development) has been financed by UNDP and implemented jointly by SWAPO, Unesco and the office of the Commissioner for Namibia on behalf of the United National Council for Nambibia. The broad objectives of this project, the first to be implemented by the United Nations system in cooperation with women of national liberation movement recognized by the Organization of African Unity were to upgrade Namibian Women's skills in politics and development. Another project "Training and information for upgrading women's roles in development" has also been taken up in Nambibia.

5. *Promoting participation of Young People in National Development*

Consultancy services, equipment and fellowships have been provided under operational youth projects carried out in Indonesia, Madagascar and the Seychelles with UNDP assistance.

RECENT UNESCO PUBLICATIONS

A manual on mass media in population and development

Population Communication Manuals, 1) 1977, 105pp., ISBN 92-3-101439-0

Methods for development planning : Scenarios, models and micro-studies

1981, 269pp., figs., tables, ISBN 92-3-101875-2.

Public Administration and management : problems of adaptation in different socio-cultural contexts
1982, 170pp., tables, ISBN 92-3-102024-2

Research in population communication
By Gloria D. Feliciano (Population Communication Manuals, 3), 1978, 84pp., ISBN 92-3-101512-5

FIFTEEN

UNESCO AND PROMOTION OF SOCIAL SCIENCES THROUGH AUDIO-VISUAL MEDIA

Photo Exhibition Celebrates IYY

As part of Unesco celebrations of the International Youth Year (IYY) 1985, a photo exhibition devoted to the theme "Youth in the 1980's" was presented at Paris headquarters (January 24-February 6) before going on view at UN Headquarters, New York, at the World Congress on Youth in Barcelona (July 8-15) and in other major cities in about 20 Member States. The exhibition was organized by Unesco in collaboration with the International Organization of Journalists, the International Federation of Photographic Art, the International Catholic Union of the Press, the Foundation for Photography-Switzerland, and the World Federation of Unesco Clubs and Associations, with technical and financial support from ILFORD. The 275 photos in the show were selected by an international jury from among over 3,000 by photographers in all regions.

New Unesco Stamps Support World Heritage Convention

In 1985 France issued three new Unesco service stamps to support and publicize the World Heritage Convention. First-day cover envelopes, souvenir sheets and stamped postcards showing the Roman Theatre in Carthage, Tunisia (1,80 F), the Plaza Vieja in Old Havana, Cuba (2,20 F) and the Temple of Anuradhapura, Sri Lanka (3, 20 F) were on sale at the Unesco Headquarters during the two days which preceded the official issue date October 28. France has put out 16 Unesco "World Heritage" stamps since the series began in 1980. Earlier series were devoted to "Human Rights", and "Environment and Natural Resources". Nearly 7,000 collectors subscribe to Unesco's regular information and sales service regarding stamps issued in favour of Unesco, the United Nations or other UN Agencies' programmes. For further details, write to Philatelic Programme, Unesco, 757000 Paris.

Man in Arid Lands : Nomads in Transition

This is a slide-tape show in Unesco's Man and the Biosphere (MAB) Programme's audio-visual series. Its 72 colour slides and 20-min cassette vividly present the human problem involved in nomadic transitions, population pressures and continuing desertification, notably in the Sahelian region. Here we see how, under MAB's Integrated Project for Arid Lands (IPAL), the management plans being developed will also be relevant to other arid zones which, in all, form one-third of the earth's surface where over 600 million people live. Another production in this series, *Man and Mountains*, takes the viewer, in 51 slides and a 15-min cassette, to places like the rice terraces in Nepal, the Andean Altiplano, or the Swiss Alps to discover the tragedy of deforestation and other problems in mountain areas which comprise another 15 per cent of the earth's surface and house over 400 million people. The slides and commentary also show how shared research and monitoring through MAB are providing a scientific basis and trained personnel to manage mountain resources in a rational and sustained manner. Both programmes, which come with bilingual English/rench cassettes and printed text for easy adaptation into other language versions, can be used on any standard slide projector-tape recorder. They can be purchased through national distributors of Unesco publications or from Unesco Press, Paris, for 220 FF/?33/$45.00 (Order code U 1361).

40th Anniversary of Unesco

Unesco came legally into being on November 4, 1946, with ratification of the Constitution by a 20th nation - Greece. Celebration of the Organization's 40th anniversary on November 3 and 4, 1986, at Paris Headquarters was marked by a series of major exhibitions, events and performances. During the opening of a central exhibition presenting the history of Unesco, French Prime Minister Jacques Chirac praised Unesco, whose objectives, framed in 1946, have become "a rich and manifold sum of practical activity forming an impressive system" and its Director General "the captain of this great undertaking". Young people from 50 countries and 60 high school students attending Unesco's system of Associated Schools joined in "Open House Day" organized by the World Federation of Unesco Clubs and Associations, and an exhibition of "40 paintings by 40-year-old artists in 40 countries" drew an enthusiastic audience from in and outside the Organization. Also on view were copies of a new Unesco/Gallimard edition of *The Treasure of Universal Poetry*, a unique summary of poetic expression from all eras and regions, edited by Roger Caillois and Jean-Claude Lambert. At the conclusion of gala November 4 evening, Director General Amadou-Mahtar M'Bow issued an appeal "to the wisdom of all countries to rise above misunderstandings...and rally round the founding principles of Unesco to guarantee the advent of lasting peace in the world".

Poster by Japanese Artist Marked International Year of Peace

A poster by Japaness master Kaii Higashiyama, a leading member of the school of traditional Japanese painting, was issued to mark the International Year of Peace 1986. Showing the moon, symbol of truth in Asian tradition, reflected in peaceful waters, it was the artist's contribution to a movement of support for Unesco by the Association of Japanese Artists, which in 1985 collected 1,148 artists'signatures for a message backing the Organization. Entitled "Two Moons", the poster was the result of collaboration between Unesco, the Japanese Federation of Unesco Associations and the International Association of Art.

Two other posters in the "Artists for Unesco" series, by Portuguese artist Vieira da Silva and French artist Benn also commemorated the International Year of Peace.

Action-oriented Education Kit on Women's Issues

A new educational kit entitled *The Key to Development : Women's Economic and Social Role* is the third in a joint UN Information Committee/Non-Governmental Organization (JUNIC/NGO) series. Building around three main themes - Women and Decision-Making, Women and Food, Women in Industry - it contains a wealth of material, including photos, reading lists, cartoons, statistics and a great number of background articles, all packed in a strong cardboard box that opens like a folder. In addition to its relevance in a wide variety of teaching situations, it will be of particular interest to voluntary organizations, government agencies and other groups working to make people more aware of the needs of women as they relate to economic and social development, and of their key role in the process. The kit, which also offers detailed guidelines on how to organize a seminar around selected themes, costs $15 or the equivalent in any convertible currency. Cheques should be made out in the name of UNESCO, and orders (for JUNIC/NGO Kit No. 3) addressed to UNESCO Co-Action Programme, Unesco, 7 Place de Fontenoy, 75700 Paris.

Unesco by night and by day

While most of Unesco's action takes place in the field, Paris Headquarters, in addition to its role as secretariat, forum and publishing house, is the constant scene of a wide variety of cultural activities. During the 1985-1986 season, these have included the art, films, photos, music and dance of over 20 countries, and performances by such illustrious artists as harpsichordist Zuzana Ruzickova, pianists Ivan Moravec, Michel Legrand, Miquel Angel Estrella, Claude Kahn and ensembles including the Organization's own Pro-Unesco chamber orchestra and philharmonic which together number 120 musicians from 35 nationalities. On June 10, 1986, the famous Buto dancer Ko Murobushi and his new troupe performed "Panta Rhei" as part of festivities celebrating Unesco's 40th anniversary. Besides attendance at these events over 30,000 people visited the Headquarters in 1985, 10,274 as part of 298 groups from 26 countries, the majority from schools and universities, who participated in the two-hour programme (featuring, in 1985, talks by 86 specialists from programme sectors) organized by the Visitors Information Centre. Others came to consult the archives (3,100), use the library (2,110) or simply to see the architecture or the art works by Picasso, Miro, Calder, Henry Moore, Noguchi, Tamayo and many others.

SIXTEEN

UNESCO AND SOCIAL AND HUMAN SCIENCES IN ASIA AND THE PACIFIC

Out of 158 Member States of Unesco, 31 belong to the vast Asia-Pacific region. Pursuing the goal of decentralization, Unesco has established Regional Offices and Units to serve the region and to effectively implement its programmes and activities. Each substantive sector - education, natural sciences, social and human sciences, culture and communication - has its regional advisers and specialists stationed in the region and they form part of a regional coordination programme.

Over the past years the Regional Unit for Social and Human Sciences in Asia and the Pacific (RUSHAP) has evolved a programme to portray the social science scene in Asia and the Pacific. This programme has three components : (1) overview of the social science situation in various countries; (ii) review of growth points of, and trends of research in, individual social science disciplines; and (iii) survey of the status of teaching of social sciences in professional education.

Portrayal of Social Science Scene in Asia and the Pacific

This programme has resulted in some useful publications. For example, four issues under the title *Social Sciences in Asia* (surveying the situation in 21 countries) have been published in the Unesco series (Paris) on "Reports and Papers in the Social Sciences" (Numbers 32,33,35, and 42). These have now been updated and brought out in a single volume under the tittle *Social Sciences in Asia and the Pacific* (1985). The monograph on Organization of Social Science Information and Documentation also forms part of

Programme Component (i). Under Programme Component (ii) three volumes, survey of individual social science discipline relating to Sociology and Social Anthropology, Political Science, International Law and Economics have been prepared. A similar exercise has been attempted for Philosophy in Asia and the Pacific.

Under Programme Component (iii), teaching of social sciences in professional education, the Unit has published the first volume, *Social Sciences in Agricultural Education* (1982), which surveys the situation in eight countries of the region.

Cross-Cultural Comparative Research

Promotion of comparative social science research is one of the major concerns of Unesco. On the intellectual plane, comparative research provides an opportunity to test existing paradigms and theories and judge the validity and reliability of methodological tools in different social settings and cultural contexts. In terms of professional growth, such research broadens the cognitive horizons of participating researchers and extends their areas of interaction beyond the national boundaries. Thus, comparative research is expected to yield valuable empirical data on urgent and vital problems of the day that will be of interest not only to theorists of society but also to policy-makers, planners, and agents of social change.

Unesco has taken a lead in this direction and has initiated and completed several cross-cultural comparative studies in Asia and the Pacific. One of its projects examined the Role of the University in National Development (1980) in Thailand, the Philippines, Republic of Korea, and Pakistan; another focussed on the interface between Doctors and Society (1980) in Malaysia, India and Sri Lanka; a third project was devoted to analyse Trends in ethnic group relations (1979) in India, Nepal, the Philippines and New Zealand. Two projects under the common theme, Vital Social Problems (VISOP), have also been completed-one of which was designed to assess the role of tradition in development, and the other to describe the role played by social sciences and social scientists in policy-making. The findings of the latter have been published under the title *Social Sciences : In Response to Policy Needs* (1980).

Research on MAB

Efforts have been also made to enhance the visibility of social science contribution in Unesco's Programme on Man and the Biosphere (MAB). In 1977, a series of seven national seminars were organized to bring face-to-face natural and social scientists for an effective dialogue and exchange of ideas. The reports of these seminars were discussed at the Second Conference of AASSREC held in Seoul. The Report incorporating these discussions was published for a world-wide distribution under the title *The Social Sciences in the Man and Biosphere Programme* (1979). A country report on "The Contribution of the Social Sciences to the MAB Programme in New Zealand 1971-83" was also published by the Unit (1983).

A five-country comparative study on Swidden Cultivation in Asia was initiated following the international symposium on the subject organized at the time of the Tenth World Congress of International Union of Anthropological and Ethnological Sciences (IUAES), which met in India in 1978. Utilizing funds made available by the United Nations Environment Programme (UNEP), the project was launched with the meeting of researchers convened in Bangkok in April 1979 to develop a comparative research design.

Human Settlements and Architecture

In close collaboration with UNEP, Unesco developed its programme of training in the management of human settlements. The first regional training seminar was held in Indonesia in 1976, following which national seminars were held in subsequent years in India, Malaysia, the Philippines and Thailand. Another regional seminar on "Management of Human Settlements in Situations of Disaster" was held in Bangkok in 1982. Under its participation programme, Unesco supported Australia in convening a subregional training seminar on the "Social Implications of Energy Management at the Local Level" in 1980.

In the area of human settlements, following studies were also carried out:

i. Legal framework for Public Participation in the Management of Human Settlements in Thailand.

ii. Andhra Pradesh (India) Cyclone Disaster of 1977.

iii. Problems related to resettlements of populations in a desert region (India).

iv. Traditional forms of rural settlements in Malaysia, Australia, Papua New Guinea and Pakistan.

v. A film study of the desert town of Jaisalmer, India.

vi. Impact of Rural exodus on the Urbanization Process in Asia.

To discuss the emerging role of the Barefoot Architects in the context of developing societies and to evolve a training strategy for this new role, a regional workshop was organized in Bangkok in 1983.

Thai architects were awarded the Unesco Prize for Architecture in 1981 on a project for the rehabilitation of a run-down district in the city of Bangkok.

Promotion and Elaboration of Social Indicators

Unesco has made a substantial contribution to the promotion and elaboration of social indicators; it has encouraged methodological discussion on them and has persuaded governments to employ the technology of indicators in planning and in evaluation, and in the preparation of social reports.

Following a Regional Meeting on the Applicability of Socio-economic Indicators to Development Planning held in Bangkok in 1974,. National or Subregional Training Workshops on the Elaboration and Use of Socio-economic Indicators were held in the Philippines in 1975, in New Zealand in 1979, in Thailand in 1980, in Nepal in 1984, and in Fiji in 1985. Two national seminars were held in 1975 in Thailand and the Philippines respectively on Territorial Indicators. A Sub-regional Training Workshop on Socio-economic Indicators was held in Australia in 1982. The proceedings of the New Zealand national workshop have been brought out for wide circulation entitled "Social Indicators for Development Planning in New Zealand by the New Zealand Social Council, Wellington (1979). A sub-regional meeting to create a network of institutions engaged in work related to development planning in South Asia was held in India in 1984.

Activities have also been carried out concerning the elaboration of indicators introducing a "thematic" approach aimed at specific areas of urgent social concern. An International Meeting on Social Indicators of the Role and Changing Conditions of Children in the Development Process was held in the Republic of Korea in 1980. Another meeting to evolve youth-related indicators was held in Sri Lanka in 1983.

Youth Programmes

The Youth constitute an important segment of society. An investment in their development is an investment in future. However, the survey of the situation of the Youth, carried out by Unesco and presented in its document, "Youth Prospects in the 1980", paints a not very bright picture. There is growing disenchantment and alienation among the young, and the incidents of the demonstration of Youth unrest are burgeoning. Unesco does not treat Youth as a problem group; it regards them as a potential force. It has encouraged programmes that are designed to utilize Youth for the fashioning of projects that are directed towards the development of the Youth, and also those that prompt Youth to actively participate in development. In the Asia-Pacific region, Unesco organized, in 1978, a meeting to discus Youth Mobilization for Development. It supported several national efforts both through its regular programme and under the participation programme. It assisted Indonesia in developing a UNDP funded project on Youth leadership training for which it is also the implementing agency.

To evolve a scheme of Youth-related indicators a Regional Seminar on the "Elaboration and Promotion of Indicators in the Analysis and Planning of Youth Programme" was held in Colombo in January 1983.

The Programme proposed by the expert group addresses itself to four major areas, namely:

i. Cross-cultural comparative research on nation building and development;

ii. Training in social science theory and methodology;
iii. Utilization of social science knowledge for policy making; and
iv. Regional information and documentation services.

Unesco organized the first Asian seminar in 1983, in Manila, to discuss the Sources, Systems and Services in Social Science Information and Documentation. The country reports presented at the seminar have been published in the Unit's Series on Occasional Monographs and Papers (8) titled '*Organization of Social Science Information and Documentation*.

In November 1984, Unesco organized the first meeting of regional institutions and foundations to exchange information about their programmes and activities designed to promote intellectual cooperation, in the area of social sciences in the developing countries of Asia. The Report on this meeting has been published and widely disseminated. In the same tenor, another meeting of representatives of governments and of academic institutions from the four countries of ASEAN-Indonesia, Malaysia, the Phillippines and Thailand-was convened in March 1985 in Bangkok to discuss the possibility of developing collaborative links among institutions of higher learning in ASEAN countries for furthering post-graduate training and research in social and human sciences.

(Adapted from *Social and Human Sciences in Asia and the Pacific 1975-1985*, Bangkok, 1985).

PART III

UNESCO AND INDIA

SEVENTEEN

UNESCO AND INDIA IN VARIOUS FIELDS

India is a founder member of Unesco and it has played an active role in its activities. In additon to paying its share of Unesco's operating budget India has made available many of its leading educators, scientists and specialists in various fields to serve as members of the Unesco Secretariat, as Unesco experts and consultants to other Member States, and as members of various international panels, conferences, advisory committees, and the Unesco Executive Board. Distinguished Indians including two former Presidents and one Prime Minister have served on the Unesco Executive Board.

India is also the first developing country to host Unesco's General Conference (9th Session, 1956). The Vigyan Bhawan in New Delhi was built specially for that Session. Because of the leading role played by India in the conference, Unesco's major project for the mutual appreciation of Eastern and Western cultural values was launched. Subsequently, India has hosted many other Unesco conferences, meetings, seminars, symposia, workshops and training courses. The first Unesco Conference on the Application of Science and Technology to the Development of Asia (CASTASIA I) was held in New Delhi in 1968, followed by CASTASIA II in Manila (Philippines) in 1982.

Unesco has collaborated with the Government of India in numerous development projects under its Regular Programme as well as with the financial assistance of the United Nations Development Programme (UNDP). Unesco provides required expertise, administers fellowships for selected Indian personnel for study abroad, and purchases imported equipment according to the agreed plan of action; the Government, which bears the main responsibility for the projects, appoints Indian staff, including a project directory; makes necessary institutional and administrative arrangements; and provides equipment and material manufactured in India. Apart from national development projects, India also participates in and benefits from many of international activities sponsored by Unesco, such as International Education Year, International Book Year, International Literacy Day, International Year of the Child, International Year of the Disabled, International Communication Year, International Youth Year, and has been an outstanding contributor to other specialized programmes which include International Hydrological Programme (IGP), Man and the Biosphere (MAB) Programme, International Geological Correlation Programme (IGCP), U.N. Science Information System (UNISIST) and Intergovernmental Oceanographic Commission (IOC), as well as regional activities, such as conferences, meetings, symposia, seminars, workshops and training courses, organized by Unesco's Regional Offices in Asia.

Unesco in the Field of Education

In the field of education Unesco has assisted India in establishing a number of central institutions to strengthen and develop its educational system. The present National Institute of Educational Planning and Administration, New Delhi, was first established in 1962 as the Asian Institute of Educational Planning and Administration and was jointly run by Unesco and the Government of India for 10 years. In 1973 it was turned over to India as a national institute. During this period the Institute trained some 300 fellows from the Asian Region, promoted research in educational planning, administration and supervision and organized educational services including adult literacy, university teaching, life-long integrated education, educational statistics and modern management techniques.

Many specialists were provided by Unesco to assist the Indian Education Commission 1964-66. India's example of including foreign specialists in a national commission has been followed by others.

In India, Unesco, under the "Secondary School Science Teaching Project", has assisted the National Council of Educational Research and Training (NCERT), New Delhi, with a team of science teaching experts in the improvement of curricula, production of science textbooks and teacher guides, developing new syllabi and samples of model school science equipment. Science equipment has been provided for almost all the teacher training institutions and science kits to nearly 30,000 schools.

Unesco has helped various programmes of book development. The Delhi Public Library was established as a joint Unesco-India project. Indian Classics have been translated and works of art reproduced in the Unesco series.

In the field of literacy Unesco has assisted India, in collaboration with FAO and UNDP, in establishing the Farmers' Training and Functional Literacy Programme. During 1970-74, more than 300,000 farmers benefited from the Government's high-yielding seeds programme. Also, in collaboration with FAO, UNDP and the Indian Council of Agricultural Research (ICAR), centres of excellence for post-graduate agricultural education research were established at 23 agricultural universities. Along with 34 central research institutes and 54 nationally coordinated research projects, these helped to bring together the functions of research, teaching and extension.

Under the National Council of Educational Research and Training, the Centre for Educational Technology was set up with technical assistance from Unesco and UNDP during 1972-80. The nomenclature of this Centre has since been changed to "Central Institute for Educational Technology". Unesco is the executing agency for this project for a period of five years (1984-1988). This centre is engaged in raising the quality of educational media utilization at the Central and State levels in India. A notable aspect of this collaboration was the pilot project SITE (Satellite Instructional Television Experiment) for large-scale use of satellite television as an educational medium.

India is a member of the Asian Programme of Educational Innovation for Development (APEID) located at the Unesco Regional Office for Education in Asia and the Pacific, Bangkok, since its very inception in 1974. The Programme is financially supported by Unesco, UNDP and voluntary contributions from participating Member States. In addition, there are contributions in kind by all the participating Member States. The main objective of the Programme is to assist the participating countries to build up their national capacities for design and introduction of educational innovations for development through relationship of equality, reciprocity and mutual learning among the leading research and development institutions of the Asia-Pacific region. In India, through this network, five Associated Centres of APEID have been established.

Among the other fields of cooperation in education are educational planning and management, low-cost school buildings, vocational and technical education, environmental education, services, and the Unesco-Unicef cooperative programme for reforming primary level curricula. UNESCO also participated in other Unicef-assisted projects in India like the Applied Nutrition Project, Children's Media Laboratory and the Community Education Project. In association with UNFPA (United Nations Population Fund Activities), Unesco has supported the National Population Education Project through advisory missions to 18 States and Union Territories in India.

India is very active in Unesco's Associated Schools Project for promoting international understanding. Presently there are 37 educational institutions all over India participating in this programme.

Unesco in the Field of Social Sciences

In the field of social sciences in India, Unesco assisted the Government of India in establishing in 1956 a Research Centre in Calcutta on Social Implications of Industrialization in South Asia. The work evolved into research in social and economic development. The Centre was shifted to Delhi and later transferred to the Institute of Economic Growth in 1967, with Unesco assistance continuing for some years.

In promoting social science development in India, Unesco has collaborated with the Indian Council of Social Science Research (ICSSR). Unesco has laid emphasis on cooperation between the social and natural sciences and mutual answers to problems arising from scientific and technological advance. Among specific problems recently addressed are the situation of women and the impact of science and technology on cultural values and the quality of life.

Unesco in the Filed of Science and Technology

In science and technology, India has close relationships with Unesco as the host of the organization's Regional Office of Science and Technology for South and Central Asia (ROSTSCA) at New Delhi which serves 11 Member States in the region including Afghanistan, Bangladesh, Bhutan, Burma, India, Iran, Maldives, Mongolia, Nepal, Pakistan and Sri Lanka.

Many of the meetings, seminars, symposia, workshops and courses organized by the New Delhi Regional Office are hosted by the Government of India at various scientific institutions in the country. Recent examples include: Unesco Regional Working Group Meeting on Metrology for South and Central Asia, New Delhi, August 9-11, 1982; Sub-Regional Workshop on Low-cost Locally Produced Equipment for Chemistry Teaching, Chandigarh, January 7-9, 1983; Second Meeting of the Asia Regional Coordinating Committee on Hydrology, New Delhi, January 10-12, 1983; Inter-Regional Meeting on Research and Human Needs, Madras, February 14-19, 1983; Unesco Regional Seminar on the Application of Informatics in South and Central Asia, New Delhi, April 13-16, 1983; International Course on Analysis and Design of Machine Foundations, University of Roorkee, February 23 to March 15, 1983; International Post-graduate Diploma Course in Hydrology and Water Resources Engineering, Anna University, Madras, August 1983 to July 1984; Workshop on Choice of Technology for Endogenous Development, New Delhi, October 24-27, 1983; Regional Training Programme on Appropriate Technology for South and Central Asian Countries, Allahabad, December 12-23, 1983; Regional Workshop on Biogas Energy Management in Rural Areas for South Asia, Hyderabad, December 27-29, 1983; and International Conference on the Role of Laboratory in Physics Education, Jaipur, December 29, 1983 to January 2, 1984; Regional Seminar on Power System Reliability: Planning, Operation and Management, Indian Institute of Science, Bangalore, March 19-23, 1984; International ICRO Unesco/Training Course on Immunogenetics, Cancer Research Institute, Bombay, March 19 to April 6, 1984; Regional Seminar on Use of Information Systems and Services on Research in Progress, Hyderabad (India), March 26-30, 1984; Regional Seminar on Management of Engineering and Technical Institutions, Indian

Institute of Technology, Kanpur, April 2-5. 1984; Regional Seminar-cum-Workshop on Small Scale Energy Systems in Rural Areas, Madras, April 19-28, 1984; Unesco Regional Course on Computer Network Design and Management, New Delhi, May 28 to June 16, 1984; Regional Training Seminar on Higher Technicians Education, Madras, December 17-21, 1984; Regional Training Course on application of Computers to Hydrological Studies, Pune, January 7-25, 1985; UGC-India/Unesco/ASPEN Workshop on TV Programmes for Science and Technology Education, Pune, January 15-31, 1985; Second Regional Training Course in Structural Geology, Dehra Dun, March 6 to April 3, 1985; Regional Meeting of Man and the Biosphere (MAB) National Committees of South and Central Asia, New Delhi, March 18-20, 1985; International Seminar on Research in Science and Technology Education (University Level), Himachal Pradesh University, Simla Hills, June 21-28, 1985; 14th International Postgraduate Diploma and Master's Course in Hydrology, Roorkee, July 1985 to June 1986; International Conference on Science and Technology Education and Human Needs, Bangalore, August 8-14, 1985; Third International Postgraduate Diploma Course in Hydrology and Water Resources Engineering, Anna University, Madras, September 1985 to August 1986; Regional Symposium on Creation of Awareness about Earthquake Hazards and Mitigation of Seismic Risks, Gauhati, October 4-5, 1985; Unesco-INSDOC Asian Regional Seminar/Workshop on Thesaurus Construction, New Delhi, Novermber 18-29, 1985; Training Course/Workshop on Modern Aspects of Monoclonal Antibody Production by Hybridoma Techniques, National Institute of Immunology, New Delhi, December 2-14, 1985.

Unesco has assisted the Government of India in its efforts to expand and improve its body of technical teachers and specialists, with the establishment of several engineering colleges and institutions in India which include Regional Engineering Colleges at Allahabad, Bhopal, Durgapur, Jamshedpur, Mangalore, Nagpur, Rourkela and Tiruchirapali. Some other institutions established with the assistance of Unesco are: Teacher Training for Engineering Colleges, Warangal; Indian National Scientific Documentation Centre (INSDOC), New delhi; Central Scientific Instruments Organization, Chandigarh; Central Arid Zone Research Institute, Jodhpur; Power Engineering Research Organizations at Bhopal and Bangalore; National Institute of Foundry and Forge Technology, Ranchi; Central Mechanical Engineering Research Institute, Durgapur; Mechanical Engineering Research and Development Organizations at Ludhiana, Madras and Durgapur; Indian Ocean Biological Centre, Cochin; School of Planning and Architecture, New Delhi; Indian Institute of Petroleum, Dehradun; Turbomachinery and Combustion Laboratory, Bangalore; Technical Teachers Training Institute, Bhopal; and Central Electronics Engineering Research Institute, Pilani. The completion in 1966 of the 10-year Unesco Project of aid to the Indian Institute of Technology, Bombay, is a milestone in the industrial and educational history of India.

Unesco Projects in India

Some Projects recently executed by the Unesco Regional Office, New Delhi,are given below:

- National Institute of Hydrology, Roorkee (India) 1979-1984.
- Post-graduate Hydrological Education and Research, Roorkee - 1981-1985.
- Special Assistance to Selected University Departments (Phase 11), University Grants Commission, New Delhi - 1979-1984.
- Post graduate Engineering Education and Research, Coimbatore - 1982-1984.
- Post graduate Engineering Education and Research, Coimbatore - 1982-1984.
- Compressibility, Viscosity and Solidification Behaviour of Liquids at Ultra-High Pressures, Department of Astrophysics, Delhi University, Delhi-1983-1985.
- Water and Power Information Systems, Central Water and Power Research Station, Pune 1982-1986.
- Study of Environmental Effect on Cultural Properties, Lucknow-1983-1986.
- Establishment of Central Institute of Educational Technology (INSAT for Education),National Council of Educational Research and Training, New Delhi-1984-1988.
- Curriculum Development for Technician Education (Phase 11),Technical Teachers Training Institutes in Chandigarh, Calcutta, Bhopal and Madras-1985-1987.

The Organization has provided assistance by way of (i) offering the services of Unesco experts of international repute and consultants, (ii) making available the services of Unesco Advisory Missions from Headquarters, (iii) supplying latest equipment for laboratories, and (iv) providing fellowships for advanced studies abroad.

In the present phase,the focus of Unesco activities is on the application of science and technology to development in fields like rural development, mineral and energy resources, biotechnology, and the biosphere, water resources, ocean and coastal marine systems and information systems and services.

Unesco in the Field of Culture

Unesco's contribution in the field of culture is quite significant. Through its various programmes of international cultural cooperation carried out by government agencies and autonomous bodies, there has been an increasing awareness of the culture of different countries of the world. India has participated in numerous cultural activities such as the 10-year (1957-66) "Major Project on the Mutual Appreciation of Eastern and Western Cultural Values" through which many works of Indian literature have now been translated into different foreign languages and published by Unesco. Unesco has assisted in the renovation and conservation of the Ranganathaswami Temple in Tamil Nadu and in the restoration of the Ajanta Cave frescoes. The Bureau of the World Heritage Committee, at its 1985 session, recommended the inclusion of Ajanta Caves, Elora Caves, Agra Fort, Taj Mahal, the Sun Temple at Konarak, and the group of monuments at Mahabalipuram in the World Heritage List. Unesco has also extended its cooperation in the building of "Auroville-international city of the future" at Pondicherry.

India on its part has contributed to Unesco's campaign to save the Nubian monuments in Egypt from the rising waters of the Nile as well as several other international campaigns to save precious-monuments.

Under the five year-(1978-1983) UNDP/Unesco Project entitled "National Research Laboratory for Conservation of Cultural Property, Lucknow", support was provided to the Government of India in the development of a National Laboratory for Conservation in the fields of museum objects made of wood, paper, metal, miniatures, textiles as well as monuments, archaeological sites and related materials and to make the laboratory a training centre for conservation in India and in the countries of the South and South East Asian Region. The Laboratory has organized many training courses on conservation of cultural property with the financial assistance of Unesco. The Organization has also been offering fellowships for each course. The conservative trainees have been drawn from several museum, art and cultural institutions in India as well as abroad.

The Unesco Literature Translation Programme, out of which has grown the "Unesco Collection of Representative Work's", has been a continuing activity of the Organization since 1948. Under Unesco's programme of "Collection of Representative Works: India Series", the Organization has so far translated and published 101 titles of different Indian languages into foreign languages including 24 (French), 62 (English), 7 (German), 2 (Spanish), 2 (Hungarian) and 4 (other languages).

Unesco in the Field of Mass Communication

In the field of mass communication, Unesco promotes the free flow of ideas by word and image. The Organization develops and improves the means and techniques of mass communication and their use for educational, scientific and cultural purposes. Unesco helps to stimulate communication as a means of democratic development. It is promoted with assistance, for example, expansion of the television network, television training and satellite instructional television through the Film and Television Institute of India, Pune, established with the assistance of Unesco and Ford Foundation.

The National Book Trust, India, at New Delhi, which produces and encourages the publication of good literature and makes such literature available at moderate prices to the public, has been assisted by Unesco. The other institutions in this field which have been assisted by Unesco include : the Southern Languages Book Trust at Madras, International Institute of Tamil Studies, Madras, and Indian Institute of Mass Communication, New Delhi.

India is a member of the inter-governmental Council of the International Programme for the Development of Communication (IPDC) which came into existence on the recommendation adopted by the Inter-governmental Conference for Cooperation on Activities, Needs and Programme for Communication Development, Paris, in April 1980. Unesco, under the International Programme for the Development of Communication, has recently supplied important equipment of a substantial amount to the Indian Institute of Mass Communication, New Delhi, in order to help and develop the Institute's programme.

The Delhi Public Library was established in 1951 in association with Unesco, as a model for public library development in South Asia. This Library was the first Unesco Public Library Pilot Project.

Unesco's public information activities are designed to promote international understanding and cooperation by making known to people what Unesco is doing for the betterment of makind. Such activities include distribution of informative literature and publications to several institutions and individuals in India. This distribution includes *Unesco Features*, *Unesco News*, *Unesco Courier*, and booklets and leaflets, giving an account of Unesco's programmes and activities. Unesco films and tapes are also supplied to interested institutions and societies in the country. *Unesco Courier* is also published in Hindi and Tamil languages with the financial assistance of Unesco.

Unesco films are also supplied to interested institutions in the country.

At the closing meeting of the 6th Session of the Council of IPDC, held in Paris (France) from March 4 to 11, 1985, the first IPDC/Unesco prize worth 20,000 dollars for Rural Communication was awarded to the Indian Kheda Communication Project which consists of a low-power television transmitter linked to a study and earth station complex that relays local programmes or central programmes received by Satellite. Community television sets enable the population to view these programmes, which are essentially development and education oriented.

The office of the Unesco Representative to India and the Regional Office of Science and Technology for South and Central Asia is responsible for liaison with the Government of India; Indian National Commission for Cooperation with Unesco, Ministry of Education and Culture; and the United Nations Development Programme in regard to Regular Programmes and UNDP activities. The Unesco Representative provides technical support for the planning and implementation of Unesco's programme of aid for development in India. Since its inception in 1949, the Indian National Commission has been closely associated with this office and all the projects are executed and implemented in consultation with the National Commission.

Assistance to Institutions in India

A number of educational and scientific institutions in India have received assistance from Unesco, in the form of technical know-how, equipment, etc. A brief account of each such institution with special reference to the help from Unesco is given below:

1. *Delhi Public Library*; It was established as a Public Library Pilot Project in 1951 by Unesco in collaboration with the Government of India, Ministry of Education. It was intended that the Library would provide a Public Library Service for the people of Delhi and that it would be a model for all public library development in India and in all countries where similar development of public libraries can be undertaken. Under the financial arrangement agreed upon, Unesco contributed a total of about $ 60,000 during the years 1951-54 and the Government of India 1,20,000 (in rupees) during the same period.

2. *Unesco Research Centre on social and Economic Development in Southern Asia, Delhi*: A Social Science Research Centre was established by Unesco at Calcutta in 1956. It was devoted to research on the impact of urbanization and industrialization in South and South-East Asia. The Centre was shifted to Delhi in 1961 and located there in the premises of the Institute of Economic Growth. After its transfer to Delhi, the centre expanded its aims and activities.

In accordance with the recommendations made by a Unesco Evaluation Commission, and with the agreement of the Government of India, the Unesco Research Centre was closed on December 31, 1966. Its Library and some other assets were transferred to the Institute of Economic Growth which organized its own Asian Research Centre during 1967 with the assistance of the Government of India and Unesco. Unesco assistance was available for four years only, ending in 1970, but the Centre continues to be run on finances made available by the Ministry of Human Resource Development, Government of India.

3. *Asian Institute of Educational Planners and Administrators, New Delhi*: The Institute was set up in 1962 by the Government of India in collaboration with Unesco under a 10-year agreement for the training of educational planers and administrators to meet the growing educational needs of the different Asian countries.

On the expiry of this agreement in 1972, the Government of India decided to merge the Asian Institute into the National Staff College for Educational Planners and Administrators.

On the recommendation of the Government of India, the NSC has been identified as an Associate Centre of the Asian Centre for Educational Innovation for Development (ACEID), which has been established in Bangkok as an integral part of the Unesco Regional Office for Education in Asia. As an Associate Centre of ACEID, the main function of the National Staff College is to cooperate with ACEID in promoting reform and innovation in India and other Member States of the Region in the field of educational management. The primary modalities of such programmes are surveys, case studies, pilot experiments, field operational and training seminars, workshops, production of instructional materials, etc. The institution is now known as the *National Institute of Educational Planning and Administration.*

4. *Centre for Educational Technology,NCERT, New Delhi*: Realizing the possibilities which educational technology can offer to education both in respect of improving its quality and extending its reach, the Centre for Educational Technology was set up as a separate institute under the National Council of Educational

Research and Training in May 1973 with a special grant from the Government of India. With this, the Centre became one of the 10 constituent units of NCERT.

The UNDP/Unesco also agreed to assist the Government of India in the initiation, growth and development of the Centre. A project known as IND/711/612-Project was accordingly formulated. The project document was signed by the Government of India and UNDP/Unesco in May 1974. On account of the initial delay, the project was extended further.

The UNDP/Unesco assistance in IND/711/612 is being given in the form of experts, equipment and fellowships for training abroad. The assistance indicated in the project document is of the order of $762,903. But as the prices of the equipment soared the figure was revised to $855,137 for the first phase from 1973 to 1976. With a view to giving a boost to the promotion of educational technology for the improvement and spread of education in the country, the Central Institute of Educational Technology (CIET) was set up in May 1984 by the merger of the erstwhile Centre for Educational Teachnology and the Departments of Teaching Aids of the NCERT. Earlier three-year UNDP Project INSAT for Education was signed by the Government of India in February, 1984.

5. *Indian National Scientific Documentation Centre (INSDOC), New Delhi*: The Centre was set up in 1952 by the Government of India with the technical assistance from Unesco to provide a full range of documentation services in the field of science and technology. The Centre is functioning under the Council of Scientific and Industrial Research. The assistance of Unesco covered the provision of experts, fellowship, equipment, etc., during the period 1952-1955. Again in 1964, INSDOC received assistance from Unesco for setting up its Regional Centre in Bangalore.

It is also actively collaborating with Unesco in its various projects and programmes. Under scientific and cultural exchange programmes, INSDOC has established exchange relationships with a number of countries in the field of scientific information.

6. *Central Scientific Instruments Organization (CSIO), Chandigarh*: It is a National Laboratory engaged essentially in research,

design and development of instruments of scientific and industrial importance. The Organization was set up in 1959 under the Council of Scientific and Industrial Research (CSIR), New Delhi.

During its infancy, the Organization was nurtured by Unesco/UNDP which provided considerable aid in the form of equipment, Unesco experts and fellowships.

7. *Central Arid Zone Research Institute, Jodhpur*: The Institute, with its strength of about 500 scientific and supporting staff, library and laboratory facilities, 15 research sub-stations in the desert regions, aerial photo-interpretation centre, solar and wind power harvesting yard and up-to-date instrumentation facilities stands today on the fringe of the great Indian desert as an evidence of the service rendered by Unesco to the international community and as its accomplishment in the field of regional development programme through aid and intellectual cooperation.

The Desert Afforestation Research Station at Jodhpur, which had been functioning since October 1952 was redesignated and reorganized as the Central Arid Zone Research Institute in October 1959 on the basis of the recommendations of a Unesco adviser. At the time of the inception of the institute, Unesco rendered aid for diverse purposes, such as (a) training of staff, (b) Providing experts, and (c) for equipping the laboratories of the different divisions under the "Major Project on Scientific Researches on Arid Lands"

8. *Films and TV Institute of India (Television Wing), Pune*: The expansion of the television network in the country was a long-felt need. A formal request by the Government of India to UNDP/Unesco in 1968 which evoked a favourable response resulted in the establishment of a Television Training Centre on August 10, 1971. This Centre which was functioning at New Delhi on a temporary basis was shifted to its permanent complex within the campus of the Film Institute, Pune, on July 6, 1974. The collaboration with UNDP which was for a period of three years ended on August 10, 1974. The UNDP asssistance to this Institute was of the order of US $1.44 million in the form of equipments, experts and fellowships.

9. *National Institute of Foundry and Forge Technology, Ranchi (Bihar)*: The Government of India in 1961 formulated a scheme to provide improved academic and practical education and training for engineers of the foundry and forge industries by creating a National Institute of Foundry and Forge Technology. In July 1965, the Government of India submitted a request to the United Nations Special Fund for assistance for the above scheme in the form of services of specialists from other countries, equipments not manufactured in India and the fellowships for training Indian counterpart staff outside the country. The NIFFT project was approved by the governing council of the United Nations Special Fund in January 1965. Unesco was designated as Executing Agency and the Ministry of Education as Government cooperating agency. The plan was signed on December 14, 1966, and Unesco was authorized to begin operation on February 16, 1967. The institute, in consultation with Unesco experts, took action to procure the equipments on a priority basis both from indigenous sources and from abroad. The equipments received through Unesco funds were worth $280,790, in addition one induction furnace was received at an approximate cost of $50,000 from Unesco.

10. *Centres of Advanced Study*: On the basis of the discussions and the report made by the Unesco Advisory Mission on Science Education which visited India and Moscow in 1962, the programme of assistance to Centres of Advanced Study Project in Indian Universities under Unesco's Technical Assistance Programme was initiated from 1963-64 with the inclusion of seven Centres/Departments. The assistance made available was in the form of (1) Services of Experts/Consultants, (11) Training Fellowships and (iii) Supply of Scientific Equipments. The Programme was again reviewed in 1967 and three additional Centres were included under this programme. The list of Centres is as follows:

1. Centre of Advanced Study in Physics, Delhi University.
2. Centre of Advanced Study in Chemistry, Bombay University.
3. Centre of Advanced Study in Chemistry, Delhi University.
4. Centre of Advanced Study in Botany, Delhi University.
5. Centre of Advanced Study in Botany, Madras University.
6. Centre of Advanced Study in Zoology, Delhi University.
7. Centre of Advanced Study in Geology, Punjab University.

8. Centre of Advanced Study in Mathematics, Punjab University.
9. Centre of Advanced Study in Mathematics, Madras University.
10. Centre of Advanced Study in Biochemistry, Indian Institute of Science, Bangalore.

This programme was completed in 1974. The new project under which the following 10 selected departments were provided UNDP assistance of $771,900 was started from October 1975: Department of Chemistry (Rajasthan University); Department of Pure Chemistry (Calcutta University); Department of Physical Chemistry (Madras University); Department of Inorganic and Physical Chemistry (Indian Institute of Science, Bangalore); Department of Geology (Jadavpur University): Department of Biochemistry (Lucknow University): Department of Physics (Andhra University): Department of Physics (Allahabad University).

11. *Indian Institute of Technology, Bombay*: Established with the cooperation and participation of Unesco, utilizing the contribution of the Government of the USSR towards building up one of the centres of higher technological education by the Government of India, the Project is a unique adventure with international cooperation in the post-independence era.

The Unesco Project at the Indian Institute of Technology, Bombay, was nomenclatured as Unesco Technical Assistance Project No. 12. Under this Project the Institute received 59 Experts, 12 Technicians and 9 Translators.

The most significant contribution made by the Unesco experts was in the preparation of course material. Lecture notes, monographs and books published by the Experts individually and jointly with the faculty staff ran to 103.

Twentyseven faculty members of the Institute received higher training in the USSR under the Unesco Fellowship Programme.

The total value of the equipments received by the Institute through Unesco stood at Rs 170,60,071.

12. *Motilal Nehru Regional Engineering College, Allahabad*: The Laboratories of all the Departments have been equipped with the latest machines and instruments. The College received assistance from the Unesco Special Fund, besides funds from the Government of India for equipment.

Four faculty members were sent abroad-three to the UK and one to the USA-for training and advanced studies by the College under the Unesco Programme for Higher Studies/Research and three for observing the educational pattern in the Western countries.

Eight Unesco experts and one guest Professor served the College for varying periods. Their contribution in the successful organization of the Industry Oriented Postgraduate courses, and the Undergraduate courses has been appreciable. They have trained some of the staff members of the college in their respective fields of specialization apart from participating in the lecture work and project and thesis guidance. Thirteen lecture notes were prepared on specialized topics.

13. *Maulana Azad College of Technology, Bhopal*: Unesco, after examining the potentialities of the College and the industrial environment in imparting post-graduate education and training in engineering, selected the College for assistance in (i) equipping its laboratories with necessary sophisticated and precision equipment especially for post graduate and research work, (ii) providing international experts to provide guidance, and train junior faculty and (iii) to train faculty members in advanced countries as summed up below:

Cost of equipment provided was $300,000. Nine members of the faculty were provided fellowship for research, training and study in the advanced countries of the world. Six experts in the various subjects of post-graduate specialization were provided for a total of about seven years.

14. *Regional Engineering College, Durgapur*: Unesco assistance has gone a long way in consolidating the existing undergraduate courses by better equipping the laboratories and improving standard of teaching by providing better training facilities to the teachers. It

has also been instrumental in developing the industry-oriented M.Tech. courses and initiating industrial research. The assistance consisted of providing the services of eight international experts, offering 10 fellowships for the training of teachers abroad and providing funds worth $0.44 million for the purchase of selected equipment.

15. *Visvesvaraya Regional College of Engineering, Nagpur*: This college, one of the first six Regional Colleges established under the scheme sponsored by the Government of India and the State Government, has been allotted three industrially-oriented post-graduate courses under the Unesco Project, and these have become popular.

Under the Unesco Scheme, the College had the advantage of the services of six Experts-four from the USSR and one each from Poland and the UAR--for the various post-graduate courses. Nine staff members of the college also got an opportunity to go abroad with a Unesco fellowship either for study tour/practical training or post-graduate studies. The College has also received substantial equipment under the Unesco scheme.

16. *Regional Engineering College, Rourkela*: The College has received substantial help from UNDP.

17. *Karnataka Regional Engineering College, Surathkal (Karnataka)*: M.Tech. Courses were started in the College as part of the Unesco Special Fund Project for development of Regional Engineering Colleges.

The College came under the "Six Regional Engineering Colleges Project" (IND-50 and IND-104) of the Unesco Special Fund Programme. Under this Project the College:

(a) received equipment for undergraduate and post-graduate courses started under this Project;
(b) received fellowships for its staff members for higher studies;
(c) started industrially oriented post-graduate courses in the following fields:

1. Industrial Structures
2. Marine Structures
3. Industrial Electronics

(d) received services of Unesco Experts to develop the post-graduate courses.

The College received equipment valued at $ 310,677. Nine staff members availed themselves of Unesco fellowships and went abroad--three to the USA, three to the UK and Italy and one each to the USSR, Japan and the UK--either for training/study tour or for post-graduate studies.

18. *Regional Engineering College, Tiruchirapalli (Tamil Nadu)*: The programme of UNDP aid to this college commenced from October 1970, with the starting of an industry oriented post-graduate degree course in Design and Production of Thermal Power Equipment.

Essential equipment for the conduct of research work and post-graduate and undergraduate laboratory work was envisaged and UNDP funds to the tune of $ 145,000 were made available.

Items of equipment purchased out of these funds are not only used in the laboratories of the departments but are also utilized by the collaborating industry (such as Bharat Heavy Electrical Limited).

Three fellowships were also made available to the college and the selected candidates obtained training experience in Germany and Czechoslovakia.

19. *Regional Engineering College, Warangal (Andhra Pradesh)*: The Unesco Programme was originally a Five-Year Project extending from 1964 to 1969 which overflowed up to 1972. This was mainly intended to introduce the new concept of industry oriented courses at the post-grduaate level and to strengthen the existing post-graduate programmes in the College. Subsequently, in 1972, a Fellowship Project was started to strengthen the U.G.C Programme on the one side and to initiate research of a high order in the form of (1) Doctoral Programmes, (2) Joint Research and Developmental

Activity between the College and Industries and (3) to develop this College as a Research Centre in certain selected fields of specialization, on the other.

It has also received equipment worth Rs 1 lakh from abroad under UNDP.

EIGHTEEN

INDIAN NATIONAL COMMISSION FOR COOPERATION WITH UNESCO

India has been a member of the United Nations Educational, Scientific and Cultural Organization since its inception in 1946. Article VII of the Constitution of Unesco requires that "each Member State shall make arrangements as suit its particular conditions for purposes of associating its principal bodies interested in educational, scientific and cultural matters with the work of the Organization preferably by the formation of a National Commission or any representative of the Government and such bodies" and further provides that "National Commissions or national cooperating bodies, where they exist, act in an advisory capacity to their respective delegations to the Central Conference and to their Governments in matters relating to the Organization and shall function as agencies of liaison in all matters of interest to it". Accordingly, an interim Indian National Commission for Cooperation with Unesco was set up in 1949, and a permanent Commission was established in 1951.

As a member of Unesco, the Government of India, in compliance with Article VII of the Constitution of the Organization, established, in 1949, the National Commission for Cooperation with Unesco to involve in Unesco's activities, various departments, agencies, institutions, organization--both governmental and non-governmental--and individuals working for the advancement of education, science, culture and communication; to collaborate with each other and Unesco's Regional Offices and Centres fostering regional, sub-regional and bilateral cooperation in education, science, culture and information, particularly through the joint formulation and execution of programmes. The Commission performs its role not only as a coordinating body at the national level but also collaborated with the National Commissions of Asia and the Pacific and with UNESCO's regional offices and centres for bringing about a better understanding of Unesco's projects and activities. Besides, the Commission identifies and recommends Indian candidates for various posts under Unesco, arrange placement of Unesco fellows from Member States in various universities, institutions, laboratories, etc., in India and helps in handling contracts offered by Unesco to experts and institutions in India for undertaking specific studies of specialized nature as well as administration of funds allocated under the Participation Programme of Unesco.

Recent Activities of the Commission

India hosted an International Seminar on Unesco--In Retrospect and Prospect at the India International Centre, New Delhi, from January 1 to 3, 1986, with financial assistance from Unesco under the Participation Programme. The Seminar was attended by four members of the Executive Board of Unesco and delegates from Algeria, Bangladesh, India, Nepal, Sri Lanka and the USSR. Eminent Indian personalities in the fields of education, science, culture, communications and social sciences also participated in the Seminar. The Seminar reviewed Unesco's work over the past 40 years, examined the nature and ramifications of its present situation and made several recommendations for the future orientation of its programmes.

The Centre for Cultural Resources and Training, New Delhi, in collaboration with the Indian National Commission, organized a Training Workshop in Documentation and Dissemination of Performing Arts at New Delhi from March 31 to April 5, 1986. The objectives of the Workshop were to evolve a methodology for research and documentation, suitable for the region; to formulate a framework of a scheme for documentation of the Performing Arts of the region; to provide guidelines on production of programmes for dissemination of information about the artistic and cultural heritage using the materials collected during documentation; and to evolve a methodology for cataloguing and indexing the documented materials collected.

Delegates from Bangladesh, Bhutan, Burma, India, Indonesia, ban, Malaysia, Maldives, Nepal, Pakistan, Sri Lnka and Thailand icipated in the Workshop. The Assistant Director General for

Coordination of Unesco Activities in Asia and the Pacific, Bangkok, and the Regional Aviser for Culture in Asia and the Pacific, Bangkok, also participated in the Workshop.

In response to a fresh appeal launched by the Director General of Unesco, a sum of US $25,000 was contributed by the Indian Government for the campaign to safeguard the monumental site of Mohenjodaro in Pakistan. With this, the total contribution made by India towards the campaign amounts to US $100,000 approximately.

Another sum of US $ 25,000 has been contributed to Unesco's International Institute for Educational Planning, a premier institute in the field of Educational Planning located in Paris.

Associated Schools Project

India joined the Associated Schools Project in 1953 with six institutions. The number has now risen to 37 which comprise 10 teacher training institutions and 27 composite schools having both primary and secondary departments. These schools work on three main themes: teaching about the United Nations and its specialized agencies ; teaching about human rights and fundamental freedoms; and teaching about other countries. The Indian National Commission for Unesco has always held the view that the Associated Schools Project is of vital importance for India and the world and that more schools and teacher training institutions should be established to increase the number of Indian Schools linked directly with Unesco Secretariat in Paris under the Associated Schools Project. The National Commission, therefore, prepared an expanded programme in India to cover a large number of schools and teacher training institutions in the country. There are about 330 institutions which have been covered under the expanded programme.

Unesco Clubs

The Indian National Commission has been promoting the establishment of Unesco clubs in various centres including universities, libraries and educational and cultural institutions. So far 133 such clubs have been established throughout the country. These clubs undertake activities like disseminating information about the aims and policies of Unesco, the UN and similar bodies and arrange various programmes in education, science, culture, etc., to promote international understanding, cooperation and world peace. The Commission has been sending publications, periodicals and other materials received from Unesco or brought out by the Commission itself to all the clubs regularly. Special kits of material are sent to the clubs to enable them to celebrate UN Day and Human Rights Day in a befitting manner.

The Unesco Courier

The Indian National Commission for Unesco gets the Hindi and Tamil editions of *The Unesco Courier* published by the Central Hindi Directorate, a subordinate office under the Department of Education and the Southern Languages Book Trust, Madras, respectively.

Unesco Coupons

The Commission operates the Unesco International Coupons Scheme designed to assist institutions and individuals working in the fields of education, science, culture and communication to import educational and scientific material from foreign countries on payment in Indian rupees.

Newsletter and Unesco Publications

The Commission brings out the quarterly *Newsletter* in English to publicize information about the activities of the Commission and Unesco in India. The Library and Documentation Unit of the Commission makes available copies of the Unesco publications/periodicals including the *Newsletter* to educational and research institutions/organizations all over India and abroad. The Unit brings out a monthly annotated list (*Current Awareness*) of publications/periodicals/reports, received from Unesco Headquarters/regional offices and Unesco's other research and planning institutions in Member States.

NINETEEN

SOCIAL SCIENCE RESEARCH IN INDIA

Social sciences in India are of recent origin. Their growth and development, which is a post-war phenomenon, is of great significance and importance. There is a virtual "explosion" of social sciences in India and as a consequence there is general awareness, acceptance and use by the laity, organizations, governmental and otherwise, scholars and researchers, business and industry and so on. In fact, there is hardly a social, economic or political problem that social scientists are not required to study and provide a solution. Social scientists help alleviate such problems through a scientific social scrutiny and evaluation. The social sciences have, therefore, become an indispensable source of guidance for administrators and professionals of all kinds. They enlighten the people on the progress of ideas and make them see things through a wider perspective. Social Sciences contribute to rational thinking, a secular outlook, free from the "disenchantment of the world" which people weave around themselves.

Expansion of the social sciences, availability of funds and opportunity of participation in large-scale empirical study and research have placed a heavy responsibility on social scientists today. The Indian Council of Social Science Research (ICSSR), a pioneer organization in the field of social sciences in India, has provided financial assistance to social sciences institutions and has brought out a number of papers dealing with social research in India.

Historical Perspective

There has been, of late, a rapid growth of social science research and training organizations in the country. A host of research organizations have come into existence outside the university system and are playing an important and significant role in the developmental activities. Their utility is being gradually realized and recognized with the progress and development of social science subjects. It is estimated that a large number of them are functioning as autonomous bodies, some receiving partial assistance, some full assistance and some getting no financial support from the Government.

The first two research institutions, outside the university system for purposes of research, teaching training and policy formulation, were formed as early as 1927; one of them worked in the field of public administration (All India Institute of Local Self-Government, Bombay) and the other had an inter-disciplinary character (Indian Council of Africa, New Delhi). In 1935 two more social science research organizations came to be set up ; one for economics and the other for statistics. Then came institutions in political science (1943), anthropology (1945) commerce (1946), management (1949), psychology (1949), demography (1956), law (1959), criminology (1961) and defence studies (1965). A good number of them are multi-disciplinary in their concern and approach. In addition to conducting research in various fields, they also function as training institutions for future researchers and administrators.

The first professional association was set up in 1919 in history, followed by anthropology (1921), geography (1926), linguistics (1928) and economics (1929). By 1947 the year when India attained freedom, there were 16 such organizations : in 10 years' time, i.e. by 1957, their number rose to 25, and in the following decade, ending 1967, as many as 22 were added. In 1970, the total number had reached 59. At present their number has gone up to 80.

Financing of Social Science Research

Broadly, the burden of assisting the social science research in India is shared by three important agencies : Government, Private Bodies and the International Organizations. The Government's contribution is the highest, i.e. about 90 per cent. As against ad hoc financing, the proportion of regular grant-in-aid by the government is also the highest. In other words, most of the social science research institutions in India receive their regular grants from government sources. However, the mode and procedure followed by each organization varies from one another. For instance, the Central Government allocates block grants to autonomous bodies which, in turn, frame their own rules and procedures for distribution of money to institutions and individuals wishing to conduct research in any branch of social sciences.

The sum spent on social sciences is meagre as compared to what is spent on scientific and technological research. According to the estimate made by J. L. Sardana, the country is spending annually about Rs.2,500 million on natural, technological and medical sciences and around Rs.25 million on research in social sciences. Similarly, the international organizations, which have bigger bodies, provide grants for social science research either directly to the Government or to research institutions after obtaining formal approval of the Government. Here too, the amount spent on social science research is small as compared to what is spent on scientific research.

The existing sources financing the social science research in the country are within the following three sectors:

I. Public/Government Sector:

(a) Ministries/Departments of Central and State Governments,
(b) Autonomous organizations, sponsored and funded by the Government, and
(c) National Banks and Public Financial Institutions.

II. Private Sector:

(a) Private Research Institutions,
(b) Professional Organizations, and
(c) Industrial Houses and Individual Companies.

III. International Sector:

(a) National Organizations sponsoring and funding research activities in the Third World countries, and
(b) International Organizations.

ICSSR conducted a study (1974-78) in respect of financing the social science research in India with the following objectives in view :

(a) to identify institutions and agencies financing the social science research;
(b) to quantify their financial inputs and assess their relative contribution;
(c) to analyse patterns and procedures of financing;
(d) to observe the nature of studies and researches emerging from the expenditure;
(e) to make suggestions for coordinating the system of providing financial support.

A brief report of the study is detailed below:

The Government plays two distinct but related roles in the research sphere, those of sponsor and user. The impetus to planned economic growth has produced an awareness of and need for social science research and consequently government sponsored research is greatly devoted to socio-economic problems facing the country and mostly is of ad-hoc nature.

The study identified 55 departments of the Central Government considered to be the possible agencies which could sponsor research and provide financial support to research organizations. The response received was encouraging. Among the Central Ministries, the following were found to be originators of a large volume of research directly and indirectly by providing financial support to research undertaken by other institutions :

(1) Ministry of Agriculture
(2) Ministry of Finance
(3) Ministry of Health and Family Welfare
(4) Ministry of Human Resource Development
(5) Ministry of Labour
(6) Ministry of Planning

Autonomous Funding Agencies

(1) Central Social Welfare Board
(2) Family Planning Foundation
(3) Indian Council of Agricultural Research
(4) Indian Council of Child Welfare

(5) Indian Council of Cultural Relations
(6) Indian Council of Historical Research
(7) Indian Council of Medical Research
(8) Indian Council of Social Science Research
(9) Indian Council of World Affairs
(10) National Council of Applied Economic Research
(11) National Council of Educational Research and Training
(12) National Productivity Council
(13) University Grants Commission

Banking Institutions

ICSSR as part of its study approached 85 banking institutions including the Reserve Bank of India to find out how far they had been able to equip themselves for the tasks assigned to them by undertaking or sponsoring research in various desired fields.

It was found that the research activities of banking institutions are problem oriented, i.e. of a functional character suiting the requirements of the institutions concerned. Their studies are short-term surveys of a particular area or region and thus are of an ad-hoc rather than of continuing nature. The Reserve Bank of India and the State Bank of India were found to be the leading institutions in social science research.

Industrial and Commercial Houses

Like the banking institutions, research projects of industrial and commercial houses were also of functional character, suiting to the requirement of the industry concerned, i.e. problem oriented and of an ad-hoc nature.

International Agencies

ICSSR conducted a similar study in respect of financing the social science research in India by the following 12 international organizations:

(1) United Nations Educational, Scientific and Cultural Organization (Unesco)

(2) United States Educational Foundation in India (USEFI)
(3) Ford Foundation
(4) World Bank
(5) British Council Division
(6) United Nation's Children's Emergency Found (Unicef)
(7) International Labour Organization (ILO)
(8) American Institute of Indian Studies (AIIS)
(9) Shastri Indo-Canadian Institute
(10) World Health Organization (WHO)
(11) United Nations Development Programme (UNDP)
(12) Food and Agriculture Organization of the United Nations (FAO)

The main objectives of the study were to identify various international agencies, which directly undertake or provide financial assistance for social science research in India, to quantify the financial inputs provided for the purpose and to analyse the patterns and procedures adopted by the various foreign funding agencies for providing financial support for social science research. These agencies were approached to supply the requisite information on a set pattern, laid down in a questionnaire, as in the case of other studies, to supply information about their basic objectives, research programmes and other facilities available with them.

It may thus be seen that there exist a number of agencies financing the social science research in the country. However lack of coordination among the funding agencies created problems, on the one hand, of duplication of research and, on the other, imbalanced research in the different branches of social sciences. Moreover, research output by various research institutions is not fully utilized.

TWENTY

INDIAN COUNCIL OF SOCIAL SCIENCE RESEARCH

The Indian Council of Social Science Research, 35 Ferozeshah Road, New Delhi, is an autonomous organization established by the Government of India in 1969.

Objectives

The objectives for which the Council has been established are:

to review the progress of social science research and give advice to its users;

to sponsor social science research programmes and projects and administer grants to institutions and individuals for research in social sciences;

to institute and administer scholarships and fellowships for research in social sciences;

to indicate areas in which social science research is to be promoted and adopt special measures for development of research in neglected or new areas;

to give financial support to institutions, associations and journals engaged in social science research;

to arrange for technical training in research methodology and to provide guidance for research;

to coordinate research activities and encourage programmes of inter-disciplinary research;

to develop and support centres for documentation services and supply of data;

to organize, sponsor and finance seminars, workshops and study groups;

to undertake publication and assist publication of journals and books in social sciences;

to advise the Government of India on all matters pertaining to social science research as may be referred to it from time to time; and

to take such measures generally as may be necessary from time to time to promote social science research and its utilization.

The Council considers for support research proposals on any subject or theme, which have a significant social science orientation. The proposal may fall within a discipline such as economics, education, geography, history, political science, psychology, public administration, sociology, social and cultural anthropology, international relations, etc., or it may be inter-disciplinary in character.

Programmes and Activities

ICSSR has been able to bring about a great deal of dynamism in the development of social sciences in India especially in terms of motivating scholars to adopt innovative approaches to research into the areas of national relevance. Over the years ICSSR, in its responsive and promotional roles, has built up a wide-ranging programme-based research enterprises at the individual, institutional, regional and national levels. The sponsored research has grown out of ICSSR's concern with the need for defining priorities in research on the basis of the following criteria : (a) adding significantly to existing knowledge or making major contributions to methodology; (b) understanding of social reality and improvement of quality of life; (c) solving the basic problems the nation is facing; (d) contributing to the study of issues leading to policy formulation; and (e) highlighting comparatively less researched areas. In its promotional role, it provides opportunities for individual scholars and teams to find utmost creative expression. In response to the developmental needs of the country, the Council has initiated a variety of research programmes such as Alternatives in Development, Women Studies, Population Studies, Analysis of Census Data, etc.

In this endeavour, importance is being given to developing methodologies of inter-disciplinary nature towards a new policy and perspective on social sciences. The linkages with medical and agricultural sciences are noteworthy in this regard. The supportive programme of assisting and bringing out publications of various kinds has helped disseminate research results widely.

An important subject being constantly debated within the ICSSR system is the issue of utilization of research. The relevant inputs towards a national debate on this issue are being documented in a series of publications planned by the Council.

International Collaboration

One of the important programmes of ICSSR is collaboration with international bodies and academic institutions abroad for promotion of research in the field of social science. The Council is also an important implementing agency for social science projects under different Cultural Exchange Programmes signed from time to time between the Government of India and those of the other countries. The Council is a member of several international bodies, namely, Association of Asian Social Science Research Councils (AASSREC), International Federation of Social Science Organization (IFSSO) and International Social Science Council (ISSC). One of the important collaborative programmes recently undertaken by the ICSSR has been the Indo-Dutch programme of Alternatives in Development. Besides, the Council has initiated and developed collaborative programmes with France. The USA, UK, Japan, Thailand, Hungary and Czechoslovakia. ICSSR also functions as the secretariat of the Indo-Soviet Commission for Cooperation in Social Sciences which has organized a number of symposia, exchange of scholars, publications, etc. The AASSREC Secretariat is located on the same premises as ICSSR with its Member Secretary as the Secretary General.

ICSSR provides financial assistance to individual scholars for visits abroad for collection of data for their research and for attending seminars and conferences in selected countries of Asia and Africa. Distinguished foreign social scientists are also invited to visit India.

Organization

The Council consists of a Chairman, 18 Social Scientists, six representatives of the Government of india and a Member Secretary. All the members are nominated by the Government. Policy matters are decided by the following functional committees of the Council.

1. Committee on Data Archives
2. Committee on International Collaboration
3. Committee on Training
4. Committee on Documentation Services and Research Information
5. Policy and Administration Committee
6. Research Committee
7. Research Institutes Committee

National Social Science Documentation Centre, New Delhi

The National Social Science Documentation Centre (NASSDOC) was set up in 1970 by the Indian Council of Social Science Research. Its activities include the following:

(1) Building up a collection of reference materials ; collecting (a) unpublished doctoral theses approved by Indian universities and foreign theses on India; (b) research reports of the projects undertaken by ICSSR and other social science research institutions assisted by ICSSR (c) working papers presented at ICSSR funded seminars and conferences; and (d) periodicals of research standard in social sciences.

(2) Providing duplicating and reprographic services.

(3) Striving for bibliographic control over social science materials by bringing out various documents under Research Information Series. 80 titles have so far been published.

(4) providing select bibliographies on request.

(5) Providing document supply services to scholars from outside Delhi.

(6) Providing bibliographical information about Indian publications in social science disciplines to international documentation agencies like International Committce for Social Science information and Documentation, Paris, *International Bulletin of Bibliography on Education*, published from Madrid and for International Geographical Bibliography published from Paris.

(7) Awarding study grants to scholars for working in libraries of their interest.

(8) Providing consultancy to social science institutions in setting up documentation and information centres.

(9) Providing facilities for staff participation in professional seminars and conferences through contributing papers as well as taking active part in their deliberations. They are also deputed to attend short duration refresher courses.

(10) Organizing training courses for Library Information Science professionals with emphasis on social science information and documentation under Continuing Education Programme.

(11) Processing project proposals for consideration of the ICSSR Committee on Documentation Services and Research Information for financial assistance in the field of documentation.

(12) Entering into exchange arrangements with national and international organizations for their publication. (At present 2,000 institutions are on the exchange list.)

(13) Supplying ICSSR publications on payment/free and participating in book exhibitions for sales promotion, also sale of Government of India publications to research institutes.

ICSSR Data Archives

Recognizing the critical role of properly organized data in improving the quality of research the Indian Council of Social Science Research (ICSSR) established the Data Archives in its secretariat at New Delhi in 1973. The main objectives of the Data Archives are:

(i) to promote and coordinate organization of data relevant for social science research in an easily processable form;

(ii) to help research scholars to have access to data gathered by governmental agencies and to act as liaison between the data gathering agencies and data users; and

(iii) to develop skills and competence among researchers in computer applications in social science research and secondary analysis of data.

ICSSR has envisaged a broader role for its Data Archives. And so, instead of establishing a huge centralized repository of data at one place, the Council has decided to follow a decentralized model in which the Data Archives is to promote and coordinate organization of existing social science data in an easily retrievable form so that it could be analysed from several perspectives. The organization of voluminous data is expected to be carried out with the cooperation of social scientists and user research institutions in the country.

These broad objectives are expected to be realized through the following functions:

1. Data repository
2. institution-based data archives
3. Grants-in-aid for data organization
4. Clearing house
5. Training
6. Guidance and consultancy Services in Data Processing
7. National Register of Social Scientists
8. International collaborations
9. Computer facilities

PART IV

SELECT UNESCO DOCUMENTS

TWENTYONE

EDUCATION FOR INTERNATIONAL UNDERSTANDING, COOPERATION, PEACE, HUMAN RIGHTS AND FUNDAMENTAL FREEDOMS (UNESCO'S RECOMMENDATION, 1974)

The General Conference of the United Nations Educational, Scientific and Cultural Organization, meeting in Paris from October 17 to Novermber 23, 1974, at its 18th session,

Mindful of the responsibility incumbent on States to achieve through education the aims set forth in the character of the United Nations, the Constitution of Unesco, the Universal Declaration of Human Rights and the Geneva Conventions for the Protection of Victims of War of August 12, 1949, in order to promote international understanding, cooperation and peace and respect for human rights and fundamental freedoms,

Reaffirming the responsibility which is incumbent on Unesco to encourage and support in Member States any activity designed to ensure the education of all for the advancement of justice, freedom, human rights and peace,

Noting nevertheless that the activity of Unesco and of its Member States sometimes has an impact only on a small minority of the steadily growing numbers of schoolchildren, students, young people and adults continuing their education, and educators, and that the curricula and methods of international education are not always attuned to the needs and aspirations of the participating young people and adults,

Noting moreover that in a number of cases there is still a wide disparity between proclaimed ideals, declared intentions and the actual situation,

Having decided, at its seventeenth session, that this education should be the subject of a recommendation to Member States,

Adopts this nineteenth day of November 1974, the present recommendation.

The General Conference recommends that Member States should apply the following provisions by taking whatever legislative or other steps may be required in conformity with the constitutional practice of each State to give effect within their respective territories to the principles set forth in this recommendation.

I. Significance of Terms

1. For the purpose of this recommendation:

(a) The word "education" implies the entire process of social life by means of which individuals and social groups learn to develop consciously within, and for the benefit of the national and international communities, the whole of their personal capacities, attitudes, aptitudes amd knowledge. The process is not limited to any specific activity.

(b) The terms "international understanding", "cooperation" and "peace" are to be considered as an individual whole based on the principle of friendly relations between peoples and States having different social and political systems and on the respect for human rights and fundamental freedoms. In the context of this recommendation, different connotations of these terms are sometimes gathered together in a concise expression, "international education".

(c) "Human rights" and "fundamental freedoms" are those defined in the United Nations Charter, the Universal Declaration of Human Rights and the International Covenants on Economic, Social and Cultural Rights, and on Civil and Political Rights.

II. Scope

2. This recommendation applies to all stages of education.

III. Guiding Principles

3. Education should be infused with the aims and purposes set forth in the Charter of the United Nations, the Constitution of Unesco and the Universal Declaration of Human Rights, particularly Article 26, paragraph 2, of the last named, which states: "Education shall be directed to the full development of the human personality and to the strengthening of respect for human rights and fundamental freedoms. It shall promote understanding, tolerance and friendship among all nations, racial or religious groups, and shall further the activities of the United Nations for the maintenance of peace.

4. In order to enable every person to contribute actively to the fulfillment of the aims referred to in paragraph 3, and promote international solidarity and cooperation, which are necessary in solving the world problems affecting the individuals' and communities' life and exercise of fundamental rights and freedoms, the following objectives should be regarded as major guiding principles of educational policy:

a. an international dimension and a global perspective in education at all levels and in all its forms;
b. understanding and respect for all peoples, their cultures, civilizations, values and ways of life, including domestic ethnic cultures and cultures of other nations;
c. awareness of the increasing global interdependence between peoples and nations;
d. abilities to communicate with others;
e. awareness not only of the rights but also of the duties incumbent upon individuals, social groups and nations towards each other;
f. understanding of the necessity for international solidarity and cooperation;
g. readiness on the part of the individual to participate in solving the problems of his community, his country and the world at large.

5. Combining learning, training, information and action, international education should further the appropriate intellectual

and emotional development of the individual. It should develop a sense of social responsibility and of solidarity with less privileged groups and should lead to observance of the principles of equality in everyday conduct. It should also help to develop qualities, aptitudes and abilities which enable the individual to acquire a critical understanding of problems at the national and international levels; to understand and explain facts, opinions and ideas; to work in a group; to accept and participate in free discussions; to observe the elementary rules of procedures applicable to any discussion; and to base value-judgements and decisions on a rational analysis of relevant facts and figures.

6. Education should stress the inadmissibility of recourse to war for purposes of expansion, aggression and domination, or to the use of force and violence for purposes of repression, and should bring every person to understand and assume his or her responsibilities for the maintenance of peace. It should contribute to international understanding and strengthening of world peace and to the activities in the struggle against colonialism and neo-colonialism in all forms and manifestations, and against all forms and varieties of racialism and apartheid as well as other ideologies which breed national and racial hatred and which are contrary to the purposes of this recommendation.

IV. National Policy, Planning and Administrative

7. Each Member State should formulate and apply national policies aimed at increasing the efficacy of education in all its forms and strengthening its contribution to international understanding and cooperation, to the maintenance and development of a just peace, to the establishment of social justice, to respect for and application of human rights and fundamental freedoms, and to the eradication of the prejudices, misconceptions, inequalities and all forms of injustice which hinder the achievement of these aims.

8. Member States should, in collaboration with the National Commissions for Unesco, take steps to create cooperation

between ministries and departments and coordination of their efforts to plan and carry out concerted programmes of action in international education.

9. Member States should provide, consistent with their constitutional provisions, the financial, administrative, material and moral support necessary to implement this recommendation.

V. Particular Aspects of Learning, Training and Action

Ethical and Civic Aspects

10. Member States should take appropriate steps to strengthen and develop, in the process of learning and training, attitudes and behaviour based on recognition of the equality and necessary interdependence of the nations and peoples.

11. Member States should take steps to ensure that the principles of the Universal Declaration of Human Rights and of the International Convention of the Elimination of All Forms of Racial Discrimination become an integral part of the developing person or adult by applying these principles in the daily conduct of education at each level and in all its forms, thus enabling each individual to contribute personally to the regeneration and extension of education in the direction indicated.

12. Member States should urge educators, in collaboration with pupils, parents, the organizations concerned and the community, to use methods which appeal to the creative imagination of children and adolescents and to their social activities and thereby to prepare them to exercise their rights and freedoms while recognizing and respecting the rights of others and to perform their social duties.

13. Member States should promote, at every stage of education, an active civic training which will enable every person to gain a knowledge of the method of operation and the work of public institutions, whether local, national or international, to become acquainted with the procedures for solving fun-

damental problems, and to participate in the cultural life of the community and in public affairs. Where possible, this participation should increasingly link education and action to solve problems at the local, national and international levels.

14. Education should include critical analysis of the historical and contemporary factors of an economic and political nature underlying the contradictions and tensions between countries, together with study of ways of overcoming these contradictions, which are the real impediments to understanding, true international cooperation and the development of world peace.

15. Education should emphasize the true interests of peoples and their incompatibility with the interests of monopolistic groups holding economic and political power, which practise exploitation and foment war.

16. Student participation in the organization of studies and of the educational establishment they are attending should itself be considered a factor in civic education and an important element in international education.

Cultural Aspects

17. Member States should promote, at various stages and in various types of education, study of different cultures, their reciprocal influences, their perspectives and ways of life, in order to encourage mutual appreciation of the differences between them. Such study should, among other things, give due importance to the teaching of foreign languages, civilizations and cultural heritage as a means of promoting international and inter-cultural understanding.

Study of the Major Problems of Mankind

18. Education should be directed both towards the eradication of conditions which perpetuate and aggravate major problems affecting human survival and well-being, inequality, injustice, international relations based on the use of force and towards

measures of international cooperation likely to help solve them. Education which in this respect must necessarily be of an interdisciplinary nature should relate to such problems as:

a. equality of rights of peoples, and the right of peoples to self-determination;
b. the maintenance of peace; different types of war and their causes and effects; disarmament; inadmissibility of using science and technology for war-like purposes and their use for the purposes of peace and progress; nature and effect of economic, cultural and political relations between countries; and importance of international law for these relations, particularly for the maintenance of peace;
c. action to ensure the exercise and observance of human rights, including those of refugees; recialism and its eradication; the fight against discrimination in its various forms;
d. economic growth and social development and their relation to social justice; colonialism and decolonization; ways and means of assisting developing countries; struggle against illiteracy; campaign against disease and famine; fight for a better equality of life and the highest attainable standard of health; population growth and related questions;
e. use, management and conservation of natural resources, pollution of the environment;
f. preservation of the cultural heritage of mankind;
g. role and methods of action of the United Nations as a system in efforts to solve such problems and possibilities for strengthening and furthering its action.

19. Steps should be taken to develop the study of those sciences and disciplines which are directly related to the exercise of the increasingly varied duties and responsibilities involved in international relations.

Other Aspects

20. Member States should encourage educational authorities and educators to give education planned in accordance with this

recommendation an interdisciplinary, problem-oriented content adapted to the complexity of the issues involved in the application of human rights and in international cooperation, and in itself illustrating the ideas of reciprocal influence, mutual support and solidarity. Such programmes should be based on adequate research, experimentation and identification of specific educational objectives.

21. Member States should endeavour to ensure that international educational activity is granted special attention and resources when it is carried out in situations involving particularly delicate or explosive social problems in relations, for example, where there are obvious inequalities in opportunities for access to education.

VI. Action in Various Sectors of Education

22. Increased efforts should be made to develop and infuse an international and inter-cultural dimension at all stages and in all forms of education.

23. Member States should take advantage of the experience of the Associated Schools which carry out, with Unesco's help, programmes of international education. Those concerned with Associated Schools in Member States should strengthen and renew their efforts to extend the programme to other educational institutios and work towards the general application of its results. In other Member States, similar action should be undertaken as soon as possible. The experience of other educational institutions which have carried out successful programmes of international education should also be studied and disseminated.

24. As pre-school education develops, Member States should encourage in it activities which correspond to the purposes of the recommendation because fundamental attitudes, such as, for example, attitudes on race, are often formed in the pre-school years. in this respect, the attitude of parents should be deemed to be an essential factor for the education of children, and the adult education referred to in paragraph 30

should pay special attention to the preparation of parents for their role in pre-school education. The first school should be designed and organized as a social environment having its own character and value, in which various situations, including games, will enable children to become aware of their rights, to assert themselves freely while accepting their responsibilities, and to improve and extend through direct experience their sense of belonging to larger and larger communities-the family, the school, then the local, national and world communities.

25. Member States should urge the authorities concerned, as well as teachers and students, to re-examine periodically how post-secondary and university education should be improved so that it may contribute more fully to the attainment of the objectives of this recommendation.

26. Higher education should comprise civic training and learning activities for all students that will sharpen their knowledge of the major problems which they should help to solve, provide them with possibilities for direct and continuous action aimed at the solution of those problems, and improve their sense of international cooperation.

27. As post-secondary educational establishments, particularly universities, serve growing numbers of people, they should carry out programmes of international education as part of their broadened function in life-long education and should, in all means of communication available to them, provide opportunities, facilities for learning and activities adapted to people's real interests, problems and aspirations.

28. In order to develop the study and practice of international cooperation, post-secondary educational establishments should systematically take advantage of the forms of international action inherent in their role, such as visits from foreign professors and students and professional cooperation between professors and experimental work should be carried out on the linguistic, social, emotional and cultural obstacles,

tensions, attitudes and actions which affect both foreign students and host establishments.

29. Every stage of specialized vocational training should include training to enable students to understand their role and the role of their professions in developing their society, furthering international cooperation, maintaining and developing peace, and to assume their role actively as early as possible.

30. Whatever the aims and forms of out-of-school education, including adult education, they should be based on the following considerations

    a. as far as possible a global approach should be applied in all out-of-school education programmes which should comprise the appropriate moral, civic, cultural, scientific and technical elements of international education;
    b. all the parties concerned should combine efforts to adapt and use the mass media of communication, self-education and inter-active learning, and such institutions as museums and public libraries to convey relevant knowledge to the individual to foster in him or her favourable attitudes and a willingness to take positive action, and to spread knowledge and understanding of the educational campaigns and programmes planned in accordance with the objectives of this recommendation;
    c. the parties concerned, whether public or private, should endeavour to take full advantage of favourable situations and opportunities, such as the social and cultural centres, community centres or trade unions, youth gatherings and festivals, sporting events, contacts with foreign visitors, students or immigrants and exchanges of persons in general.

31. Steps should be taken to assist the establishment and development of such organizations as student and teacher associations for the United Nations, International Relations Clubs and Unesco Clubs, which should be associated with the preparation and implementation of coordinated programmes of international education.

32. Member States should endeavour to ensure that, at each stage of school and out-of-school education, activities directed towards the objectives of this recommendation be coordinated and form a coherent whole within the curricula for the different levels and types of education, learning and training. The principles of cooperation and association which are inherent in this recommendation should be applied in all educational activities.

VII. Teacher Preparation

33. Member States should constantly improve the ways and means of preparing and certifying teachers and other educational personnel for their role in pursuing the objectives of this recommendation and should, to this end:

a. provide teachers with motivations for their subsequent work commitment to the ethics of human rights and to the aim of changing society, so that human rights are applied in practice; a grasp of the fundamental unity of mankind; ability to instil appreciation of the riches which the diversity of cultures can bestow on every individual, group or nation;
b. provide basic interdisciplinary knowledge of world problems and the problems of international cooperation, through, among other means, work to solve these problems;
c. prepare teachers themselves to take an active part in devising programmes of international education and educational equipment and materials, taking into account the aspirations of pupils and working in close collaboration with them;
d. comprise experiments in the use of active methods of education and training in at least elementary techniques of evaluation, particularly those applicable to the social behaviour and attitudes of children, adolescents and adults;
e. develop aptitudes and skills such as a desire and ability to make educational innovations and to continue his or her training; experience in teamwork and in interdisciplinary studies; knowledge of group dynamics; and the ability to

make educational innovations and to continue his or her training; experience in teamwork and in interdisciplinary studies; knowledge of group dynamics; and the ability to create favourable opportunities and take advantage of them.

f. include the study of experiments in international education, especially innovative experiments carried out in other countries, and provide those concerned, to the fullest possible extent, with opportunities for making direct contact with foreign teachers;

34. Member States should provide those concerned with direction, supervision or guidance-for instance, inspectors, educational advisers, principals of teacher-training colleges and organizers of educational activities for young people and adults-with training, information and advice enabling them to help teachers work towards the objectives of this recommendation, taking into account the aspirations of young people with regard to international problems and new educational methods that are likely to improve prospects for fulfilling these aspirations. For these purposes, seminars or refresher courses relating to international and inter-cultural education should be organized to bring together authorities and teachers; other seminars or courses might permit supervisory personnel and teachers to meet with other groups concerned such as parents, students, and teachers' associations. Since there must be a gradual but profound change in the role of education, the results of experiments for the remodelling of structures and hierarchical relations in educational establishments should be reflected in training, information and advice.

35. Member States should endeavour to ensure that any programme of further training for teachers in service or for personnel responsible for direction includes components of international education.

36. Member States should encourage and facilitate educational study and refresher courses abroad, particularly by awarding fellowships, and should encourage recognition of such courses

as part of the regular process of initial training, appointment, refresher training and promotion of teachers.

37. Member States should organize or assist bilateral exchange of teachers at all levels of education.

VIII. Educational Equipment and Materials

38. Member States should increase their efforts to facilitate the renewal, production, dissemination and exchange of equipment and materials for international education, giving special consideration to the fact that in many countries pupils and students receive most of their knowledge about international affairs through the mass media outside the school. To meet the needs expressed by those concerned with international education, efforts should be concentrated on overcoming the lack of teaching aids in improving their quality. Action should be on the following lines:

   a. appropriate and constructive use should be made of the entire range of equipment and aids available, from textbooks to televisions and of the new educational technology;
   b. there should be a component of special mass media education in teaching to help the pupils to select and analyse the information conveyed by mass media;
   c. a global approach, comprising the introduction of international components, serving as a framework for presenting local and national aspects of different subjects and illustrating the scientific and cultural history of mankind, should be employed in textbooks and all other aids to learning, with due regard to the value of the visual arts and music as factors conducive to understanding between different cultures;
   d. written and audio-visual materials of an interdisciplinary nature illustrating the major problems confronting mankind and showing in each case the need for international cooperation, and its practical form should be prepared in the language or languages of instruction of the country with the aid of information supplied by

the United Nations, Unesco and other Specialized Agencies;

e. documents and other materials illustrating the culture and the way of life of each country, the chief problems with which it is faced, and its participation in activities of worldwide concern should be prepared and communicated to other countries.

39. Member State should promote appropriate measures to ensure that educational aids, especially textbooks, are free from elements liable to give rise to misunderstanding, mistrust, racialist reactions, contempt or hatred with regard to other groups or peoples. Materials should provide a broad background of knowledge which would help learners to evaluate information and ideas disseminated through the mass media that seem to run counter to the aims of this recommendation.

40. According to its needs and possibilities, each Member State should establish or help to establish one or more documentation centres offering written and audio-visual material devised according to the objectives of this recommendation and adapted to the different forms and stages of education. These centres should be designed to foster the reform of international education, especially by developing and disseminating innovative ideas and materials, and should also organize and facilitate exchanges of information with other countries.

IX. Research and Experimentation

41. Member States should stimulate and support research on the foundations, guiding principles, means of implementation and effects of international education and on innovations and experimental activities in this field, such as those taking place in the Associated Schools. This action calls for collaboration by universities, research bodies and centres, teacher-training institutions, adult education training centres and appropriate non-governmental organizations.

42. Member States should take appropriate steps to ensure that teachers and the various authorities concerned build interna-

tional education on a sound psychological and sociological basis by applying the results of research carried out in each country on the formation and development of favourable or unfavorable attitudes and behaviour, on attitude change, on the interaction of personality development and education and on the positive or negative effects of educational activity. A substantial part of this research should be devoted to the aspirations of young people concerning international problems and relations.

X. International Cooperation

43. Member States should consider international cooperation a responsibility in developing international education. In the implementation of this recommendation they should refrain from intervening in matters which are essentially within the domestic jurisdiction of any State in accordance with the United Nations Charter. By their own actions, they should demonstrate that implementing this recommendation is itself an exercise in international understanding and cooperation. They should, for example, organize, or help the appropriate authority and non-governmental organizations to organize, an increasing number of international meetings and study sessions on international education; strengthen their programmes for the reception of foreign students, research workers, teachers and educators belonging to workers, teachers' associations and promote reciprocal visits by schoolchildren, and student and teacher exchanges; extend and intensify exchanges of information on cultures and ways of life; arrange for the translation or adaptation and dissemination of information and suggestions coming from other countries.

44. Member States should encourage the cooperation between their Associated Schools and those of other countries with the help of Unesco in order to promote mutual benefits by expanding their experiences in a wider international perspective.

45. Member States should encourage wider exchanges of textbooks, especially history and geography textbooks, and should, where appropriate, take measures by concluding. if

possible, bilateral and multilateral agreements for the reciprocal study and revision of textbooks and other educational materials in order to ensure that they are accurate, balanced, up-to-date and unprejudiced and will enhance mutual knowledge and understanding among different peoples.

TWENTYTWO

SOCIAL SCIENCES IN MAN AND BIOSPHERE (MAB) PROGRAMME

(Report on Seven Seminars - 1977)

Introduction

Seven national seminars were held between June and October 1977. The financial support for the national seminars came from the Social Science Sector's "Division for Human Settlements and their Socio-cultural Environment" (ENV, for short), and for the regional meeting from the "Division of Ecological Sciences" (ECO) of the Science Sector. In the organization of the national seminars, both the MAB committees and the key social science funding agencies were involved. The programme of seminars was the first not only in Asia, but the world.

The national seminars were organized with the following objectives in view:

i. to make Unesco's MAB programme known to the academic community;
ii. to establish a dialogue between natural and social scientists so that they could jointly initiate activities pertaining to MAB;
iii. to interest social scientists in the MAB programme and ensure their participation;
iv. to identify researchable topics that are relevant to the country, and also those which may be taken up for cross-cultural comparative study.

More specifically, the seminars were expected to accomplish the following:

1. Review of researches in various social science disciplines that

have a bearing on the MAB programme, with a view to finding out:

(a) What themes have interested the social scientists?
(b) What geographical areas have been studied?
(c) What methodologies have been employed ? and
(d) What insights and hypotheses exist which can be utilized for further research in this area?

2. A review of the MAB Programme in the country to find out:

(a) Which areas have been chosen for research?
(b) What social science inputs have already been made?
(c) What problems exist in involving social scientists in the MAB programme? and
(d) How social scientists can be involved in the future projects and programmes of MAB?

The national seminars organized in seven countries of the region, as also the special sessions of MAB at the second conference of the Association of Asian Social Science Research Councils (AASSREC) held in Seoul, Republic of Korea, have served a useful function of disseminating information about MAB, and of generating interest amongst the social scientists in biosphere related research themes.

Participants in all the seminars and meetings felt that the concern with environment is universal and the scholarly community must immediately address itself to the several vexing problems concerning man's relationship with environment.

The participants felt that efforts should be made to restore the focus of MAB, which should be Man. Unless this is done, it will be difficult to stop Man's march toward disaster. Man, through his several acts-intended as well as unintended-has been engaged in the process of "colonizing the future". It is the task of the MAB committees to deal with the problem of "Survival of Man" and not merely with the problem of "conservation of environment". In the MAB programme, it is Man who should be at the "Core", and the question of biosphere ought to be tackled from that vantage point. Research that disregards Man and his culture, and focuses solely on the non-human aspects of biosphere, was viewed as non-relevant and a dispensable luxury. The seminars gave ample support for what may be called a "non-disciplinary" orientation to MAB research.

A review of the recommendations made by the various seminars suggests that there is an urgent need for Unesco to activize its efforts to promote the work on MAB. It should be stressed that it is not only researches on the "social" aspect of MAB that are lacking, even in the sphere of natural sciences researches need to be promoted in several countries. In a way, this is advantageous: such a situation makes it possible to introduce pluridisciplinary orientation to the entire programme right from the beginning.

The seminars clearly brought out the need for a better collaboration and coordination amongst various agencies interested in the problems of environment-either its management, or research on it. One major function performed by the seminar was to make MAB known to the scholarly community and to stimulate among its members an interest in problems related to biosphere; the seminars thus helped bridge the communication gap that existed between the officials of the MAB Committees and the researchers located in the academia came to know that there is a programme like MAB, that the governments have set up national committees to develop a plan of action, that researchers can make use of this forum and get the much needed funding support. Participants also requested for the reconsideration of the composition of national committees to ensure that the natural as well as social scientists are duly represented.

The concrete suggestions for immediate action thrown up by the seminars are summarized below:

1. Need to carry out stock-taking exercises.

Almost all the seminars suggested the need for a systematic stock-taking of the available researches in various social science disciplines relative to Man-Environment relations. These were proposed to be done at two levels:

(a) Global level: Eminent scholars representing the key social science disciplines may be invited to prepare small monographs on contributions made by their respective disciplines towards the understanding of Man-Environment relations. These scholars would be preparing 8-to 100-page monographs "On the state of the arts" which can be used by all countries. Initially, such global reports may be commissioned in the following disciplines: sociology\anthropology; economics; geography; psychology; law; public administration, and political science.

(b) National level: In cooperation with the National MAB Committees and the Social Science Councils, stock-taking exercises in the above-mentioned disciplines may be commissioned for different countries. These reports will contain extensive annotated bibliography and a review of the theories and concepts utilized in the studies, methodologies employed for investigation, and available generalizations and hypotheses. These reports are also expected to identify research gaps and suggest priorities.

2. **Fellowship and ad-hoc grants**

The seminars suggested that Unesco might consider encouraging students to undertake their Ph.D. work or problems related to MAB by instituting research fellowships. These fellowships may be awarded through either the national MAB committees or through the social science research councils. A Ph.D fellowship given for a period of two years would ensure that the recipient scholar would be devoting his full time to carry out research on a theme that is of interest to MAB. Because of his first involvement in research and because of his personal interest in obtaining a degree, the fellowship incentive might be the most economical means of ensuring completion of a study and of generating a life-long interest in the young researcher.

Similarly, the seminars suggested that students writing their dissertation for the M.A. degree may also be encouraged to do work on MAB-related themes. For this, a small subsidy to cover the costs of field work, and also of typing the manuscript, may be given.

In addition, Unesco might consider "buying the time" of senior faculty members for a year or two so that they can devote their entire time to the pursuit of research on MAB-related themes. The concept of "buying time" involves reimbursement of the salary that the scholar receives from his employers. He may, in addition, be given some grant with which to hire a research assistant, obtain secretarial services, and to cover his field expenses.

A provision may also be made for giving an ad-hoc grant to scholars who might approach Unesco for a publication grant, or a grant for field trip, or for some other secretarial assistance.

3. Training programmes and workshops

The seminars also recommended to Unesco to organize national level training seminars on one or more of the following themes:

(a) Trends in environmental research
(b) Systems approach in various disciplines
(c) Management of environment and of human settlements
(d) Social Science perspective in environmental research

For these seminars, one or two specialists may be recruited to serve as faculty. It will be ideal if the recruited faculty could cover more than one country so that the cost of travel may be reduced.

Provision may also be made for the organization of national level workshops in which scholars working on the same theme may be invited to develop a common research design, and exchange experience.

The Seminars also suggested that some advanced level training seminars or workshops may be organized at the regional level.

4. National seminars on MAB and social sciences

Some other countries in the region may like to organize seminars at the national level to discuss social science inputs into the MAB programme. Unesco was requested to encourage such proposals.

5. Proposals for cross-cultural research

Several topics were suggested by the seminar participants for further research through active involvement of the social scientists. Those which were recommended by more than one seminar, and were assigned priority, are listed below:

(i) Urban-industrial systems and environmental crisis

The themes under this heading which were recommended are:

(a) uncontrolled growth of habitation
(b) slum cultures
(c) industrial wastes
(d) pollution

(ii) Forest eco-systems with particular reference to shifting (Swidden) cultivation
(iii) Agricultural development and environmental problems with special reference to:

(a) irrigation and drainage
(b) chemical fertilizers
(c) bio-gas
(d) animal husbandry and fisheries

(iv) Water management
(v) Perception of environmental quality
(iv) Human migrations, including the problem of tourism (international migration)
(vii) Communities in disaster: Natural hazards and human response.

6. Need for a documentation centre

During the discussions, several participants mentioned the need for a centre-regional or sub-regional which would collect all the available literature on Environment, and serve as a clearing house. It may also become a centre for research where scholars from different countries may come for short durations on study leave to consult the literature and do the writing.

TABLE

Seminars on MAB and Social Sciences
held in Asia in 1977.

Country and Venue	Organizing Agency	Dates	Number of Partici-pants
Thailand, Sakaerat Biosphere Reserve Station	National Research Council	June 26-29 1977	43
Nepal, Kathmandu Planning Commission	National MAB Committee	July 19 1977	21
Bangladesh, Dacca Atomic Energy Commission	Unesco Nat. Com. & MAB Committee	July 21-22 1977	30
The Philippines, Manila, Midtown Ramada Hotel	National MAB Committee & PSSC	Aug. 4-5 1977	70
Pakistan, Peshawar Forest Research Institute	National MAB Committee	Aug. 13-15 1977	25
India, Delhi Department of Anthropology, Delhi University	Indian Council of Social Science Research	Sept.16-17 1977	42
Malaysia, Penang Palam-Beach Hotel	National MAB Committee	Oct. 4-5 1977	34
Republic of Korea, Unesco National Commission	Association of Asian Social Science Research Councils (AASSREC)	Oct. 4-8 1977	28

TWENTYTHREE

YOUTH MOBILIZATION FOR DEVELOPMENT

(Meeting of Youth-September 1978)

The concept of "youth" and the series of problems to which it gives rise, far from being homogeneous, vary with the socio-economic conditions obtaining in the different countries and regions and reflect their values and their history. The Kathmandu meeting (1978), instead of focussing narrowly on youth's problems and aspirations, placed these in a much broader social, economic and particularly cultural perspective, viewing young people not as a problem group apart from society but as a force for change within society.

In pursuance of Resolution 3.161 adopted by the General Conference at its 19 th session, an Asian Regional Meeting (Category VI) was organized by Unesco, as part of its youth programme, in Kathmandu, from September 17 to 27, 1978, to consider "Youth Mobilization for Development in Asian Settings".

Thirtythree participants from 18 countries, including seven women, took part in the 1978 Kathmandu meeting, which was also attended by 18 observers from governmental and non-governmental agencies in or concerned with the Asian region, as well as representatives of five agencies of the United Nations system. There were participants with experience in the governmental and non-governmental sectors; there were adult specialists in the youth field and young people themselves; and levels of responsibility ranged from high-ranking officials to grass-roots workers.

The participants in the Asian Regional Youth Meeting divided their Recommendations into three groups: General principles; Recommendations addressed to governments; and Recommendations addressed to Unesco and other international organizations.

General Principles

Youth is an overwhelming part of the population in Asia. Present problems and future perspectives of Asia can be observed through the needs of the young generation.

There are many complex problems confronting young people today. They endeavour to obtain recognition of their elementary right and to have a full share in social, economic, political and other aspects of life.

Millions of youth continue to suffer from the gap between the rich and the poor. It is a foremost duty of Asian governments to ensure social justice and basic minimum necessities of life and education for the young generation.

Asian development and mobilization of youth are closely interrelated in terms of carrying out projects and plans of national development and achieving future prosperity of the region's nations.

The solution of the problems of youth, varying from eradication of illiteracy, poverty and unemployment to securing all indispensable rights of children and youth as a whole, which are proclaimed and recognized by numerous internationally acknowledged charters and covenants, should be achieved as quickly as possible. Development of Asian nations is inseparable from the fulfilment of the aspirations of youth and the expression of its creative energy. The aims of Asian development and mobilization of youth for it can be achieved only in peace and through international cooperation.

The mobilization of youth for the development of Asia should be linked with efforts to establish a New International Economic Order, which would ensure to the developing countries of Asia the ownership of their natural resources and enable them to use these resources for the overall development of a society inspired by social justice.

The youth of Asia should be given an appropriate place in governmental policy. Youth has to be considered as a most important part of overall national policy. Strong emphasis must be laid on the recognition of democratic rights of youth. The vast range of youth rights and their implementation in Asia should be provided for; among them is the right to education without distinction of social, cultural and national backgrounds of youth.

The mobilization of youth cannot be brought about without the complete elimination of illiteracy, unemployment, ill-health, poor nutrition and other social problems which still exist in Asian countries. Poor sections of the population should be given preference in achieving those standards of education which are adopted for involvement in different projects and development programmes.

Asian countries will have to assign youth problems the highest priority if the general problems of economic, technological and social progress are to be solved.

Development is very considerably affected by the situation of youth in the present and in the future. In this respect, deep concern must be accorded to the situation and economic conditions and needs of rural youth. The burning issues of rural youth must be given full consideration in national programmes.

The governments of Asian nations are called upon to spare more funds for educational programmes and to consider this expenditure as an investment in a key project in their strategic and long-term planning. Youth programmes should be acknowledged by respective governments as the crucial issue of national development. Meaningful education reform should be introduced to make education a right and not a privilege and to divert funds from unproductive expenditure to education.

The mobilization and education of youth should be achieved together with the preservation of traditional cultural values, behaviour and attitudes.

The continuation of the brain drain seriously challenges Asian societies and youth itself. Nationwide programmes and persuasive campaigns should be carried out to stop it and bring the energies of young talents back home to involve them in the process of development of their respective countries.

It was proposed that vast programmes for youth activities should be initiated in Asian countries. Asian governments and Unesco Member States in general are called upon to assist in the fulfilment of different forms of youth activities.

Recommendations addressed to governments

1. *Formulate comprehensive national youth policies*

   These should take into consideration the objective reality of each country and specific Asian values.

2. *Sponsor leadership and skills training programmes*

   Participants : Youth trainers, youth workers, out-of-school young adults, young parents. *Content*: work skills, citizenship awareness, population education, family planning, sanitation, nutrition, health care, conservation, child-rearing, non-formal education.

3. *Foster community development services*

   Participants: adults, young parents, community in general. *Content*: infrastructural development, agriculture, training and non-formal education (training has the same content as above, see 2 above).

4. *Promote local youth exchange*

   Exchange of young people from different parts of the country. *Purpose*: to reinforce national integration through exchange of skills, arts and crafts.

5. *Issue publications*
   Magazines with articles written by, for and on youth. Reports

on youth programmes through mimeographed or printed news bulletins.

6. *Encourage local resource development*

   Identification and use of local resource persons, local cultural institutions and premises for youth projects, e.g. skilled workers and artisans, shadow plays for disseminating progressive values, use of public places and school premises for youth meetings.

7. *Undertake research*

   More money and facilities should be provided for research on youth and preferably by youth. Stress should be placed on particular problems affecting youth such as unemployment, drug abuse, prostitution, child abuse, child labour, etc.

8. *Promote allocation*

   By developed countries in Asia and other regions of more funds and expertise in their assistance programmes to the projects proposed above, to be implemented in all Member States of the region, developed and developing. Member States are invited to contribute to the Special Fund for Youth created by Unesco in 1977.

9. *Asian Member States are invited*

   To express, in appropriate ways, their solidarity with Vietnam's reconstruction efforts, particularly in the field of youth.

Recommendations Addressed to Unesco and other International Organizations

1. Promote exchange of personnel at the middle and grassroots levels
   Purpose: Sharing skills and information.
2. Sponsor exchange of teams of experts

Purpose: Advice and cooperative evaluation.

3. Hold intra-regional and inter-regional meetings
Purpose : Share experience and information.
Participants: Youth leader youth experts, youth delegations from governmental and non-governmental organizations.

* As for as possible, delegation members must be from the grassroots level.

* It is advisable to have one youth expert and one youth leader from each country, for future meetings of this type.

Retionale: Experts have the experience but usually cannot fully express the sentiments and do not possess the creativity and openness of the younger generation. Vice versa for the youth delegates.

* Asian delegates must also to invited to youth conferences outside the region, to prevent inbreeding.

4. *The United Nations System*

should continue and intensify its efforts to encourage governments in Asia to implement a policy of minimum wages for industrial workers in relation to their economic and social realities.

The World Health Organization

5. should use its resources to monitor information, and undertake research through independent individuals or organizations, on occupational diseases, problems of workers in slums and squatter areas and on environmental issues affecting young workers.

6. *Foster Youth Festivals (sports, arts, music)*
7. *Encourage discount rates for youth, students and young workers' travel*

Rationale: If travel is considered one of the best forms of international understanding, Unesco and other agencies should assist student organizations in securing discounts for travel, the simplification of formalities for visas and passports.

8. *ensure coordination*

Retionale: The lack of coordination of the various international programmes in the region is of concern to this Meeting. The agencies of the United Nations system and NGOs are all developing programmes. We believe that it is important for appropriate senior officers of these agencies to discuss and coordinate their programmes. We suggest this could be organized by Unesco Regional Offices within the next 12 months and ask that an outline of the coordinated programmes be circulated to Member Governments and organizations for their consideration and comments.

9. *Offer more opportunities to Asian youth*

in the organizations of the United Nations system and the Regional Offices

10. *Increase information exchange about youth*

through Unesco, UNDP, FAO, WHO, ESCAP, UNICEF, RCCIVS, and other organizations, with Unesco as the clearing house.

11. *Issue an Asian Youth Magazine*

as a vehicle for information exchange:

- articles and news reports from youth leaders and youth experts.
- to be founded by Unesco.

12. *Issue a Journal on Youth*

containing findings of research of various youth projects as well as throwing light on experiments and ongoing programmes in different countries.

13. *Promote projects*

for stressing young women's rights and responsibilities.

14. *Ensure that the unesco Regional Office for Education in Asia and Oceania (Bangkok)*

accords greater attention throughout its activities to youth activities. The Regional Adviser for Social Sciences in Asia should follow up this recommendation.)

15. *Submit Recommendations of this Meeting*

to the 20th (1978) session of the Unesco General Conference and to the next United Nations General Assembly.

16. *Give stress to;*

- providing early opportunities for youth to participate fully in every sphere of development
- informing young women of their rights and responsibilities.

17. *Promote population education*

and provide more information on IPPF and the problems of rising population among youth, since youth are the most productive part of the society not only in economic terms, but also in terms of fertility.

18. *Help form a body on voluntary youth service*

to give greater information, organize seminars, cooperation and free flow between the non-governmental organizations of Asia. In this respect, the Coordinating Committee for International Voluntary Survey (CCIVS) should be encouraged to regionalize, and sub-regionalize when necessary, its activities in Asia. Steps should be taken to ensure that activities of CCIVS benefit governmental as well as non-governmental agencies.

19. *Welcome the proclamation*

by United Nations of an International Youth Year and invite governments and NGOs to devote best of their efforts to its celebration.

20. *Invite Unesco*

to study the elaboration of a Charter of Rights and Responsibilities of youth in a changing world so that this Charter may be adopted by Member States in the future.

TWENTYFOUR

DYNAMICS OF NATION-BUILDING WITH PARTICULAR REFERENCE TO THE ROLE OF COMMUNICATION

(Meeting of Experts-1979)

Most countries of the Asia-Pacific region have recently attained their independence from colonial rule and have become sovereign States. The leadership of these countries, which trained itself in the politics of iconoclasm during the period of freedom struggle, by arousing the spirit of nationalism among the masses and engineering rebellion against the alien regime, suddenly came face-to-face with the practical problems of governing the country and building the nation. Depending upon individual country situations-both the internal structure and the ties of the country with the outside world-the leadership evolved its own strategies of nation-building. These strategies have their own stories of successes, and of failures, to tell. They are important not only as items of readable literature, but as significant empirical evidence for the construction of a theory of political development.

It is now accepted that both in the rise of nationalism and emergence of new nations, and in the process of modernization and political development following it, communication plays a vital role. It is the onslaught of information that is claimed to have weakened the walls of tradition and stirred a tide of rising expectations. It is the infrastructure of communication created by the colonial regimes which not only helped the establishment but became "counter-productive" in as much as it served the cause of "freedom fighters". While the "rulers" played the game of insulating the people from vital sources of information, leaders of the freedom movement succeeded in breaking some of those barriers, and also effectively utilized traditional means of communication for new purposes. The attainment of independence put the same leaders into the saddle of power giving them considerable control over the entire communication system. But the communication channels, particularly the mass media, did not only spread the message and ideology of the ruling elite, they also amplified people's complaints and frustrations. The leadership got the message once again that the mass media do not propagate only pledges and platitudes; they also diffuse failures and frustrations. Communications serve a dual function, similar to a polyandrous wife, of meeting the demands of the government and responding to the "overtures" of the people.

It is, thus, the overall structure of communication, understood in broader terms as an all-pervading phenomenon of social life, that ought to be comprehended by a student of nation-building. This is, of course, not to deny the role of mass media, which are relatively recent, compared to the phenomenon of social communication that characterizes all social systems-big or small, formal or informal. But it will be a narrow view of communication if only mass media were considered. The statistics about literacy, number of TV and radio sets, newspaper readership, movie-going, etc., is important but not enough as an indicator of nation-building. One has to consider the entire sphere of transactions in a given society while assessing the extent of its integration an outcome of the dynamic process of nation-building. In order to keep the nation independent and autonomous, cohesive, and internally legitimate, deployment of effective communication strategy is needed.

In the societies of Asia and the Pacific, one can identify a fascinating array of questions and problems related to the process of nation-building. Consider the case of Indonesia: a country of about 13,000 islands with a rich and colourful variety of subcultures has remarkably succeeded in forging a single national language. The roaring sea between the islands could not submerge the linguistic bridge. And contrast this with India, a country with a contiguous geographic terrain, which became independent almost at the same time as Indonesia and yet the question of national language is still burning hot. While the advocates of English in India ceaselessly plead for its continuance in the interest of "progress and development", the Japanese case offers a brilliant example of industrial advancement through the national language. There is also ample evidence available in the region that neither religion nor language alone succeeds in cementing the bonds of cohesion. internally, the coexistence of diverse ethnic groups, with different timings of their arrival, along with the indigenous, autochthonous population has posed problems of nation-building in countries that are described as "plural societies". A study of nation-building focussing on communication, ought to identify the mechanisms operating in society that tend to isolate and insulate sub-groups from each other by reducing the volume of transaction flows between them and the other groups. At the same time, strategies employed by the government and other agencies to keep the "apertures" open should also be properly understood. The flow of communications across the national boundaries is yet another dimension of the problem to be reckoned with. The external milieu of nation influences its internal politics, and its internal politics, in turn, guides the pattern of relations with other nations. A communication model particularly the transaction flow analysis can be employed to understand this international dimension of the nation-building process.

Since 1968, Unesco has promoted global discussion and dialogue on the theme of nation-building. It organized the first European regional workshop in Sweden to discuss the question of state-formation and nation-building. It was followed by an international meeting of experts held at Crissy-la-Salle (France) in 1970 where questions related to conceptual framework and methodology were discussed at length. In 1971, Unesco convened an Asian Working Party in Singapore to consider the process of State and Nation Building from a Third World perspective. Unesco's fourth regional training seminar in Asia held in 1975 on the Sociology of Development focussed also on nation-building.

1979 Meeting

The expert meeting on the Dynamics of Nation-Building with special reference to the role of communication, organized in collaboration with the Asia-Pacific Institute for Broadcasting Development, took place in Kuala Lumpur from September 24 to 28, 1979.

Held in accordance with the provisions of the Programme and

Budget for 1979-1980 (paragraph 3301 of 20 C/5 approved) the meeting was attended by 15 experts from 11 countries in Asia and Oceania. Also represented at the meeting were representatives from the Social Welfare Development Centre for Asia and the Pacific (SWDCAP), Asia-Pacific Institute for Broadcasting Development, and the University of Malaya.

The purpose of the meeting was as follows:

1. to take stock of, and examine, theoretical and methodological developments and trends as well as data available in the study of nation-building and the role of communication therein; and

2. to develop a research outline for a cross-national and comparative study on the subject.

The following were thought worthy of reflection in any proposed study of nation-building and communication:

1. The role of artists (i.e. poets, novelists, etc.) and of institutions such as universities in achieving nationhood;

2. External forces, including those with interests likely either to inhibit nation-building or to give it a direction not necessarily intended by newly independent peoples themselves;

3. Class and the nature of the State, especially where the media, for instance, might reflect class goals and aspirations and not the hopes of the majority of the population;

4. Group versus individual rights, particularly in culturally fragmented societies;

5. The perceptions of the task of nation-building as well as the functions of the nation and the prerequisites of these in order to achieve integration between the masses and their rulers;

6. While all opportunities must be provided to newly independent peoples to develop in their own way, using their own traditions and values, there should be some caution on their

part in case this led to a state of introspection which excluded an awareness of the world environment; nevertheless while one might guard against possible parochialism it was essential to remember that the magnitude of foreign imposition in some areas made this term irrelevant because of the need to redress gross imbalances;

7. The capacity of the media to influence people in subtle and covert ways, not always for positive ends.

TWENTYFIVE

TRAINING AND RESEARCH AND DOCUMENTATION IN SOCIAL SCIENCES IN ASIA AND THE PACIFIC

(Report of the Programme Meeting-1982)

Introduction

Responding to the suggestions and recommendations of Unesco national commissions in the region, Unesco prepared a draft document for a Regional Cooperative Programme in Social Sciences for development in the Asia-Pacific region for submission to UNDP for financial support. Six Member States communicated to UNDP and to Unesco their agreement to support this proposal.

Consequently, it was decided to convene a consultation meeting of experts to formulate the substantive and operational elements of the Programme and prepare a detailed project document for submission to Unesco and UNDP.

The meeting was held in New Delhi from August 9 to 13, 1982. It was jointly hosted by ICSSR and the Indian National Commission for Cooperation with Unesco.

The meeting was attended by representatives from India, the Philippines, Republic of Korea, Thailand and the Socialist Republic of Vietnam. Besides, there were representatives from the United Nations Asian-Pacific Development Centre, UNDP/New Delhi, Association of Asian Social Science Research Councils (AASSREC), and the Indian Council of Social Science Research (ICSSR).

Development Objectives of the Programme

The Programme of Regional Cooperation in Social Sciences aims at:

(a) enhancing the national capacities for extending the range and improving the quality of social science research and its contribution to balanced social and economic development of the member countries;

(b) promoting exchange and dissemination of social science knowledge and information to ensure their effective utilization for development;

(c) assisting policy-makers and planners in gauging the impact of science and technology on societies and cultures;

(d) promoting better understanding of different cultures and societies in the region.

Outputs

The activities under the programme are expected to produce the following:

(a) greater participation of social sciences in the programmes and activities connected with national development;

(b) increased awareness among social scientists, policy makers and administrators about new developments in social science theories and methodologies and about significant experiences and experiments;

(c) exchange of social science findings between the countries of the region;

(d) establishment of interaction and dialogue between policy-makers, administrators and social scientists;

(e) collaborative research on specific problems of social development which are common to the countries in the region thereby enhancing the understanding of the problems involved in policy making;

(f) development of documentation and information services and preparation and dissemination of inventories and other relevant documents on social sciences in the countries of the region;

(g) enlargement of cadres of trained personnel for social science research on problems of development and nation-building; and

(h) establishment of various regional networks for exchange of expertise and information, and for the promotion of TCDC.

Four Major Areas

The Project will develop its activities around four major areas, namely:

(i) cross-cultural comparative research on nation-building and development;
(ii) training in social science theory and methodology:
(iii) utilization of social science knowledge for policy-making; and
(iv) regional information and documentation services.

Project Activities

The main modes of action in the Regional Programme are:

(a) regional and sub-regional consultations and joint programming;
(b) network of institutions engaged in social science information documentation and data archives:
(c) cross-cultural comparative research projects and case studies;
(d) training programme for young social scientists in quantitative research methodology, and orientation workshops for administrators and policy-makers;
(e) faculty development through inter-country study visits and at-

tachments; and

(f) publication of abstracts and support for publication of important research monographs.

The four clusters of activities are:

Cluster A : Cross-Cultural Comparative Research on Nation-building and Development

Cluster B : Training in Social Science Theory and Methodology

Cluster C : Utilization of Social Science Knowledge for Policy-making

Cluster D : Regional Information and Documentation Services.

Cluster A : Cross-Cultural Comparative Research on Nation-Building and Development

1. Rural Transformation
2. Role of Tradition and Culture in Development
3. Language and National Integration
4. Migrant Groups and the Processes of Their Accommodation and Assimilation

Cluster B : Training Programme in Social Science Theory and Methodology

The four clusters of training activities are:

1. Foundation courses in research methodology.
2. Quantitative analysis in social sciences including computer applications.
3. Social science information management and retrieval.
4. Recent advances in social science theory and research on development.

Cluster C : Utilization of Social Science Knowledge for Policy-Making

The activities proposed under this Cluster are as under:

1. National surveys to ascertain to what extent social science research is put to use in different areas in the academia, in

administration, in planning and implementation of development activities, in courses of general education.

2. Dialogues between social scientists and the users of social science research.
3. Strengthening infrastructures for the dissemination of research findings for different types of users.

Methods of Action

(a) Preparation of national studies on utilization of social science knowledge and on factors which hinder exchange of information:
(b) Regional workshops to exchange experiences and analyse problems of utilization of social science knowledge in policy-making and development work; and
(c) Clearing house facilities to promote awareness about availability of social science knowledge and data potentially useful for policy purposes.

Cluster D : Regional Information, Documentation and Clearing House Services

The information, documentation and clearing house services are intended to provide support to cross-cultural research on development, to disseminate social science knowledge generated through research and to ensure its utilization through better communication. At present the support services are scattered in different institutions and there is no regional focal point or clearing house for assisting member countries in location and collection of relevant information.

The Unesco Office of the Regional Adviser for Social Sciences in Asia and the Pacific, along with UN Asian and Pacific Development Centre and other relevant regional institutions, will develop appropriate information reports, thematic surveys and abstracts and distribute them to the Member States and their institutions. Effort will also be made to encourage setting up of national social science documentation and data archival centres, and to establish a regional network of such centres to promote exchange of data and information.

Methods of Action

(a) Preparation of bibliographies;
(b) Promotion of indexing and abstracting services;
(c) Exchange of specialists and documents:
(d) Preparation of inventories;
(e) Training of resource persons at national and regional levels;
(f) Identification of focal points for documentation activities at national and sectoral levels and coordination of these services through the regional mechanism;
(g) Translation activities; and
(h) Increasing the availability of gray and rare literature through microfilming and reprographic services.

Expected Outcomes

(a) Indexing and abstracting services to Member States on a continuing basis;
(b) Augmentation of social science information services in the region to ensure their better utilization;
(c) Increased national capacities in information and documentation services; and
(d) A regional network of national social science documentation and data archival centres.

TWENTYSIX

WOMEN'S STUDIES AND SOCIAL SCIENCES

(Meeting of Experts-1982)

Introduction

As foreseen in its Regular Programme and Budget for 1981-1983, paragraph 3252, and as a contribution to the implementation of activities within the framework of its Medium Term Plan Objective 6.B concerning "the improvement of the status of women and their participation in development", Unesco organized a meeting of experts on "Women Studies and Social Sciences" for countries of the Asian region in collaboration with the Indian National Commission for Cooperation with Unesco, the Indian Council of Social Science Research. and the Centre for Women's Development Studies. This meeting was held from October 4 to 8,1982, at the India International Centre, New Delhi.

The meeting was attended by representations from Bangladesh, India, Republic of korea, Malaysia, the Philippines and Thailand.

Observers were present from the Ministry of Education (Government of India), Indian Council of Social Science Research, Indian Statistical Institute, Centre for Women's Development Studies (New Delhi), SNDT Women's University (Bombay), Institute of Social Studies Trust (Delhi), National Council of Educational Research and Training (NCERT, New Delhi), Regional Institute of Higher Education and Development (RIHED, Singapore), Association of Southeast Asian Institutions of Higher Learning (ASAIHL, Bangkok), and the Association of Asian Social Science Research Councils (AASSREC). The meeting was also attended by representatives from FAO, ILO, UNICEF and WHO.

Unesco was represented by Dr. Yogesh Atal (Unesco Regional Adviser for Social Sciences in Asia and the Pacific) Ms. Carrie Marias (Division of Human Rights and Peace, Sector for Social Sciences and their Applications) and Ms. Koto Kanno (Associate Expert, office of the Regional Adviser for Social Sciences in Asia and the Pacific).

Recommendations

1. The meeting appreciates the initiative taken by Unesco in promoting research and teaching on women and lends its support for further work in this area in the Asia-Pacific Region.

2. The meeting strongly recommends that Unesco should mobilize its resources and also explore the possibility of developing collaborative links with other regional and international agencies for developing a programme of cross-cultural studies on women. The meeting invites the attention of Unesco to consider the topics for research as listed at the end of the recommendations.

3. There is also an urgent need for promoting exchange of information and of scholars across countries. This would require setting up of regional networks or similar mechanisms. As a component of this programme, action is also needed to create and strengthen national capabilities and national infrastructures for which support, both material and intellectual, is needed from agencies much as Unesco. The meeting invites Unesco to assign it priority in its future programming. Countries of the region, including their National Commissions for Unesco universities, research institutes as well as the respective government (or national) bodies in charge of women's affairs, are invited to join in these efforts, providing technical and financial support, in order to strengthen national research and teaching capacities.

4. It is encouraging to learn that some efforts have succeeded in setting up regional professional associations of women

researcners. It will be desirable that such initiatives are encouraged and necessary support for them is provided so that they could effectively function and ensure regional collaboration.

5. The review of the existing studies on women in Asia and the Pacific region attempted at this meeting indicates the need for organization at the national and regional levels of a series of workshops and symposia. These may be organized for purposes of:

    i. Curriculum development for university courses.
    ii. Development of reading and teaching materials related to women.
    iii. Promotion of utilization of research for policy and for faculty development.

6. To develop social science research on Asian and Pacific women, in a way which could promote greater regional cooperation and understanding of inter-cultural issues on women, the meeting recommends that national and regional workshops be organized to examine conceptual frameworks and evolve relevant research methodologies.

7. The meeting recommends that national directories of institutions engaged in research on women be compiled, that similar directories of women researchers may also be compiled. Countries should be encouraged to prepare annotated bibliographies of research on women.

8. The meeting welcomes the growth of the Association of Asian Social Science Research Councils (AASSREC) and suggests that this forum should be utilized for the promotion of social scientific research on women.

9. Technical and financial support from international and regional organizations like Unesco, RIHED, ASAIHL, AASSREC should be provided to enable academic institutions and organizations to strengthen the quality of teaching, learning and training within a multi-disciplinary perspective.

10. As an essential basis for undertaking cross-cultural research, meetings of researchers should be held periodically to ensure effective monitoring and evaluation of the ideological and conceptual framework which have been adopted.

11. Orientation programmes to develop greater understanding and cooperation between academicians and government and semi-government agencies should be developed to promote women's issues as a vital area of concern in development planning.

Ten Major Research Areas

The meeting considered several research topics of an innovative and priority nature that could be examined through cross-cultural studies. Ten major research areas were identified with sub-themes indicating specific research projects that were considered feasible. These are as follows:

1. **Women in the Development Process**

The focus of this research area will not be development plans as such but actually implemented programmes, both governmental and non-governmental. These programmes will be studied in their various phases: their origin and rationale, the process and the extent of implementation, the impact of the changes (intended, unintended) brought about.

Specific sub-themes for research will include: analyses of the impact of minimum wage legislation, of the introduction of new technology on the existing socio-economic structures, and of the effectiveness of leadership training programmes.

2. **Changes in Land Relations including Land Reforms and Land Rights and their Impact on Women in a Historical Perspective.**

3. **Women and Religion**

   i. Examination of religious ideologies and practices and their implications for women in society,

ii. the impact on women of revivalist trends in religions.

4.Women and Law

i. Critical examination of women's rights under customary, personal and statutory laws, including laws in the economic sector.
ii. Evaluation of problems and processes in the realization of women's rights under the law (e.g. awareness of legal rights, attitudes and practices of the judiciary and the legal profession, the mechanisms for enforcement).
iii. Comparative studies of women's efforts (especially contemporary) to change the laws to better their position in society.

5. **Interlinkages between Kinship, Family Structures and Production Systems, with Special Reference to Change (technology and other development processes).**

These may include:

i. Ideological dimensions of family structure,
ii. Studies of families and women's work and work patterns
iii. Authority patterns
iv. The socialization process (e.g. cross-cultural comparative studies on socialization practices with a view to promoting more egalitarian models).

6. **Women and People's Movements**

An analysis of women's participation and roles in protest movements, peasant movements, trade union movements, peace movements, women's movements to uncover and highlight women's participation in them in the historical and contemporary context. The studies could cover such aspects as:

(a) Initial motivation
(b) Nature and extent of participation by various strata of women
(c) Impact on women of the aftermath of these struggles
(d) Any changes effected in the wider society.

7. **Industrial Development and Utilization of Women's Labour**

Since considerable material is available on this theme, the first task would be of collating the material and preparing synthetic reports.

8. **Women and Language Use**

It was considered important to study language use as it reflects and perpetuates ideology, conception of roles and statutes, and certain behaviour patterns.

9. **Women and Media**

Some of the areas that could be examined are:

i. Women's position in media structures and images projected by the media.
ii. Policy guidelines concerning the media's responsibility in presenting a balanced interpretation of sex roles, and
iii. The use of media by women.

10. **Women and the Academia**

Six themes under this topic are suggested for research:

(i) Patterns and trends of women in higher education.
(ii) Equality of opportunity for Women students and researcher's education.
(iii) Study of recruitment and promotion patterns and policies on women in higher education.
(iv) Socio-economic factors affecting the status of women in higher education.
(v) The structure of higher educational institutions and the effect on women and women's studies.
(vi) Role of women's colleges as change agents.

TWENTYSEVEN

YOUTH RELATED INDICATORS

(Report of the Workshop-1983)

Introduction

In pursuance of Resolution 3/05 titled "Role of Youth" adopted by the Unesco General Conference at its 21st session, which provides the policy and guidelines for the preparatory work for the International Youth Year (IYY), and in accordance with Unesco's Approved Programme and Budget for 1981-83 related to objective 6.C, Unesco organized a regional Workshop on Elaboration and Promotion of Indicators in the Analysis and Planning of Youth Programmes in Asia. In its organization, the Asia-Pacific Centre of the Commonwealth Youth Programme collaborated with Unesco by providing additional funding support. The workshop was hosted by the national Youth Services Council of Sri Lanka, and was hall in Hotel Taprobane (Colombo) from January 10 to 14, 1983.

Participants from four of the Commonwealth countries in the region, namely, Bangladesh, India, Malaysia and Singapore were invited by the Commonwealth Youth Programme's Asia-Pacific Centre. Unesco invited participants from Indonesia, Japan, Republic of Korea, Malaysia, Nepal, Pakistan, the Philippines, Sri Lanka and Thailand.

The meeting was attended by observers from the United Nations Economic and Social Commission for Asia and the Pacific (ESCAP), Food and Agriculture Organization (FAO), United Nations Children's Fund (Unicef), World Health Organization (WHO) and United Nations Volunteers (UNV).

Unesco was represented by Dr Yogesh Atal (Regional Adviser for Social Sciences in Asia and the Pacific) and Ms Koto Kanno

(Associate Expert for Social Science Development).

The Asia-Pacific Centre of the Commonwealth Youth Programme was represented by its regional Director, Mr. W. de S. Ratnaweera, and a staff member, Mr. Devendra Agochiya.

Recommendations

1. The group recommends that Unesco, CYP and other UN and international agencies should encourage the Member States to prepare national profiles on the situations of youth, according to the scheme of indicators suggested at this meeting. This would ensure comparable information across countries. Such profiles will be a significant contribution to the International Year of the Youth.

2. While working on the scheme of indicators the group realized that on a number of relevant indicators, information in quantifiable terms is not presently available. Further, there are certain indicators which require systematic empirical investigation so as to be able to construct simple as well as composite indicators specially concerning perceptions, attitudes, values and aspirations of the youth. The group strongly recommends that efforts should be made to encourage such studies. In particular, the following themes may be assigned priority:

   1. Youth and unemployment
   2. Youth in slums
   3. Political socialization of the youth
   4. Drug abuse among the youth.
   5. Youth attitudes and aspirations.

3. Knowing that considerable data on youth are available in several countries of the region which can be fruitfully utilized for the construction of indicators, the group feels concerned about the fact that these are vastly scattered and that there is little coordination between the agencies generating them. It recommends that steps be taken to promote a system of coordination and a retrieval of these data. It further suggests the

need to review and evaluate existing national statistical systems (i) to ascertain the extent to which they can provide material for construction of indicators related to youth participation, and (ii) to explore the possibility of integrating the task of development of these indicators within the national information system, in a phased manner. This would involve creation of a suitable mechanism at the national level for collating existing data relevant to youth and for generating additional data needed for the purpose of constructing relevant indicators.

4. The group appreciated the fact that in the convening of this meeting Unesco was able to collaborate with other regional and international agencies, in particular ESCAP, the Asia Pacific Centre of the Commonwealth Youth Programme, FAO, UNICEF and WHO. This is a welcome trend and the group wishes that in future such collaboration could be further strengthened.

5. The group recognizes the need for further work on the scheme of indicators proposed by this workshop. It is felt that a manual of detailed guidelines for preparing national profiles of youth, model designs for carrying out scientific investigation concerning priority areas of research on youth, and detailed framework of indicators, especially concerning youth and developmental programmes, would go a long way in promoting the indicator movement for youth. Unesco may, for this purpose, consider the possibility of (i) convening a meeting of two or three experts, or (ii) commissioning the necessary work to a consultant, or (iii) collaborating with ESCAP and other agencies of the UN system interested in youth programmes.

EXCERPTS FROM THE TECHNICAL NOTE ON THE WORKSHOP PREPARED BY UNESCO SECRETARIAT

1. The youth constitute an important segment of society. An investment in their development is an investment in future. The importance of youth in a country's development is widely recognized and efforts are being made in almost all the countries to tap this poten-

tial and to utilize it for shaping the future world. Programmes are being implemented for the development of youth and for the involvement of youth in development of the country. There is worldwide concern for the youth, and concerted action is called for at the national, regional and international levels to meet their needs and aspirations.

A survey of the situation of the youth, carried out by Unesco and presented in its document, *Youth Prospects in the 1990's*, paints a not very bright picture. Chronic economic uncertainty, prevailing poverty and growing scarcity of resources will affect the humanity in the coming years, and the youth will have to bear their brunt. With improvement in health and nutrition, the death rate among the infants and youth has come down and thus the size of the young population is growing in the countries of the Third World. With some betterment in the system of education, a relatively higher percentage of these young is literate and educated, although in absolute numbers the size of the young illiterate population is continuously rising. The existing educational infrastructure cannot accommodate all those who are eligible and willing to go to school, and the economy is finding it difficult to provide the kind of employment that the educated young are seeking. The growing disenchantment and alienation among the young, and the burgeoning incidents of the demonstration of youth unrest, are causing concern.

It is, however, believed that youth should be treated not as a problem group, but as a potential force, and the programmes be designed to utilize them for the good of the society. Both for designing programmes and for evaluating and monitoring them, social sciences have a role to play. They assist in developing conceptual apparatus and approach, and in fashioning tools and techniques. In the field of planning, they have provided a useful tool in the form of Social Indicators, which goes beyond compilation of simple statistics, by providing a frame and identifying various components of a given phenomenon for which quantifiable measures are developed. A composite of these measures gives a better profile of the phenomenon and helps in identifying changes. It is also used to transform subjective and qualitative aspects into quantitative variables. Thus social indicators are used in improving descriptive social reporting, measuring the provision, distribution and effectiveness of social services, and analysing social conditions and changes in them. Social indicators are important instruments in policy analysis, planning and implementation.

Unesco has made a substantial contribution in the promotion and elaboration of social indicators; it has encouraged methodological discussion on them and had persuaded governments to employ the technology of indicators in planning and in evaluation, and in the preparation of social reports.

As an extension of the same programme, Unesco has organized this workshop to review the situations as regards the use of indicators in the area of youth in various Member States, and to synthesize this experience to evolve a systematic framework of social indicators for wider use.

2. Unesco is not alone in the field of social indicators. Almost all agencies of the UN system have found this tool useful and contributed to its refinement and sophistication; in this, Unesco has joined hands with them and provided the needed methodological and theoretical input.

In the area of youth, the United Nations Economic and Social Commission for Asia and the Pacific (ESCAP) organized an expert group meeting in December 1980 in Manila (the Philippines) on "The Development of relevant indicators for planning, monitoring and evaluation of country efforts for promoting youth's role in development". The meeting provided a useful list of indicators. Following this, ESCAP initiated a programme of country monographs on the profile of youth which is being carried out in five countries of the region : Bangladesh, the Philippines, Malaysia, Sri Lanka and Thailand. These monographs would deal with (i) the situation of youth : main problems, major trends and aspirations of youth; (ii) available services and opportunities for youth; and (iii) suggestions for enhancing the role of youth in national development.

Definition of Youth

Despite so much work on youth, the term still suffers from lack of consensus on definition. While the core age group 15-24 seems to have universal agreement, age groups on the peripheries of this core are also included in different countries : thus variations exist as regards the lower and upper limits of age for inclusion in the category of youth.

Sociologically speaking youth is a category and not a group per se. There is a need to identify problems that pertain to the category as a whole, and to the specific groups. A category is transformed into a group when the individuals have a sense of belonging to it and when they interact in it as members.

This would require classification of youth by categories and by groups, and identification of problems associated with each of them.

Following categories seem to be relevant:

i. by age groups
ii. by marital status
iii. by religions or ethnic groups
iv. by education (illiterate, student, educated)
v. by employment
vi. by residence (urban/rural)
vii. by class (rich, middle class, poor)
viii. by sex

It will be seen that a young man or woman can be classified along all of these variables; developing composite categories by merging of various variables pose several methodological problems. But treating each one separately results in a series of overlaps.

Groups Related to Youth

Both governmental and non-governmental groups are to be found that are set up by youth and or for youth. These may operate at local, regional, or national level. Some of these may be part of the international network, or of a national organization (such as political party, trade union, or a cultural society). The typology of groups may be developed taking into account their goals and objectives, target groups, types of activities, and area of their operation. An analysis of membership may be a useful device to find out who participates in them.

Location of Youth in the Economy

Unemployment among the youth is said to be constantly rising, but there is widespread disagreement about indicators of unemployment and the statistics related to it.

Questions such as the following deserve attention:

1. How many are unemployed? Who are they?
2. Is unemployment seasonal? Volitional?
3. How to distinguish underemployment and misemployment from unemployment?
4. How to define the concept of time lag between completion of education and getting a job?
5. How reliable are statistics of employment exchanges?

In addition, questions should also be asked about the activities the unemployed engage in while waiting for employment. Who supports them? What do they do during unemployment? Are the unemployed politically more active? Are there agencies which look after the welfare of the unemployed?

It is equally important to analyse employment statistics to find out where do the youth get absorbed in the economy - this will provide a differentiated profile for different age groups, both sexes, and different categories of education. This will also give an idea of job avenues. Analysis of data on migration to the West Asia will also be of particular interest.

Data on Health and Nutrition

How is the general health of the youth in a country? What is the percentage of the disabled, and what kinds of disablement are more frequent? Educational and employment status of the disabled youth will be of special interest.

Involvement of Youth in Development Work

To answer the general question regarding the contribution made by the youth in the country's development, information on following indicators may be useful:

1. Young people engaged in the promotion of family planning
2. Number of young doctors, nurses and health workers
3. Youth leadership in the prevention of drug abuse
4. Proportion of youth working in employment oriented programmes in the area
5. Youth participation in community development work
6. Youth contribution to educational programmes
7. Youth in trade unions
8. Membership in the youth wings of political parties
9. Other activities

Programmes for Youth Development

In this area, only evaluative indicators are to be identified and elaborated. This would, first of all, involve indentification of areas in which programmes for youth development exist in the Member States, and content analysis of goals and targets against which the programmes are to be evaluated both in terms of implementation rate and reach of benefits to the young.

The principal areas in which such exercise may be attempted are the following:

i. Education
ii. Vocational training
iii. Employment-oriented programmes including vocational guidance
iv. Social welfare programmes, including social work activities among delinquents, drug abusers and the like
v. Sports and recreational activities
vi. Programmes for the special groups
vii. Others

Attitudes and Aspirations of Youth

This may be divided into two parts : (i) collective expressions and (ii) individual profiles.

There are several ways through which youth are mobilized to give expression to their feelings. Such expressions are indicative both of their involvement and commitment to the society, and of the articulation of their frustration, alienation and resentment vis-a-vis the system. A typology of campaigns, protests and riots can be constructed and their frequency tabulated over a period of time. Such mass movements may have specific youth referrent, or the youth may form part of a society-wide movement either in favour of status quo or against it.

Individual profiles of attitudes and aspirations of youth are hard to construct at the national level. These can be the subject-matter of sample surveys. In the filed of sociology and political science one can find numerous examples of index-construction using the concept of property-space. Some such constructs are communication exposure index (based on indicators of habits of newspaper reading, cinema-going and radio-listening). Index of the Sense of Political Efficacy, Political Participation Index, Opinion and Attitude and correlated with the Socio-Economic Status (SES) Index, and other basic identification indicators. Cross-index comparisons are also attempted.

TWENTYEIGHT

TEACHING AND RESEARCH IN PHILOSOPHY IN ASIA AND THE PACIFIC

Introduction

In its 20th General Conference, held in 1978, Unesco decided to launch a series of surveys on teaching and research in Philosphy throughout the world. During the biennium 1979-80, such surveys were conducted for the African region. In the triennium 1981-83, a similar exercise was undertaken for the Asia-Pacific region. Sixteen Member States of the region responded to the invitation and designated scholars to prepare country status reports on teaching and research in the field of Philosophy. Based on the guidelines provided by the Unesco secretariat, the status reports cover the following : (i) a brief history of the discipline of Philosophy in the country; (ii) present situation and current trends of teaching and research in Philosophy; (iii) problems of the profession; and (iv) perspectives and agenda for the future.

The present meeting was convened to review these reports, exchange experience and identify areas for priority action to promote teaching and research in Philosophy and to encourage regional and international cooperation among philosophers, and institutions engaged in philosophical research.

The meeting was held at the Unesco Regional Office for Education in Asia and the Pacific, Bangkok (Thailand), from February 21 to 25, 1983.

Participation

The authors of the country status reports were invited to participate in the meeting. However, participants from Australia, Afghanistan, Malaysia and Vietnam expressed their inability to attend. Thus, following countries sent the participants: Bangladesh, People's Republic of China, India, Iran, Republic of Korea, New Zealand, Pakistan, the Philippines, Democratic Socialist Republic of Sri Lanka, Thailand and Turkey.

Besides, there were observers from the Regional Institute of Higher Education and Development (RIHEAD), International Labour Organization (ILO), Chiang Mai University, Thammasart University (Bangkok) and International Federation of Philosophical Societies (IFPS).

Three resource persons assisted the meeting: Prof. D.P. Chattopadhyaya (Chairman of the Indian Council of Philosophical Research), Prof. Daya Krishna (University of Rajasthan, Jaipur India) and Prof. Richard Dyche (Chulalongkorn University, Bangkok).

Discussion

The main issues on which the discussion focussed are the following:

1. Understanding

There was difference of opinion regarding the definition of right understanding. How to define what is right, and from whose point of view? How to distinguish between explanation, understanding and interpretation? What is the task of the philosopher: to explain, to interept, or to understand? Or all the three? It was argued that understanding is multiform, and works where explanation fails. The distinction between "truth" and "validity of judgement" also figured in the discussion and it was asserted that while truth may be important, it does not occupy a central position in the scheme of thought. What is problematic is the plethora of validities of judgements.

2. Cultural Identity

Two strong views prevailed in the discussion. There was a view that each society has the task of establishing its identity and that philosophy should be culture specific rather than a mere implantation of external, mainly western philosophy. They posited traditional philosophy in contrast to the Western philosophy, but there was no agreement in regard to what is "traditional". Even in Western philosophy one can distinguish between the traditional and modern elements.

The other point of view was expressed in the question : why should cultural identity be treated as a problem or an issue? Can there be as many philosophies as there are Member States in the world political map? Does creation of a separate political State make it possible for the system to have its distinctive philosophy as part of a new and separate cultural identity? Is not the human being more valuable than culture? How does one seek cultural identity by means of a cognitive enterprises? The object of reflection is universal, trans-temporal and trans-historical. If philosophy is a cognitive enterprise, how does it respond to the demand of cultural identity?

Replying to this query, it was mentioned that even in the West philosophy was not considered by all as a purely intellectual activity. There are Western traditions coming from Plato and Plotinus, through Augustine and Anselm, Pascal and Kierkegaard, to Bergson and Karl Jaspers, which consider philosophy to be either vision or conscious faith. Truths, in fact, are also accessible through methods other than reason and logic.

3. Fact-Value Dichotomy

Recognizing the need to dichotomize facts and value, the group was of the view that values must be the subject matter of philosophy because the idea of action is germane to philosophy itself. In a theoretical sense, value is problematic.

4. Modern and Traditional Philosophies

There was a major discussion on the extent to which teaching and research in philosophy should attend to traditional philosophies (including philosophical system). Considerable difficulty with the terminology emerged. Some participants preferred to distinguish sharply between philosophy on the one hand and culture, ideology and religion on the other. Others wished to include within the scope of philosophy questions about the interpretation of the traditional systems. However there was general agreement that philosophy is primarily an analytical, argumentative and conceptual enterprise. Considerable amount of the traditional material is not, in this sense, philosophical, although it can properly be subjected to philosophical analysis.

The question was raised whether a philosophy can be translated from one language into another without thereby suffering important changes-whether traditional philosophies can be understood in terms other than their own, without immersion in their languages and practices.

It was suggested that languages embed unarticulated conceptual frameworks; that even "philosophies" contain argumentative and conceptual elements; that there is a continuum between traditional and modern philosophies; that attempt at definition will collapse.

5. The Problem of Relevance

The question was raised, in just what sense of "relevance" ought philosophical teaching and research be relevant? A somewhat justified complaint against much philosophy is that, without continuous interactions with other disciplines, it becomes excessively speculative. Such interaction should, therefore, be fostered, in order to bring philosophy close to the social, natural and life sciences, and to make philosophical works more accessible to non-philosophers.

It was agreed that while philosophers in Asia are familiar with Western philosophy they know little about the philosophical traditions of their neighbouring countries within the region. Familiarization with each other's philosophies is as important as familiarization with the Western philosophy. This would require freer and frequent interaction among philosophers within the region.

It was complained that a real intellectual atmosphere in many universities is indeed rare; that it can be fostered by means of daily seminars on texts, and also by means of open-ended, open-entry seminars. The use of works of fiction as a means of bringing the human predicament to the foreground was advocated. It was also suggested that philosophers contribute to practical affairs by subjecting to philosophical scrutiny the ideological presuppositions of public policies.

Finally, it was suggested that philosophers themselves set an example by holding conferences, writing books and monographs, mounting audiovidual philosophical exhibitions, and initiating mixed seminars to highlight the interdisciplinary character of philosophy.

Recommendations and Suggestions

Having considered the various aspects of teaching and research in Philosophy in the Asia-Pacific, this Meeting makes the following recommendations to the Director General of Unesco:

1. To promote mutual understanding and cooperation among the philosophers of the Asia-Pacific region and to disseminate knowledge of the philosophies of this region throughout all its Member States in particular, and in all the countries of the world, we recommend that steps may be taken (a) to convene periodic meetings of philosophers of Asia and the Pacific, and (b) to promote academic exchange of teachers and students in this region. Towards the realization of this objective existing institutions and organizations may be strengthened and new ones established.

2. An institute for the study of philosophy in Asia may be established in one of the countries of this region.

3. Member States should be encouraged to establish suitable courses in philosophy at schools, colleges and universities. For this purpose, it would be helpful to get model syllabi and suitable books prepared.

4. (i) Translation of the classical as well as important modern works in philosophy, (ii) starting a journal, (iii) publication of books, and (iv) preparation of a Directory of Research Work carried on in this region may be encouraged.

5. In tune with the Unesco objective of safeguarding and

promoting indigenous cultures, indigenous philosophical research may be encouraged, so that independent philosophical thinking on world problems may be promoted.

6. The country status reports on teaching and research in philosophy prepared as background material for this meeting may be published in a book form at an early date Support may be provided to the Member States for translation and publication of it into other languages.

7. Philosophers of the region may be encouraged to initiate and carry out furtner interdisciplinary studies relating to human, natural and social sciences.

TWENTYNINE

TRAINING OF "BAREFOOT" ARCHITECTS

(Report of a Working Group-1983).

Organization of the Workshop

A week-long workshop was organized at the Unesco Regional Office for Education in Asia and the Pacific, Bangkok, from May 30 to June 4, 1983, to examine the emerging concept of a "barefoot architect" and to consider the possibilities for the preparation of this new role.

Done in accordance with the approved budget and programme in 21C/5 (para 3146), the Workshop was attended by representatives from Australia, India, Maldives, Nepal, the Philippines and Thailand. In addition, there were observers from the Asian Institute of Technology, National Housing Authority of Thailand, Department of Town and Country Planning of Thai Government. Japanese Volunteer Centre based in Bangkok, United Nations Centre for Human Settlements (UNCHS, Nairobi), UN-ESCAP, and the United Nations University. In all, 22 persons (including Unesco staff) attended the workshop.

Scope of the Conference

The Workshop was convened to discuss the merging role of the "barefoot" architects in the context of developing societies and to discuss the possibility of training people to perform this role. It focussed on the following:

1. Sharing of experience on the improvement of marginal settlements and rural housing where local people with limited training have made a major contribution.

2. Examination of existing architectural curricula of various institutions and identification of elements that might be included in the syllabi for the training of barefoot architects.

3. Suggestions for further activities in the area of training of trainers, organization of national level short-term courses; and preparation of teaching materials.

The Secretariat note specifying the context and scope of the Workshop is reproduced below:

"It is being increasingly realized that solutions to many developmental problems can be sought from within the society, and much work can be carried out by the people themselves with little external support. Such a strategy is both economical and appropriate.

"Attention to the effectiveness of this model of endogenous development has been drawn by the social workers operating in local communities, who devised ingenious ways to tackle local problems. There are instances of people who employed such a model in their work related to the improvement of both marginal urban settlements and rural habitats. There are also examples in the Asia and Pacific region where multilateral and bilateral projects have successfully worked for the improvement of such settlements applying this philosophy of local involvement in development. Furthermore, one may also find cases where the community people, under their own initiative, have managed to find sensitive and apt solutions to their housing and social needs by using their own resources. Indeed, some of the world's finest built environments have been produced through these local initiatives.

"On the other hand, the number of successful habitats coming from spontaneous endogenous development is limited. Examples of housing and social facilities which are unhealthy, unsafe, and socially degrading places in which to live, abound in the rural setting as well as in the urban slums.

"The question which poses itself is : how can the experiences from the successful settlements be communicated to the less successful?

"One answer is that the systematization and diffusion of information on these experiences would help. Yet we know that barriers such as lack of funds for such a programme and the great number of local languages used throughout Asia, and the situation where many people who live in these settlements are not literate even in their own language rule out such an approach.

"Another possible answer is to provide these settlements and villages with professional architects, engineers, and community development advisers. The hopelessness of this approach, however, is even more evident than that of the information blitz suggested above. The large number of villages and marginal settlements far exceeds the supply of professionals available; few governments in the region could afford to send out high salaried professionals in large numbers; and finally, the training of most professional architects and engineers suits them poorly as village workers.

"A third approach is through providing the services of a special kind of person whom we shall call the 'barefoot doctors' developed and promoted in the People's Republic of China during the 1960. These doctors...provided a basic level of health services to remote and rural areas in China. These people had received training in medicine and public health which was sufficient only to enable them to deal with the most common health problems in the villages. One great advantage to this approach was that their simplified training was of relatively short duration and thus, with limited resources, large numbers could be trained.

"The 'barefoot' architect would be someone who would spend his energies on solving the major problems of marginal urban settlements or of villages. He or she would be able to deal with a variety of issues including roadways, water supply, and drainage as well as the construction of houses, and community buildings such as schools. He or she would be able to guide local people in the introduction of simple technologies which enhance the use of locally available resources.

"Above all, this person would be able to mobilize community support for the various projects which would be undertaken to physically improve or expand such a settlement.

"Such a person might best be drawn from the community itself and be specially trained for this work. He would be armed with information on other successful experiences and the results of research on life in villages or urban communities."

Suggestions for Future Activities

Given that the workshop participants were from a number of professions and that the subject had taken on a fairly wide scope, the suggestions put forth cover several of Unesco's sectors.

In identifying areas for possible future actions by Unesco, it was decided to relate these to the following groups : community opinion leaders, and indigenous builders, external facilitators, construction managers, and professional architects. These are the persons who are either members of low-income groups themselves or are most directly linked with them.

1. People at the Community Level

Popularize information on shelter and basic services. There exists in some Asian countries and elsewhere considerable information on human settlements which is aimed at servicing people. Information for popular consumption should be developed in such a way as to be of practical use to recipients and presented in a way as to be understandable. The media to be applied will vary according to that which is best understood by the recipients. This information may also be disseminated for use by other people in other countries. Unesco can promote the exchange of information between countries and its adaptation to local situations.

2. Introduction of Information on the Built Environment into Primary School Curricula

Following the example of introducing an understanding of population issues through schools, a similar effort could be undertaken to provide curricula development centres with basic concepts on human settlements developments. Considering that children in these areas who attend school may drop out at an early age, this introduction should be given in the earlier years of schooling.

3. Research on Local Level Innovations

A non-formalized "research and development" process takes place at village level whenever a new idea is tried out and modified in subsequent applications. Studies on this process of innovation would provide information which could help in the development of any future activity in this area.

4. At the Level of Village Leaders

Encourage non-formal training in specific skills required for village people who have responsibilities for certain human settlements' tasks. These should be communicable through distance education means.

5. At the Intermediate Level of External Facilitator (e.g. community development workers or building technician)

Encourage the development of training programmes which give a broader based technical education including community organization and developments, technical and management skills. Such a programme should be flexibly structured, based on self-contained modules and also have the potential of being disseminated through "open university" type distance learning techniques. A large number of formal training programmes already exist for the preparation of intermediate-level technicians and community development workers which could be modified in this direction. Existing networks, such as those under the Asian Programme for Educational Innovation for Development (APEID), could be utilized in accomplishing this.

6. At the Formal Higher Education Level

Support of studies on the specific needs of particular areas and communities which are particularly in need of improvements in human settlements in order to understand their specific needs and thus identify which kinds of skills might be imparted to people living in that area. This might be incorporated into the curricula of schools of architecture as a means of creating more awareness on the part of students of the needs of the poorer people in their society.

7. At all Levels of Training

Continuing education. The concept of providing new and updated information at all levels needs to be encouraged. Thus programmes of continuing education can be drawn up in a variety of ways ranging from one-day programmes to more exhaustive treatment of selected topics as an extension activity of the formal structured courses.

THIRTY

INTELLECTUAL COOPERATION BETWEEN DEVELOPING COUNTRIES IN ASIA

(Report of a Regional Workshop-1984)

Introduction

Intellectual cooperation is needed for the development of national capabilities to tackle complicated and challenging tasks of nation building and for the enhancement of social sciences. As part of Unesco's programme relating to "Development and International Relations", the primary aim of various activities is to consolidate the bases of endogenous development and to lay the foundations for regional and sub-regional integationan essential component of intellectual international cooperation.

Organization of the Workshop

The Chulalongkorn University Social Science Research Institute (CUSRI) organized, under a contract with Unesco, this consultative meeting of regional and sub-regional institutions to discuss and further enhance intellectual cooperation among the developing countries in Asia. The meeting was held from November 20 to 23, 1984.

The meeting was attended by representatives from 16 institutions/organizations/funding agencies. These included the Association of Developing Institutes of Asia and the Pacific (ADIPA), Asian and Pacific Development Centre, Institute of Developing Economies (IDE), Institute of Library Science of the University of the Philippines, Regional Institute of Higher Education and

Development (RIHED), Institute of South East Asian Studies (ISEAS), Asian Mass Communication Research and Information Centre (AMIC), Association of Southeast Asian institutions of Higher Learning (ASAIHL), Social Research Institute of Chulalongkorn University (CUSRI), International Development Research Centre (IDRC), Asia Foundation, Agricultural Development Council (ADC), South East Asian Ministers of Education Secretariat (SEAMES), ILO, UNICEF and ESCAP. Unesco was representated by its Regional Unit for Social and Human Sciences in Asia and the Pacific (RUSHSAP).

The Agenda

The agenda is given below:

1. Inaugural session
2. Election of office-bearers
3. Adoption of agenda
4. Briefing about Unesco's activities in social sciences in the Asia-Pacific region
5. Statements by representatives of different organizations
6. Discussion of issues related to regional intellectual cooperation
7. Suggestions and Recommendations
8. Adoption of the Report
9. Closing session

Summary and Conclusions

1. The meeting recognized the need to strengthen intellectual cooperation both between national and regional institutions, and between scholars. The present meeting is the first of its

kind to bring together various agencies and institutions engaged in the task of enhancing the role of social sciences and promoting intellectual cooperation in the region. For this, Unesco's initiative is indeed commendable. The meeting also welcomed the Unesco proposal for holding an intergovernmental Conference on Social Sciences for the Asia-Pacific region in 1986-1987. It also appreciated the steps being taken by Unesco to create a regional network of social science information and documentation centres.

2. The contribution made by donor agencies, foundations and UNDP to develop national capabilities was acknowledged. However, it was felt that adequate support for the growth of social sciences in the region has not been forthcoming; it also expressed concern over UNDP's reduced support to regional efforts in this direction. It needs to be emphasized that social sciences are directly relevant to development. As long as social science capabilities are not helped to be developed within the developing countries, the aims of endogenous development will remain unfulfilled, and the principles of TCDC unattended. UNDP is requested to reconsider its policies towards social sciences and to provide funding support for regional cooperation in social sciences in its next programming cycle. The preparatory work done by Unesco to mount such a cooperative programme, which has received support of several Member States, should pave the way for a favourable UNDP action.

3. Work in the area of social science information and documentation deserves priority. This may include:

i. Setting up a regional network (for which Unesco has already commissioned a feasibility study);
ii. Joint efforts by concerned institutions to prepare union catalogues of publications;
iii. Encourage reorientation of individual institutions so that information is widely disseminated and scholars and institutions can have access to it on a regional basis;
iv. Develop translation facilities to make available literature from national languages into an international link language,

and vice versa;

v. Organization of short-term courses for senior officials and policy-makers to introduce them to newer developments in the field of information.

4. Efforts should be made to develop a programme of internships of shorter duration, on a cost-sharing basis, for younger social scientists.

5. To facilitate further regional cooperation, it would be advisable to utilize existing structures and facilities. For example, the newsletters published by various agencies can carry information about programmes and activities of other agencies on a reciprocal basis.

6. To facilitate further regional cooperation, it would be advisable to utilize existing structures and facilities. For example, the newsletters published by various agencies can carry information about programmes and activities of other agencies on a reciprocal basis.

7. There is a need for developing cultural awareness programmes. Modalities for this will have to be explored.

8. There is a need to encourage research by scholars in countries of the region other than their own so that a comparative perspective to contemporary problems can be developed.

9. The meeting also agreed to promote relationship between institutions operating at the regional level through some sort of networking arrangement.

10. There are various international donor agencies such as Asia Foundation, IDRC, Friedrich Ebert Stiftung, DANIDA, NORAD, SAREC, SIR, and local foundations such as Lee and Toyota Foundations which could assist regional institutions. Efforts may be made to contact these agencies and foundations and seek funding support for regional cooperation. Reports of regional workshops, seminars and con-

ferences should also be sent to these agencies and foundations so that they are kept informed of the developments and the new needs in the region.

11. The meeting recommended that studies be commissioned on the following topics:

    i. Management of maintenance crisis by regional institutions
    ii. Conceptual analysis and review of existing regional networks
    iii. Review of schemes of exchange of scholars on a cost-sharing basis as an aspect of TCDC.

THIRTYONE

AN ASIAN PATTERN OF POLITICAL SCIENCE

A Dynamic Process

The divergent and complex issues that confront political science as an academic discipline appear to defy an attempt to draw a clear picture of the discipline in Asia. The evolution of political science is a dynamic process, and issues may constantly change as time goes by, making it difficult and less meaningful to try to arrive at an "Asian pattern" of political science. Furthermore, it would be necessary to look into and compare other patterns of political science in different world regions to define Asian characteristics of political science. In spite of these limitations and difficulties, it seems helpful to identify the main elements that constitute an Asian pattern, particularly a desirable pattern as perceived by the Asian political scientists.

A. Objective

One such element is concerned with the objective of the discipline itself. Political science was introduced in the Asian countries primarily to train government officials and was synonymous with public administration. The American impact on political science was largely responsible for the broadening of the scope of the discipline to include the investigation into the political process and the interactions among[1] different political actors. Introduced into different political systems in Asia, the American influence helped political science in Asia to critically examine the power relations and to demystify the

1. (Adapted from RUSHAP Series on Occasional Monographs and Papers 10, edited by Takeo Uchida, Bangkok-1984.

established political ideas and institutions. In short, it has become a critical science. There exists a tense relationship between the technocratic and critical aspects in all social sciences. Political science may be the discipline that stands on a most delicate and fragile balance between the two aspects because it addresses itself to the question of power most directly than any other discipline.

It is not, however, a choice between the two functions. The majority of political thinkers seems to favour a more active participation in and contribution of political science to policy making, mostly at the national level. The policy-relevant political science might be considered a synthesis of technocratic expertise and critical analysis in its best. The emphasis on policy relevance can be partly explained by the fact that the social scientists in the Third World in general believed, and still believe, that it was their mission to build up and develop their young nations. There was a widespread expectation that the social sciences could play significant roles in national development in the 1960s and 1970s in particular.

As nation-building involves social transformation, the role of political science cannot simply be technocratic in managing the functions of the State.

Political scientists' first obligation is scientific education and research in its own right and that unless they succeed in this endeavour, their service to policy making and society will be severely restricted. The relationship between political science and society is not only conditioned by the kind of political system that the political scientists find themselves at a given time but is also a function of the development of the discipline itself. The Asian social scientists should be able to set a common objective of developing and refining the concepts, theories and methods of political science which are more reflective of, and responsive to, the Asian scene and needs.

B. Scope

There exists a fair amount of agreement as to the content and scope of political science in the countries in Asia. The original emphasis on public administration and the consequent American influence on Asian political science have probably provided a common general framework for the content of the discipline. The following four areas can be said to constitute political science as taught and researched in the universities and research institutes in the countries in the region:

a. political theory and thought
b. comparative government
c. public administration
d. international relations

Political science appears on the surface as an interdisciplinary area of teaching as, for instance, international relations study requires knowledge about history, economics and law, to say nothing of comparative government. In most countries, however, the synthetic understanding and linking the areas are left to the students to tackle while professors tend to specialize in one of these areas. The emergence of political sociology and social psychology has not improved the situation as little systematic endeavour has taken place towards interdisciplinarity. There is a need to go beyond the building up of a model curriculum to place political science properly in relation to other social sciences.

Political theory and thought can be safely identified as the area which calls for the greatest attention and work of political scientists in Asia and the Pacific. Political thought courses are usually devoted to the classical Western political thinkers from Plato to Rousseau, although some attempts have been made to introduce the ideas of political philosophers in the respective countries in the region. In Indonesia, there was a conscious effort to introduce Indonesian political thought from the very beginning. "Modern Indonesian Political Thought is a required course of all political science curricula" and Islamic Political Thought is also offered. The efforts in introducing major political thinkers of the countries are also undertaken in several other countries including Bangladesh, India and the Philippines. It would appear that more Asian Political philosophers could be taught as the relevant teaching materials become readily available. This presupposes a greater research in this area by Asian political scientists.

Political theory, including methodology, is probably the least developed area in political science in Asia, and for that matter in political science as we know it today, courses offered in political theory and methodology introduce the works of Western theoreticians but do not seem to attract many students. Empirical research and quantitative approach have never become as popular as in the United States despite the strong American influence on Asian political science. In India, for example, it was the Indian Council of Social Science Research and the University Grants Commission rather than the university departments that took the initiative to train the young teachers and students in research methodology, while "most of the older political science teachers find the modern quantitative research methods rather distasteful and look askance at the empiricist presumption".

Scepticism and reservation about quantitative methods may have good reasons in the Asian context. Certain research techniques such as questionnaires and interviews are more relevant in a culture which values self-expression. At the same time, some concepts and theories employed by Asian political scientists might not be found useful in the analysis of political phenomena in Asian countries. Under such a circumstance, any attempt to employ a particular method, in separation from the theory, may be meaningless. The challenge for Asian political scientists will then be to develop endogenous concepts and theories and devise the methods appropriate to them. The existing "gap between theory and empirical research" will have to be bridged first in this endeavour.

C. Regional Cooperation and Perspectives

There is a great need for developing regional cooperation among Asian political scientists. There exists already the basic national level infrastructure of political science which should enable collaboration at a regional level. In all countries there are national social science councils or associations, and political science associations except in Indonesia and Malaysia. Six Asian political science associations are either full or associate members of IPSA. Furthermore, Asian political scientists have already been actively participating in regional collaborative research sponsored by Unesco, the United Nations University, and by the regional associations such as the Association of Asian Social Science Research Councils (AASSREC) and the Association of Development Research and Training Institutes of Asia and the Pacific (ADIPA).

Regional cooperation is, of course, part of international scholarly cooperation. Efforts to "indigenize" social sciences could be encouraged by regional collaboration by broadening the communication flows among political scientists in Asia whose main counterparts are still found in North America and Europe rather than in the neighbouring countries. The call for indigenization has passed through the state of reaction to the Western social sciences and it now constitutes part of the globalization process of the social sciences. Regional cooperation is a means and not an end in itself. Cooperation will be meaningful to the extent that a common objective is shared by those involved. It will be necessary to identify specific tasks and to develop the mechanism to that end.

THIRTY TWO

TEACHING AND RESEARCH IN INTERNATIONAL LAW IN ASIA AND THE PACIFIC

(Report of a Regional Consultation Meeting-1984)

Introduction

In accordance with its Budget and Programme for 1984-85, Unesco convened a meeting of experts on Teaching and Research in International Law for countries of the Asia-Pacific region, in collaboration with the Korean Association of International Law and the Korean National Commission for Unesco. This meeting was held from October 10 to 13, 1984, at the International Conference Hall of the Korean National Commission for Unesco, Seoul, Republic of Korea.

The meeting was attended by participants from Australia, India, Indonesia, Japan, Republic of Korea, Pakistan, the Philippines and Thailand.

Observers were present from the Ministry of Education, Government of Korea, Korean Association of International Law, Various Korean Universities, Association of Southeast Asian Institutions of Higher learning (ASAIHL), and Korean Social Science Research Council (KOSSREC).

Unesco was represented by Dr. Yogesh Atal, Unesco Regional Adviser for Social Science and Human Sciences in Asia and the Pacific.

Suggestions for Promoting Regional Cooperation in International Law

The Regional Consultation Meeting was deeply appreciative of the initiative taken by Unesco in organizing this meeting. It also recorded its appreciation to the local hosts-the Korean National Commission for Unesco and the Korean International Law Association for joining Unesco in convening this meeting, which was the first of its kind to be held in the Asia-Pacific region. It gave an opportunity to scholars from various countries to learn about the trends and developments in international law in neighbouring countries, and to reflect together on the ways and means to promote further regional cooperation.

The intensive discussion carried out in the various sessions led the meeting to make certain concrete suggestions for furthering regional cooperation among scholars and institutions devoted to international law. These are listed below :

1. The meeting proposed that the Report on this consultation be published by Unesco and distributed widely in the region among universities and departments and institutes of international law. It recommended inclusion of the full country papers in the Report.

2. It was agreed that bilateral exchanges between the countries of the region in respect of information on the development of international law should be promoted. These may include exchanges of publications on international law, exchange of scholars and teachers of international law. The programme of these bilateral exchanges may be organized through National Associations of International Law if they exist in a country. In the absence of such an organization, some other institution or agency performing similar functions may be approached for this purpose. It is suggested that the possibility of including this item in cultural agreements between governments be explored.

3. The meeting noted the positive initiative given to students of international law by the American Society of International Law's Jessup Competition which invites teams of interna-

tional law students from all over the world to participate in its moot court competition. An effort to institute a similar moot court competition at the Asia-Pacific level may be one way to encourage study and research in international law in the region. Alternatively, countries of a particular sub-region may hold a sub-regional final for the Jessup Competition in an appropriate language (whether or not a team can be sent to the international final in Washington.

4. Because of the increasing use of national languages as the medium of instruction and for scholarly writing in most of the countries of Asia, the need is urgently felt for translation of works-from national languages into international languages and vice versa. Unesco may be approached to provide financial assistance under its Participation Programme for such efforts as would assist in breaking down communication barriers. The possibility of a regional documentation and abstracting service may also be explored, seeking support from the developed countries within the region.

5. The success of the Meeting, and the common problem it revealed in the countries represented, gave rise to suggestions for some regional mechanism for the exchange of information about research, teaching and other international law developments in each country. It may not be practical at this stage to set up any formal organization or structure. But a brief newsletter, distributed two or three times a year to a national contact organization, is a real possibility. The contact organization would be responsible for the further distribution of the newsletter (if necessary in translation) to interested members within the country in question. In each case it would be possible to nominate the most appropriate international law association or organization (if more than one) in each country. For countries with no such association, an individual scholar might accept responsibility for distribution. Responsibility for the preparation of the newsletter would rotate between institutions in different countries, on an annual or biennial basis. The Unesco Regional Unit for Social and Human Sciences in Asia and the Pacific agreed to write to the appropriate organizations in each country seeking their agree-

ment to participate in it. This would involve only:

i. the designation of a local scholar who would write to the current newsletter editor at appropriate intervals with a short note on local developments
ii. agreements to distribute the newsletter (with other communications made by the organization) to interested persons.

Upon receipt of responses, efforts may be made to find volunteers who can take up the responsibility to edit and publish the newsletter.

6. The problem of access to international law materials produced in the region is indeed serious. It was proposed that there should be a free exchange of materials particularly yearbooks of national/international law societies, law school journals and book reviews. It was agreed that initially Unesco's Regional Unit for Social and Human Sciences should facilitate such an exchange by contacting the respective national law associations proposed by the participants.

7. A variety of topics presently of interest to the international law scholars emerged from the papers and discussions at the meeting. These are: statehood and state succession; status of the Antarctica, law of the sea, self-determination and decolonization, nuclear non-proliferation and disarmament, human rights, sovereign immunity, minority rights, relationship between international law and municipal law, status and treatment of refugees, neutrality and non-alignment, air and space law, international administrative law and international terrorism, North-South dialogue and the new international economic order, international humanitarian law, international commercial arbitration, peaceful settlement of international disputes, national development and international law, and indigenous parallels of international law.

The group suggested that for future research it will be desirable to give priorities to the following topics for research, and for regional seminars and symposia:

i. International Refugee Law and Asia
ii. National and International Perspectives of Human Rights
iii. Newly emerging nations and International Law
iv. National Development Planning and International Law
v. Environment and Resources Law
vi. Asia-Pacific Contribution to International Law
vii. Compatibility of International Law and National Law.

The group also recommended that Unesco should consider organizing of a seminar in the biennium 1986-87 on Asia-Pacific Contribution to International Law as part of its regular programme.

THIRTYTHREE

YOUTH AND HUMAN UNITY

(International Seminar 1985)

Organization of the Seminar

To launch the International Youth Year 1985, the First International Seminar was organized by the Auroville Trust at Auroville (India) from February 21 to 28, 1985. The Seminar was sponsored by the Department of Sports and Youth Affairs, Ministry of Education, New Delhi, Indian Council of Philosophical Research, Indian Council for Cultural Relations and Unesco. The seminar began with a plenary session on the "Crisis of Contemporary Man". This was followed by an intensive discussion by three sub-groups on the topics "Unity, Uniformity and Diversity". "Free Grouping of Mankind" and "Science and Spirituality".

Delegates came from 50 countries of the world and many Indian States.

Declaration

Declaration of the International Youth Year International Seminar on Youth and Human Unity held in Auroville from February 21 to 28, 1985.

Motto

"It is the unity of all in the solidarity of a common manifestation that will allow the creation of the new and divine world upon the earth. Each will bring his part, but no part will be complete except as a power in the solidarity of the whole". **Sri Aurobindo**

We, the representatives of 50 nations of the world, welcome the important initiative by the Government of India, Unesco and Auroville to invite the youth of the world to the first International Seminar of the International Youth Year which has the theme of Youth and Human Unity. This represents a significant and timely contribution to the fulfilment of the goals and objectives of the IYY-Participation, Development, Peace.

We, the youth of the world, firmly believe in the oneness of humanity and that the entire world is our family and we want it to be a happy home where the bonds of love join and unify human beings in their harmonious interaction with each other and with nature.

The themes discussed during the seminar (a) Unity, Uniformity and Diversity, (b) Science and Spirituality, and (c) Free Grouping of Mankind have provided a stimulating focus for the exchange of opinions and experiences with regard to our common destiny in our contemporary world. In spite of cultural and national differences, the spirit of youth triumphed over the deliberations and brought about a convergence of opinions and analyses expressed by the delegates.

The following resolutions emerged from the discussions:

1. The Member States of the United Nations and the international community are strongly urged to regard the International Youth Year as a process, starting in 1985 and continuing into the future and thus should provide supporting resources and structures for carrying out definitive programmes inspired by the views already expressed at this International Youth Year 1985 Seminar in Auroville.

2. Auroville has provided us with a valuable experience towards human unity and, therefore, we suggest that this Seminar should be at the starting point for a series of international meetings in Auroville to be held on a regular basis in the years to come.

3. To make human unity a reality and ensure lasting peace and integral development throughout the world, we strongly insist on:

   (a) immediate ban on the arms race and progressive and complete disarmament;

(b) cessation of conflict and tension among nations and within nations;
(c) funds now used for armaments should be redirected to the process of world development;
(d) constructive cooperation in the fulfillment of all national vital needs and possibilities;
(e) recognition and upholding of the right of self-determination;
(f) abolition of apartheid and any other kind of discrimination and oppression;
(g) support for all UN Resolutions to this effect, and within this context, we stress the right for the self-determination of the peoples of the world. We demand the total withdrawal of forces from all the occupied territories immediately, and respect for international laws.

4. We agree that an important and essential step towards human unity is the furthering of one's own self-perfection through the development of consciousness in all its integrality. We stress the importance of facilitating this growth process for all the youth of the world by providing:

(a) essential vital needs;
(b) universal education for the free and full development of each individual based on respect for, and appreciation of, the rich diversity of the human race;
(c) using science for the advancement of mankind rather than for threatening of our very existence;
(d) free exchange of human knowledge.

5. It was concluded that human unity can best be achieved through maintaining diversity and avoiding uniformity such that each nation can make its own specific contribution towards the progress of humanity, and therefore we appeal for the increase of multicultural exchanges.

We welcome the efforts of all youth organizations which strive for peace, human unity and mutual understanding.

We wish to express our profound gratitude to all those who have made this Seminar both possible and successful. We affirm that this positive experience and exchange and the spirit of Auroville will remain with us upon our return to our respective countries and will inspire us to take practical steps towards the realization of the goals we have all proposed for human unity.

We urge world youth to join us and participate in achieving these goals and find ways in which their unique abilities and talents can contribute to the emergence of peace and human unity. Diversity exists so that human unity may be achieved.

THIRTYFOUR

WOMEN'S PARTICIPATION IN DECISION MAKING IN PUBLIC LIFE

(Meeting of Researchers-1985).

Introduction

In order to launch, according to the programme and budget approved by the General Conference of Unesco at its 22nd session (22C/5 Approved para 13424-26), a cross-cultural comparative research project on Women's Participation in Decision Making in Various Aspects of Public Life, a meeting of researchers was convened at the Unesco Regional Unit for Social and Human Sciences in Asia and the Pacific, Bangkok. Held from April 1 to 5, 1985, the meeting accomplished the following objectives:

1. Exchange of country experiences in regard to women's participation in decision making in various aspects of public life;
2. Identification of common research focus and development of a framework for comparative study;
3. Formulation of a research design; and
4. Decision on organizational matters related to the project, report format, time-table, coordination and budgeting.

The following were invited to attend the meeting, in their personal capacity:

1. India : Dr. Govind Kelkar
2. Indonesia : Dr. Toeti Heraty Noerhadi
3. Malaysia : Dr. Noraini Abdullah
4. Thailand : Dr. Chancha Suvannathat

Besides, there were representatives from UN-ESCAP (Social Development Division) and FAO.

Unesco was represented by Dr. Yogesh Atal, Regional Adviser for Social and Human Sciences in Asia and the Pacific, Ms Koto Kanno and Mr Luca Dall' Oglio, Associate Experts attached to the Regional Unit for Social and Human Sciences in Asia and the Pacific.

Emerging Key Issues Reviewed

Presentation of statements by scholars from the four countries was concluded with a review of key issues emerging from them. Dr Yogesh Atal summarized the discussion and brought up the main points for further consideration and examination. This summary is reproduced below:

1. Women's participation in public life is limited in terms of areas and the levels of decision making. This phenomenon is observed in all four countries. Religion, cultural millieu and socialization were pointed out as important factors influencing women's (non) participation in public life, in particular their contribution to decision making. Socialization plays an important role in inculcating culture-specific "ideology of gender", which in these country contexts is characterized by dependency on, and subordination to, men, and rigid division of labour by sex. This ideology of gender appears to be reinforced, in recent years, by the revivalistic tendencies such as resurgence of religion and reinvigoration of traditions alongside of the process of modernization.

2. The group felt that tradition and modernity need not be regarded as contradictory concepts. Tradition can exist in modern society, and may even play an important role in development and modernization.

3. While appreciating the gains of technological innovations, the researchers recognized that technology does not always have positive consequences for all sections of society. There is, thus, a need to review the "net balance of consequences" of technological innovations on the lives of women.

4. Questions regarding perception were also raised. The meeting agreed that examination of women's self-perception is relevant to this study on women's participation in decision making in public life. The group, however, admitted that there is a difference between self-perception and by others, and that this may not be lost sight of.

5. "Participation in public life" is regarded both as an indicator of development and an instrument for development. It can also serve as an indicator of the "democratization" process.

6. The group discussed as to what "Participation in public life" means. Activities, in general, are divided into those taking place inside the house and those undertaken outside the house. By "public life", the group agreed to mean "activities outside the house" In this sense, activities in public life do not always involve crucial decision making. The group, however, was of the opinion that activities inside and outside the house influence each other in a variety of ways, and are not mutually exclusive in determining women's socio-economic roles and positions.

7. The concept of "dual role" was regarded crucial in the analysis of women's participation. The concept, as elaborated in the group, goes beyond the usual sense of the term which meant domestic and non-domestic roles; it was indicated that "dual role" be understood as an element of androgynous development in which women are socialized and trained to take on some of the roles that are traditionally defined as "masculine". Consideration should be given to the pressure on women to perform the dual role as if she were a "super human being".

8. Participation in public life was identified in three areas economic, political and socio-cultural. Participation in economy means employment, running business, etc. Participation in politics may mean such activities as voting, holding position (elected) in legislative bodies or in political parties, organizations, and performing various other political roles. Social participation may imply membership of religious organizations, clubs, or other non-profit voluntary organizations. (These are only illustrative cases.

9. With regard to "decision Making", the following points were

discussed:

(a) Participation and decision making : The group raised the question whether one can fully and substantially participate in anything without having the responsibility of decision making, and reached the opinion that participation involving decision making should be distinguished from passive participation.

(b) Selectivity, capability and knowledge are regarded as main pre-conditions for holding a decision-making post. Since skills and capabilities vary from individual to individual, a keen competition is found for higher positions of decision-making, which are, of necessity, limited. Thus the process of selectivity is an important dimension in social placement.

(c) Typology and hierarchy of decision-making : There are many types/kinds of decision-making. The types and areas of decision making relate to level of decision-makers. The top level decision makers will take decisions on policy matters, middle rank decision-makers will decide administrative matters and lower rank decision-makers will handle operational matters.

(d) Spatial element in decision making : Urban centres, where policy-making bodies are located, make decisions on planning and policy-related matters, while rural peripheries can make decisions at administrative and implementation levels.

(e) Manifest/Hidden decision making : The way decisions are made differs from situation to situation. Though, in general, the superior would make decisions for her/his subordinates, there are cases where the subordinate de facto makes the decision for the superior; but de jure (i.e. manifestly) it is attributed to the superior, who only accords his approval. Thus, the real decision-makers may be different, and may remain anonymous and unknown. In this respect, even housewives may also influence the decisions of their husbands that relate to their public offices. However, there are methodological problems to document this process.

10. Women in the Third World are facing particular problems

which are different from those of women in the First World. Sheer application of a model for women's participation in decision-making in public life imported from the First World to the Third World will not work. "Third World Feminism" may, therefore, be examined in the socio-economic and cultural contexts of the Third World. In this respect, it is fundamentally important to see women not in confrontation with men as two opposing groups, but as actors in a social milieu whose needs and aspirations have to be understood in terms of their historical and social experiences, and in terms of the changes that are occurring at the family level.

THIRTYFIVE

YOUTH UNEMPLOYMENT

(International Meeting of Experts 1984 and 85)

Nature and Objectives of the Meeting

In observance of the programme mandate (para. 08150 of the Approved 22 C/5 Programme and Budget for 1984-1985), a series of exploratory regional, subregional and national studies on the causes and consequences of youth unemployment was undertaken from September 1984 to September 1985. Several international and national research centres took part in this exercise whose common task was to analyse the existing social sciences literature concerning in particular three major subjects: (a) social status of youth in society, highlighting problems related to education, employment profiles and technological change; (b) socio-cultural implications of youth unemployment, taking into consideration youth aspirations and expectations; (c) responses of youth to the problem of unemployment, including "coping strategies" and "strategies of survival"

In pursuance of the programme mandate, an international meeting of experts, category VI, was held at Unesco headquarters from September 18 to 20, 1985, in order to examine the results of the studies and to formulate recommendations to Unesco on future research and action programmes concerning the promotion of youth employment and youth participation.

Participants and Observers

The meeting was attended by 14 participants, five of them from industrialized countries and nine from developing countries. Observers from the following organizations also attended: International Social Science Council (ISSC), International Labour Organization (ILO), World Federation of Trade Unions. Several members ot Unesco's

Secretariat were also present.

Agenda of the Meeting

The agenda of the meeting, as prepared by the Secretariat, provided for the following subjects and for the following organization of the work of the meeting: Wednesday the 18th: general presentation of the findings of the studies; evaluation of the findings of the studies (i) social sciences and youth unemployment/employment problems; Thursday the 19th: evaluation of the findings of the studies; (ii) the consequences of youth unemployment; (iii) the causes of youth unemployment; Friday the 20th: reflection on alternative policies to cope with the problem of youth unemployment; formulation and adoption of recommendations to the Director General.

Conclusions and Recommendations

Based on all the previous debates, during the third day of the meeting the participants worked on the conclusions and recommendations. At the end of the debate, they agreed upon and approved the following text:

"The International Meeting of Experts on Youth Unemployment held from September 18 to 20 gave rise to the following recommendations:

A. Research

1. Unesco is strongly recommended to promote future research on the theme of youth and unemployment/employment which not only takes into account the importance of economic factors but highlights the crucial role of cultural, social and political dimensions affecting the degree of participation of young people in society. The research activities should be undertaken in close cooperation with established research institutes and international research associations with a multidisciplinary perspective, emphasizing, whenever possible, longitudinal/time series research designs in order to scrutinize causal dynamics of the factors impacting on working conditions and unemployment of youth.

Taking into consideration the pronounced differences among youth with respect to genders, social class, place of living, ethnic background, Unesco is advised to pay special attention to research in the following areas:

Consequences of economic and technological change taking place in the industrialized countries affecting the living conditions of young people in developing countries both with respect to interdependencies in the economic and the cultural sector;

evaluation at national and regional levels of existing youth employment and participation programmes on the local level, with special consideration given to the changes taking place in the role of work and education for youth in different societies;

living conditions of youth related to special working status such as unpaid work in households or associations, extremely low-paid jobs as apprentices or unqualified workers;

the role of educational programmes for the promotion of young people, ability for self-help and the establishment of cooperatives and other forms of self-employment and of collective organization of work in the various fields of society;

youth attitudes, aspirations and images about employment and the future of societal development in comparison to other relevant population groups.

B. Operational programmes and activities

Unesco is advised to promote operational programmes and activities which are directed to:

the creation of alternative youth employment initiatives in the field of culture and education at local and national levels, with special emphasis on programmes which are organized, administered and evaluated by youth itself;

the establishment of cooperatives and other forms of self-employment and of collective organization or work aimed of facilitating the employment of young people in the various fields of society;

support youth employment initiatives coming from other United Nations agencies such as ILO, and also initiatives based on the interlinkage of the public and private sectors of society for the promotion of youth employment and youth participation.

C. Implementation strategies

Unesco is advised to strengthen its function as an active inter-mediator between the young people, the policy-makers and the researchers. This aim could be reached by:

providing for the participation of concerned young people in both research and operational activities;

organizing seminars, round-tables or other forms of international exchange which bring together involved young people, policy-makers and researchers;

an active cooperation with other international, regional and national bodies engaged in the issue of youth and employment and other connected issues. In regions where research and training centres related to this area already are existing, Unesco should intensify the joint organization of activities; in regions where such centres are missing, Unesco should promote the establishment of a similar network of institutions and programmes;

supporting the dissemination of information on youth unemployment and employment issues and value-changes related to those themes among young people, decision-makers and the public at large.

The participants in the meeting expressed their satisfaction with and support for Unesco's activities in such an important area as the struggle against youth unemployment and expressed their hope to contribute to its successful realization.

THIRTYSIX

UNESCO'S ROLE IN IMPROVING THE SITUATION OF YOUNG PEOPLE AND ITS CONTRIBUTION TO INTERNATIONAL YOUTH YEAR (RESOLUTION NOVEMBER 1985)

(Resolutions adopted on the report of Commission V at the 36th plenary meeting on November 8, 1985.)

Cultural exchanges between young people

The General Conference

Considering the interest of the younger generation in the problems facing the world today,

Recognizing the legitimate aspiration of the young to be able to meet one another and travel in order to get to know the world,

Emphasizing the importance of a follow-up to International Youth Year 1985,

Having regard to the provision in the Draft Programme and Budget (23C/5, paragraph 05221(a) concerning out-of-school science and technology education for young people,

Considering that meetings in the fields of music, fine arts and other areas of culture in the broadest sense contribute to the strengthening of international understanding,

Invites the Director General:

(a) To develop summer camps for young people in Unesco's various fields of competence (scientific, musical, linguistic, artistic):
(b) To encourage National Commissions for Unesco to take the initiative in these inter-cultural exchanges which promote international understanding;
(c) To ensure generally that young people are still more closely associated with activities of Unesco.

Unesco's contribution to International Youth Year and to the Promotion of its Future Objectives

The General Conference,

Recalling its resolutions on the role of youth, and, in particular, resolutions 3/05 and 3/06 adopted at its 21st session, and resolution 22 adopted at its 22nd session,

Recalling the provision contained in the Second Medium-Term Plan (1984-1989) in the note on the lines of emphasis with regard to young people (22C/4).

Taking into account the recommendations of the Final Report adopted at the World Congress on Youth (Barcelona, July 8-15, 1985), and the Barcelona Statement, reflecting the aspirations of young people to live freely and in peace and seeking to come to terms with their problems and challenges, which are in fact those of contemporary society,

Taking note of resolution 36/28 of November 25, 1981, in which the General Assembly of the United Nations endorsed the Specific Programme of Measures and Activities to be undertaken prior to and during the International Youth Year, and resolution 37/48 of December 3, 1982, in which the United Nations General Assembly invited the Specialized Agencies, in particular Unesco, to support the implementation of the United Nations Programme for the International Youth Year and its follow-up,

Reaffirming the fact that young people represent a substantial and ever-growing section of the world population and have an increasingly important role to play in the solution of the major problems facing mankind, and that it is, therefore, necessary to offer them even broader opportunities of playing an active part in all aspects of the social, economic, political, educational and cultural life of the society to which they belong,

Convinced that effective functioning of channels of communication between Unesco, youth and youth organizations is a basic prerequisite for the proper information and active involvement of young people in the work of Unesco,

Mindful of the fact that Unesco is in a paramount position, through its activities within its fields of competence, to make valuable contributions to the specific interests of youth,

Taking note with satisfaction of the report of the Director General of Unesco's role in improving the situation of young people and the contribution of Unesco to the International Youth Year (23C/21),

Also taking note of decision 5.1.4(II) adopted by the Executive Board at its 122nd session,

1. *Recommends* to Member States and all the institutions concerned:

   (a) to pay attention to the recommendations adopted by the World Congress on Youth, held in Barcelona in 1985 in cooperation with the Spanish Government;
   (b) to contribute, in the years to come, to the activities resulting from the implementation of the objectives of the International Youth Year: "Participation, Development, Peace";

2. *Invites* the Director General:

   (a) to continue to devote particular attention to, and strengthen within the Approved Programme and Budget, Unesco's youth activities, laying particular emphasis upon concrete activities not only for, but also with and by, young people;

(b) to continue to cooperate with the United Nations system, in particular with the ECOSOC Commission for Social Development and with the United Nations Centre for Social Development and Humanitarian Affairs in order to ensure a comprehensive and coordinated approach to youth policies and programmes within the United Nations system, and taking into account in future action the results of the United Nations World Conference for International Youth Year;

(c) to consult, in carrying out these activities, the main international non-governmental youth organizations, making use of the Unesco collective consultations, in cooperation with structures such as the Geneva Informal Meeting and other appropriate mechanisms;

(d) to undertake these activities within a coherent youth policy based on an active inter-sectoral cooperation, while ensuring a clearly unified management of this policy;

(e) to give priority within the Approved Programme and Budget (1986-1987) and in future programmes to the topics examined by the World Congress on Youth (Barcelona, July 8-15, 1985), namely, "Youth, education and work", "Youth and cultural development and "Youth, mutual understanding and international cooperation";

(f) to assist Member States in the elaboration of appropriate youth policies and youth programmes, especially with a view to ensuring the participation of the youth in all the sectors of society;

(g) to disseminate widely the Final Report and the Statement adopted by the World Congress on Youth;

(h) to inform the General Conference at its 24th session on the follow-up and implementation of this resolution.

THIRTYSEVEN

GLOBAL PROBLEMS OF SOCIAL CHANGE AND SOCIAL SCIENCES

(International Federation of Social Sciences Organizations-Report 1985)

A gist of the views expressed by eminent scholars at the VII General Conference of IFSSO held at New Delhi is given below:

Prof Chavdar Kiuranove of the Bulgarian Academy of Sciences, speaking at VII General Conference of the International Federation of Social Sciences Organizations, held at New Delhi in 1985, observed that during the second half of the 20th century, social change was becoming more and more important because human society was facing specific types of problems the so-called global problems. He remarked, "They concern *all of us*, all human beings. But even this is not enough to characterize them. What is more important is that *their solution is possible only with the participation of all*-all countries, all people, all classes, all individuals". According to him, the major reasons for the globalization of these problems were the growing world-wide network of *communication*, the limitless spread, accumulation and velocity of *information* and the element of *world consciousness*.

Prof. Kiuranove identified three major global problems as being of significant importance to the social sciences:

1. Development,
2. Employment and
3. Peace and Disarmament.

Prof Niels Amstrup, Treasurer, IFSSO ,pointed out five aspects of social change in the context of Western European countries. These are: black economy, revolt among the youth, influences of foreigners, changing role of women in society and the questioning of the foundations of a Welfare State.

Prof. Amstrup felt that the role of the social scientists was very moderate on account of two reasons. First, the social scientists are bad as predictors due to the fact that human societies are far too complex to make predictions possible. The second reason is that politicians do not listen to social scientists, simply because our research fields are often hot issues in political terms.

Prof. Josef Blahoz, Vice-President, IFSSO, enumerated five problems which he found of global dimensions-danger of wars fought with nuclear weapons of mass destruction, neocolonialism and the policies of cold war, the growing gap between the developed and the developing worlds, the depletion of non-renewable energy resources and the far-reaching deterioration of the global environment, and the social dimensions of scientific and technological change.

Prof. Sung-Chick Hong, Vice-President, IFSSO, listed 19 social problems of unsurmountable difficulties in the world: (1) population explosion, (2) poverty, (3) population, (4) Urban-rural gap, (5) prejudice and discrimination, (6) alienation, (7) unemployment, (8) youth revolt, (9) public health, (10) class conflict, (11) illiteracy, (12) trade imbalance, (13) international debt, (14) ethnic tensions, (15) value conflict and confusion, (16) information, explosion and gap, (17) nuclear armament, (18) trade protectionism, (19) labour unrest.

Social research has become an important tool for determining public policy as it can provide the decision makers and planners with current, objective and reliable data to adopt sound policies in different spheres of society. Not only that, development and social changes are also determined by the extent of knowledge and information about a society, which are gathered systematically and with expertise by the social scientists. The role of research and consequently of the expertise of social scientists have thus become more significant in view of the complexities of social activities and the increasingly growing governmental intervention in the hitherto unknown region of the society. Policy makers everywhere want to formulate and execute a policy which is based as much as possible on scientific knowledge, while the social scientists analyse problems scientifically from different perspectives.

In the Third World countries, social science research receives its funds from different sources, which could be government, non-government organizations, foundations and foreign and international agencies. However funds for social sciences research are very inadequate and more resources in terms of money, training facilities, trained personnel, equipment, etc., are very necessary for the overall development of social science research.

Research Areas in Social Sciences

Following research areas were mentioned by the participants of the VII General Conference of IFSSO (1985):

The representatives of the Third World mentioned such areas as Poverty and its Eradication, Rural Development, Development Policies, Theory and Planning, Population Questions, Women Studies, Youth, Environment, Application of Modern Technology, Urbanization, Energy and Water Resources, Income and Wealth Distribution, Crime and Corruption, Industrial Relations, Labour Movements, the Political Process, Questions related to the State, Political Regime and Institutions, Citizenship, etc., Foreign Aid Dependency, and the Comparative Research on Development Experiences in the Third World.

The representatives of the Second World indicated as high priority areas : Development and Management of Science, Economic and Social Development of Society, Perspectives of the Scientific and Technological Revolution, Positive Development of International Relations, Disarmament and Peace, Problems of the Social and Demographic Structure, Environmental Protection, Status of Women, Development of the Family and Education and Cultural Development.

The representatives of the First World gave a number of examples of the research areas considered of great importance in their respective countries. Some of these were related to the Welfare State, Technological Development, Labour and Labour Market Issues, Demographic Issues, Women Studies, Environment and Energy Issues, the Administrative and Political Process, Science Policy Issues, the Family in Modern Society, Minority Groups, Bilingualism and Multiculturalism.

THIRTYEIGHT

ASIA-PASIFIC PROGRAMME OF EDUCATION FOR ALL APPEAL

(Regional Experts Meeting 1986)

Background

The Fifth Regional Conference of Ministers of Education and Those Responsible for Economic Planning in Asia and the Pacific (Bangkok, March 4-11, 1985) had recommended (Recommendation No. 10) to the Director General of Unesco to study the possibility of launching a regional programme, to eradicate illiteracy and to universalize primary education in Asia and the Pacific before the end of the century.

The Twenty-Third Session of the Unesco General Conference (Sofia, 1985) by it Resolution 2.3 had authorized the Director General to launch a regional programme for universal provision and renewal of primary education and eradication of illiteracy in Asia and the Pacific. To develop the programme, a technical meeting of experts was convened by the Unesco Regional Office for Education in Asia and the Pacific in January 1986.

Guided by its deliberation, the programme was prepared and submitted to the Regional Experts Meeting on the Regional Programme for Universalization and Renewal of Primary Education and the Eradication of Illiteracy in Asia and the Pacific (Bangkok, May 20-27, 1986).

The Meeting unanimously endorsed the programme under the title "Asia-Pacific Programme of Education for All", acronym AP-PEAL, and recommended to the Director General to launch it on

November 4, 1986, on the occasion of the 40th Anniversary of Unesco.

APPEAL is built on the premise that education is a fundamental human right, and that it is a critical means for development. In the context of the problems of illiteracy and the need for universalization of primary education, it is realized that education cannot be treated as a closed system. It should be regarded as a sub-system of the wider society, having interfaces with the economic, political, social and cultural domains; actions should be planned taking into account all these domains.

The Programme acknowledges the rich cultural and civilizational heritage of the region. The existence of indigenous languages and the long literary tradition of many of them is another unique feature. There is also a renewed assertion of cultural identity by the Nation States. Furthermore, there is an increase in the tempo of development and strong emphasis on enhancing the absorptive capacities of their economies.

Education is expected to support these trends and contribute to national development. Rather than being a goal by itself, education is to be treated as a means for development. This newer role requires not only to enlarge the existing structures to impart conventional education, but to create new ones-both within and outside the education system and to fashion new curricula with contents relevant to the nationally defined goals for development. The technological breakthroughs made in recent years provide newer tools and techniques which could be fruitfully and imaginatively utilized for the Programme.

The Programme is a response to the resolution of Member States to eradicate illiteracy and to universalize primary education. It is intended to backstop national efforts and promote intra-regional cooperation so that inequalities in literacy profiles are wiped out, and prophylactic action be taken against the possibility of lapse into illiteracy.

Its focus will primarily be on the children and the younger age-groups of the adult population who have somehow remained outside the catchment area of the existing educational system. The Programme would initiate research to investigate the factors that were responsible for their neglect, and encourage Member States to evolve suitable strategies to ensure their involvement and participation.

Aim, Objectives and Tasks of APPEAL

The aim of APPEAL is to facilitate, through regional cooperation, the national efforts of the Member States in Asia and the Pacific with a view to:

(a) achieving universal primary education;
(b) eradicating illiteracy; and
(c) providing continuing education in support of (a) and (b) above.

Objectives of APPEAL would be to promote and strengthen mutual cooperation among the Member States in the Region to fulfil their resolve to:

i. continue and intensify their effort to eradicate illiteracy by the year 2000 by adopting effective policies and strategies;
ii. consider literacy programmes as an integral part of socio-economic development plans of the countries, especially of local development efforts;
iii. link universal primary education (UPE) to literacy programmes by facilitating and strengthening their potential complementarity;
iv. create appropriate infrastructures for effective planning, management, and research and development supports for attaining the goals of eradication of illiteracy and UPE;
v. strengthen training programmes for all types of literacy workers from central to field levels;
vi. mobilize on the widest possible basis the human, material and financial resources;
vii. encourage community participation and utilization of local resources involving all sectors of society including local leaders, industries, religious and social organizations in the planning and implementation of literacy programmes;

viii. develop special programmes for women and disadvantaged population groups to ensure that they derive full benefit from them;
ix. promote and strengthen post-literacy and adult education programmes to check lapsing into illiteracy and to upgrade general and vocational skills of youth and adults to make them more employable and productive;
x. take appropriate measures for achieving universal enrolment and retention at the primary level to meet the target of universal primary education well before the year 2000; and
xi. give special attention to the problem of quality, the renewal of educational content and raising the levels of learning achievement.

In support of achieving the above objectives, the Fifth Regional Conference of Ministers of Education and those Responsible for Economic Planning in Asia and the Pacific (MINEDAP) also indicated the following as among the tasks to be undertaken by APPEAL:

i. provide increased technical and other necessary assistance to the Member States to strenghten their national capabilities or the eradication of illiteracy and the achievement of UPE within the century, and to promote exchange of experiences, expertise and information;
ii. undertake comparative studies on the effective strategy for linking education and the world of work in literacy and UPE programmes;
iii. focus, to an increasing extent, on programmes of education, innovation in science and technology within the programme of UPE in view of the changing environment; and
iv. mobilize international resources from international organizations and development banks to promote programmes for universal access to, and retention and quality in, primary education in the Member States, and to eradicate illiteracy, especially to assist the least developed countries and disadvantaged sectors of the people in the region.

Principles and Strategies Guiding Actions of APPEAL

To achieve the above objectives and undertake the stated tasks

APPEAL has identified specific principles and strategies for action.

The overriding principle governing APPEAL is its actions for inputs into, and in support of, national activities for UPE and the eradication of illiteracy.

APPEAL would attempt to enhance national capabilities, leading to self-sufficient growth and independent development.

This enhancement of national capabilities is to take place using the strategy of mobilizing regional cooperation, including technical cooperation among developing and developed countries in the region.

This would involve:

1. The maximal mobilization of existing national and regional structures, within the education sector and outside it, and their appropriate coordination to encompass innovation, and implementation on a mass scale against quantitative and time targets;

2. The conjoining of quantitative expansion and quality improvement and renewal, including the redefinition of curricular specifications and incorporation of technological breakthroughs in support of both quantitative expansion and quality improvement; and

3. The special attention on population groups such as women, the primary school child populations in poverty environments, out-of-school early drop-out youth populations, minority groups, displaced and nomadic groups, and groups living in remote areas.

The regional attributes of this Programme, thus, are:

(a) the sharing of common objectives for universalizing primary education and eradicating illiteracy; and
(b) the shared determination of Member States to achieve these objectives.

Action Areas of APPEAL

Eradication of illiteracy (EOI) through:

* development of appropriate and viable literacy strategies'
* development of programmes designed to serve the needs of women, out-of-school children and youth and/or other defined disadvantaged groups;
* development of post-literacy activities;
* mobilization of community support and resources;
* strengthening of programmes in critical areas such as production of learning materials and resources training of instructors, research and evaluation;
* linking literacy with development.

Universalization of Primary Education (UPE) through:

* enrolment and retention of girls;
* enrolment and retention of defined disadvantaged groups;
* improvement of the quality and/or relevance of primary education;
* provision of preparatory, complementary or supplementary education to primary school-age children;
* planning and management of UPE at the micro level.

Continuing Education for Development (CE) through:

* parental education;
* improved linkages between formal and non-formal education;
* continuing education and its applications to work.

Modalities of Regional Cooperation

* 1. mobilization of public and resources through dialogue and discussion.
* 2. exchange information, experiences and expertise.
* 3. conduct joint consultation, research evaluation and other actions.
* 4. train personnel at national, regional and sub-regional levels.

PART V

UNESCO PUBLICATIONS

UNESCO PUBLICATIONS

A. Books on Social Sciences

Administrative management for development

A reader Edited by Yves Chapel. 1977, 200 pp., ISBN 92-3-101176-6. Co-published with the International Institute of Administrative Sciences, Brussels, which shares exclusive sales rights with Unesco throughout the world.

The Aetiology of psychoactive substance use

A report and critically annotated bibliography on research into the aetiology of alcohol, nicotine, opiate and other psychoactive substances used by C. Fazey. With the financial support of the United Nations Fund for Drug Abuse Control (UNFDAC).

1977, 226 pp., ISSBN 92-3-101508-7

Apartheid : A teacher's guide

By Godfrey N. Brown 1981, 104 pp., Illus., tables, ISBN 92-3-101896-5

Apartheid and social research

Edited by John Rex
1981, 199 pp., tables, ISBN 92-3-101898-1

Apartheid : power and historical falsification

By Marianne Cornevin
(Insights, 3)
1980, 144 pp., ISBN 92-3-101769-1

Applicability of indicators of socio-economic change for development planning

(Socio-economic studies, 7)
1984, 128 pp., illus, ISBN 92-3-102214-8

Approaches to the science of socio-economic development

Edited by Peter Lengyel
1971, 383 pp., ISBN 92-3-100924-9 (limpbound);
ISBN 92-3-100923-0 (hardbound)

Arkisyst feasibility study

Final report
(Reports and papers in the social sciences, 45)
1981, 65 pp., tables, ISBN 92-3-101795-0

Armaments, arms control and disarmament

A Unesco reader for disarmament education
Edited by Marek Thee
1981, 446 pp., figs., tables, ISBN 92-3-101920-1

Becoming aware: human rights and the family

By Margaret Gallagher
1984, 102pp., ISBN 92-3-102178-8

Bibliographic guide to studies on the status of women, development and population trends

(Women in a world perspective)
1983, 292 pp., ISBN 92-3-102122-2. Co-published with Bowker Publishing Company, Epping, and Unipub, New York, who have exclusive sales rights in the United Kingdom and United States respectively.

Bibliography of mono and multilingual vocabularies, thesauri, subject headings and classification schemes in the social sciences

Prepared by the Aslib Library in collaboration with Jean Aitchison and C.G. Allen.
(Reports and papers in the social sciences, 54)
1983, 101 pp., ISBN 92-3-102072-2

Biology and ethics

Reflections inspired by a Unesco symposium
by Bruno Ribes (Insights, 2)
1978, 202 pp., ISBN 92-3-101568-C

Can equity be organized?

Equity, development analysis and planning by Bernard Schaffer and Geoff Lamb, 1981, 166 pp., ISBN 92-3-101843-4. Co-published with Gower Publishing Company Ltd, Aldershot, who have exclusive sales rights in the United Kingdom

The challenge presented to cultures by science and technology
By Jean Ladriere
1977, 165 pp., ISBN 92-3-10148-8

Community development

Comparative case studies in India, Republic of Korea, Mexico and United Republic of Tanzania.
Editors : Ronald Dore and Zoe Mars 1981, 446 pp., figs., tables, ISBN 92-3-1101877-9.

Co-published with Croom Helm Ltd., London, who have exclusive slaes rights in the United Kingdom

The concept of international organization

Edited by Georges Abi-Saab
1981, 245 pp., illus., ISBN 92-3-101742-X

Consensus and peace

Amadou-Mahtar M'Bow, Mario Amadeo, Gerald Antoine, Rachid Daker, Asbjorn Eide, Mihajlo Javorski, Joaquin Ruiz-Gimenez and Abdoulaye Wade.
Edited by Beseat Kifle Selasssie
1980, 231 pp., ISBN 92-3-101851-5

The conservation of cities

1975, 186 pp., ISBN 92-3-101087-5. Co-published with Croom Helm Ltd, London, who have exclusive sales rights in the United Kingdom

DARE information management system

A condensed system description
(Computer design version 2)
(Reports and papers in the social sciences, 31)
1975, 23 pp., ISBN 92-3-101256-8

Data archives for the social sciences: Purposes, operations and problems

(Reports and papers in the social sciences, 26)
1973, 126 pp., tables, ISBN 92-3-101052-2

Data-based teaching in the social sciences

International Federation of Data Organizations/Unesco Invitational Seminar, Waterloo, Ontario, November 1979.
In memory of Stein Rokkan (1921-79)

Reports and papers in the social sciences, 50)
1983, 46 pp., tables, ISBN 92-3-102113-3

Different theories and practices of development

1982, 258 pp., tables, ISBN 92-3-2002-6

Domination of sharing?

Endogenous development and the transfer of knowledge(Insights 5)p 1981, 288 pp., figs., ISBN 92-3-101842-6

Ecological data in comparative research

Report on a first International Data Confrontation Seminar
By Jerome M. Clubb
(Reports and papers in the Social Sciences, 25)
1970, 37 pp., ISBN 92-3-100845-5

Ecosocial systems and ecopolitics

A reader on human and social implications of environmental management in developing countries
Edited by Karl Deutsch.
1977, 368 pp., ISBN 92-3-101450-1

Employment-oriented national youth programmes in Africa: situations, problems and prospects

(Reports and papers in the social sciences, 44)
1982, 61 pp., tables, ISBN 92-3-101777-2

Ethnicity and the media

An analysis of media reporting in the United Kingdom, Canada and Ireland
(Race, ethnicity and the media)
1977, 376 pp., ISBN 92-3-101454-4

Evaluating social action projects

Principles, methodological aspects and selected examples
(Socio-economic studies, 1)
1980, 161 pp., illus., ISBN 92-3-101807-8

Evaluation manual

By Sven Grabe
(Socio-economic studies, 6)
1983, 84 pp., figs., ISBN 92-3-102099-4

Evaluation research and social change

By Alexander Weilenmann
1980, 104 pp., illus, ISBN 92-3-101699-7

History in black and white ; an analysis of South African school history texbooks

By Elizabeth Dean, Paul Hartmann and May Katzen
1983, 137 pp., ISBN 92-3-102092-7

Human rights, questions and answers

By Leah Levin
1981, 86 pp., illus., ISBN 92-3-101957-0

Human rights aspects of population programmes with special reference to human rights law

1977, 154 pp., figs., ISBN 92-3-101487-0

Human rights in urban areas

1983, 169 pp., tables, ISBN 92-3-101983-X

Immigrant workers in Europe: their legal status

A comparative study by Eric-Jean Thomas, Study Director
1982, 245 pp., tables, ISBN 92-3-101867-1

The impact of microelectronics and information technology

Case studies in Latin America by Juan F. Rada
1982, 108 pp., figs., tables, ISBN 92-3-102004-8

Indicators of environmental quality and quality of life

(Reports and papers in the social sciences, 38)
1978, 96 pp., figs., tables, ISBN 92-3-101593-7

Indicators of social and economic change and their applications

Reports and papers in the social sciences, 37)
1977, 95 pp., ISBN 92-3-101493-5

International congress on the teaching of human rights

September 1978, Vienna
1980, 259 pp., tables, ISBN 92-3-101-781-0

The international dimensions of human rights

General editor: Karel Vasak
Revised and edited by Philip Alston, 1982, 755 pp., ISBN 92-3-101477-3
(2 hardbound volumes, not sold separately)
Co-published with Greenwood Press, Inc., Westport, Conn., who have exclusive sales rights in the United States

Islam and the race question

By 'Abd-al' -Aziz Abd-al-Qadir Kamil
1970, 65 pp., ISBN 92-3-10033-1

Islam, philosophy and science

Contributors: Muhammad Hamidullah,
Jean Jolivet, Jacques Berque, Rahat Nabi Khan and Roshdi Rashed.

Preface by Amadou-Mahtar M'Bow
1981, 168 pp., ISBN 92-3-101951-1

It is time to begin

The human role in development: some further reflections for the seventies by Malcolm S. Adiseshiah
1972, 182 pp., ISBN 92-3-100954-0

living in two cultures

The socio-cultural situation of migrant workers and their families
1982, 325 pp., tables, ISBN 92-3-101869-8

Co-published with Gower Publishing Co. Ltd. who have exclusive sales rights in the United Kingdom

Main trends of research in the social and human sciences

Part One: Social sciences (op)

Part Two: Anthropological and historical sciences; Aesthetics and the sciences of art; Legal science; Philosophy under the editorship of Jcques Havet. Contributors: Maurice Freedman, Sigfried J. De Laet, Geoffrey Barraclough, Mikel Dufrenne et al., Victor Knapp and Paul Riceur.
1978, 1, 591 pp., (2 vols),
ISBN 92-3-101013-1

A manual on evaluation of population communication programmes

Population communication manuals (2) 1981, 129 pp., ISBN 92-3-101559-1

A manual on mass media in population and development
(Population communication manuals, 1)
1977, 105 pp., ISBN 92-3-101439-0

Methods for development planning
Scenarios, models and micro-studies

1981, 269 pp., figs., tables, ISBN 92-3-101875-2

Moving towards change

Some thoughts on the new international economic order
1976 (2nd impr, 1978), 137 pp., ISBN 92-3-101365-3

New approaches to rural youth and development in Latin America and the Caribbean

(Regional youth meetings, 4)
1981, 103 pp., ISBN 92-3-101910-4

A new concept of development

Basic tenets
By Francios Perroux
1983, 224 pp., ISBN 92-3-102057-9

Obstacles to disarmament and ways of overcoming them

Edited for Swadesh Rana (Insights, 7)
1981, 223 pp., tables, ISBN 92-3-101879-5

Planning methods and human environment

By Gberete C. Gallopin (Socio-economic studies, 4)
1981, 68 pp., ISBN 92-3-101894-9

Project evaluation: problems of methodology

1984, 141 pp., ISBN 92-3-102132-X

Public administration and management: Problems of adaptation in different socio-cultural contexts

1982, 170 pp., tables, ISBN 92-3-102024-2
Co-published with Abhinav Publications, India, who have exclusive sales rights in Asia and the Gulf States

Quality of life: problems of assessment and measurement

(Socio-economic studies, 5)
1983, 177 pp., ISBN 92-3-102096-X

Race and biology

By L.C. Dunn
(The race question in modern science)
1985 (7th impr., 1965), 48 pp., ISBN 92-3-100436-0

Race and class in post-colonial society

A study of ethnic group relations in the English-speaking Caribbean, Bolivia, Chile and Mexico
(Race and society)
1977, 458 pp., figs., tables, ISBN 92-3-101445-5

Rece as news

(Race, ethnicity and the media)
1974, 176 pp.; ISBN 82-3-101191-X

Race mixture

By Harry L. Shapiro
(The race question in modern science)
1960 (2nd impr., 1961), 48 pp., ISBN 92-3-100444-1

Racism and apartheid in southern Africa

South Africa and Namibia
1974, 156 pp., ISBN 92-3-101199-5

Racism, science and pseudo-science

Proceedings of the Symposium to Examine
Pseudo-Scientific Theories Invoked to Justify Racism and Racia
Discrimination (Athens, March 30 to April 3, 1981) (Insights, 8)
1983, 158 pp., figs., tables, ISBN 92-3-101993-7

Readings on population for law students

Edited by L.T. Lee and P. Saney
1977, 123 pp., ISBN 92-3-101364-5

Reporting southern Africa

Western news agencies reporting from Southern Africa
by Phil Harris
1981, 168 pp., ISBN 92-3-101700-4

Research in population communication

By Gloria D. Feliciano
(Population communication manuals, 3)
1978, 84 pp., ISBN 92-3-101512-5

Review of research trends and an annotated bibliography

Social and economic consequences of the arms race and of disarmament
(Reports and papers in the social Sciences, 39).
1974, 44 pp., ISBN 92-3-101552-4

Scientists, the arms race and disarmament

A Unesco/Pugwash symposium, General Editor : Joseph Rotblat
1982, 323 pp., figs., tables, ISBN 92-3-102021-8.
Co-published with Taylor & Francis Ltd. Who have exclusive sales rights in the United kingdom

Selected applications of the Unesco educational simulation model

(Reports and papers in the social sciences, 34)
1977, 74pp., ISBN 92-3-101358-4

Selected studies on the dynamics, patterns and consequences of migration

Mexico City: Industrialization, migration and the labour force, 1930-1970
By Humberto Munoz, Orlandina de Oliveira and Claudio Stern.

(Reports and papers in the social sciences, 46)
1983, 87 pp., figs., maps, tables, ISBN 92-3-101855-8

Migration and development : major features of migratory movement in India

By Biplab Dasgupta
(Reports and papers in the social sciences, 52)
1983, 39 pp., tables, ISBN 92-3-102011-0

Medium-sized towns in Nigeria: research and policy prospects

by Aderanti Adepou
(Reports and papers in the social Sciences, 53)
1983, 56 pp., tables, ISBN 92-3-102035-8

Selective inventory of information services

World social science information services, 3)
1985, 247 pp., ISBN 92-3-002343-4
Trilingual: English/French/Spanish

Social implications of the peaceful uses of nuclear energy

Edited by Otto Klineberg
1964, 169 pp., ISBN 92-3-100553-7

Social implications of the scientific and technological revolution :

A Unesco symposium
1981, 408 pp., index, ISBN 92-3-101664-4

Social science methods, decision-making and development planning

(Socio-economic studies, 8)
1984, 104 pp., ISBN 92-3-102207-5

Social science organization and policy: first series

Belgium, Chile, Egypt, H ingary, Nigeria, Sri Lanka

Introduction by A.B. Cherns
1974, 352 pp., ISBN 92-3-101084-0
Co-published with Mouton, The Hague, who have exclusive sales rights in the Netherlands

Social science research and women in the Arab world

1984, 250 pp., ISBN 92-3-102140-0. Co-published with Frances Pinter (Publishers) Ltd, who have exclusive sales rights in the United Kingdom (and from whom the hardbound edition is available)

Social Sciences in Asia

Vol. I: Bangladesh, Iran Malaysia, Pakistan, Thailand
Reports and papers in the social Sciences, 32)
1976, 54 pp., ISBN 92-3-101324-6
Vol. II : Afghanistan, Indonesia, Japan Republic of Korea, Nepal
(Reports and papers in the social sciences, 33)
1977, 70 pp., ISBN 92-3-101403-X
Vol. III.: Burma, Mongolia, New Zealand, the Philippines, Singapore
Reports and papers in the social Sciences, 35)
1977, 111 pp., ISBN 92-3-101510-9
Vol. IV: Australia, Fiji, Hongkong, India, Papua New Guinea, Sri Lanka.
(Reports and papers in the social sciences 42)
1980, 98 pp., figs., tables, ISBN 92-3-1017117-9

Social sciences in Asia and the Pacific

1984, 612 pp., tables, ISBN 92-33-102148-6

Social sciences in Latin America and the Caribbean

I-Social science needs and priorities
(Reports and papers in the social sciences. 48)
1982, 54 pp., ISBN 92-3-101962-7

Socio-economic indicators for planning; methodological aspects and selected examples

(Socio-economic studies, 2)
1981, 122 pp., ISBN 92-3-101892-2

Sociological theories, race and colonialism

1980, 500 pp., ISBN 92-3-101635-0

Sociology and social anthropology in Asia and the Pacific

1984, 720 pp., ISBN 92-3-102172-9
Co-published with Wiley Eastern Ltd, New Delhi, who have exclusive sales rights in India

Southern Rhodesia

The effects of a conquest society on education, culture and information by Marion O'Callaghan with a contribution by Reginald Austin
1977, 293 pp., ISBN 92-3-101393-9

Study on the dynamics, evolution and consequences of migrations

II-Three centuries of spatial mobility in France
By Daniel Courgeau, Institut National d'Etudes Demographiques, Paris
(Reports and papers in the social sciences, 51)
1983, 64 pp., maps, ISBN 92-3-102086-2

Suicide or survival?

The challenge of the year 2000
(Insights, 1)
1978, 192 pp., ISBN 92-3-102124-9

Teaching and research in philosophy: Africa

(Studies on teaching and research in philosophy throughout the

world, 1)
1984, 287 pp., ISBN 92-3-102124-9

Thinking and doing

Youth and a new international economic order by Barbara Bruhl Day with illustrations by Garry Apgar
1980, 96 pp., illus, ISBN 92-3-101841-8

Threat of modern warfare to man and his environment

An annotated bibliography prepared under the auspices of the International Peace Research Association (IPRA)
(Reports and papers in the social sciences, 40)
1979, 25 pp., ISBN 92-3-101608-3

Time and philosophies

H. Aguessey, M. Ashish, Y.F. Askin, Boubou Hama, H.G. Gadamer, L. Gardet, A. Hasnaoui, T. Honderich, A. Jeanniere, S. Karsz, S. Ohe, P. Ricceur, A.J. Toynbee and J. Witt-Hansen
(At the crossroads of cultures)
1977, 256 pp., ISBN 92-3-101396-3

Time and the sciences

Edited by Frank Greenaway with Contributions by J.M. Abraham, Ahmed M.
Abou-Zeid, F. N. Sougan Agbelmagnon,
Paul Fraisse, Mubeccel Kiray, John
McHale, A. Neelameghan, S.L. Piotrowski,
Frederic Vester and Gerald J. Whitrow.
(At the crossroads of cultures)
1979, 182 pp., ISBN 92-3-101657-1

Tourism: transnational corporations and cultural identities

By Francois Ascher
ISBN 92-3-102095-1

Towards a new international economic order

By Mohammed Bedjaoui
(New challenges to international law)
1979, 287 pp., ISBN 92-3-101670-9
Co-published with Holmes & Meier, New York and London, who have exclusive sales rights in the United States and share rights throughout the rest of the world

Transnational corporations and endogenous development

By Jean-Louis Reiffers with Andre Cartapanis, William Experton and Jean-Luc Fuguet
1982, 280 pp., ISBN 92-3-101603-2

Trends in ethnic group relations in Asia and Oceania
(Race and society)
1979, 292 pp., tables, ISBN 92-3-101603-2

Two studies on ethnic group relations in Africa: Senegal, the United Republic of Tanzania

(Race and society)
1974, 156 pp., ISBN 92-3-101101-4

Two studies on unemployment among educated young people

Part I: Unemployment among educated young people in the developed market-economy countries
by Simone Morio
Part II: Unemployment among educated young people in the French-speaking developing countries
by Yarrise Zoctizoum
1980, 133 pp., tables, ISBN 92-3-101618-0

Unesco yearbook on peace and conflict studies 1980

1981, 311 pp., ISBN 92-3-101254-1

Unesco yearbook on peace and conflict studies 1981

1982, 396 pp., ISBN 92-3-102032-3

Unesco yearbook on peace and conflict studies 1982

1983, 269 pp., ISBN 92-3-10211-2

Unesco yearbook on peace and conflict studies 1983

1985, 285 pp., ISBN 92-3-102282-2
Co-published with Greenwood Press Inc., Westport, Conn., who have exclusive sales rights in the United States and Canada.

United Nations lawmaking : cultural and ideological relativism and international law making for an era of transition

By Edward McWhinny
1984, 200 pp., ISBN 92-102147-8
Co-published with Holmes & Meier, Inc., New York, who have exclusive sales rights in the United States.

The use of socio-economic indicators in development planning

1976 (2nd impr., 1979), 282 pp., ISBN 92-3-101329-7

Using folk entertainments to promote national development

(Population communication manuals, 4)
By H.K. Ranganath
1980, 45 pp., ISBN 92-3-101773-X

Violations of human rights : possible rights of recourse and forms of resistance

1984, 236 pp., ISBN 92-3-102114-1

Violence and its causes

Methodological and theoretical aspects of recent research on violence

(Insights, 40)
1980, 269 pp., ISBN 92-3-101809-4

Why people move

Comparative perspectives on the dynamics of internal migration
By Jorge Balan
1981, 342 pp., figs., tables, ISBN 92-3-101909-0

Women and racial discrimination in Rhodesiaa

By A.K.H. Weinrich
1979, 143 pp., figs., tables, ISBN 92-3-101621-0

Women and work in Uruguay

By Graciela Taglioretti
(Women in a world perspective)
1984, 80 pp., ISBN 92-3-102110-9

Women as heads of households in the Caribbean

Family structure and feminine status by Joycelin Massiah
(Women in a world perspective)
1983, 69 pp., ISBN 92-3-102047-1

Women in the villages, men in the towns

(Women in a world perspective)
1984, 526 pp., illus., ISBN 92-3-102039-0

Women on the move: contemporary changes in family and society

(Women in a world perspective)
1984, 324 pp., ISBN 92-3-102157-5

World directory of peace research institutions

(Reports and papers in the social sciences, 55)
1984 (5th ed. rev.), 228 pp., ISBN 92-3-102261-X

World list of social science periodicals

6th ed. rev.
(World social science information services, 1)
1983, 446 pp., ISBN 92-3-002058-3
Trilingual: English/French/Spanish

Young people and cultural institutions

A Unesco survey
Eight young people give their views on the cultural institutions in their countries
1980, 87 pp., ISBN 92-3-101698-9

Youth in the 1980s

1981, 320 pp., ISBN 92-3-101885-X

Youth mobilization for development in Asian settings

(Regional youth meetings, 2)
1984 (2nd impr.), 136 pp., ISBN 92-3-101686-5

Youth, tradition and development in Africa

(Regional youth meetings, 3)
1981, 146 pp., tables, ISBN 92-3-101918-X

B. Refereence Books

Bibliography of publications issued by Unesco or under

Its Auspices

The first twenty-five years: 1946 to 1971
1973, 385 pp., ISBN 92-3-001037-5

Index Translationum

International bibliography of translations

Vol. 30 : 1977
1981, 1,024 pp., ISBN 92-3-001911-9
Vol. 31: 1978
1983, 1, 024 pp., ISBN 92-3-001912-7
Vol. 32, 1979
1984, 1,024 pp.,ISBN 92-3-102205-5
Multilingual, with trilingual
(English/French/Spanish) introduction

Index translationum lists world translations published in a single year. Compiled with the help of librarians in many countries, it enables readers to follow, year by year, the flow of translations from one country to another and to trace the works of individual authors as they appear in translation. Volume 31 gives data on over 50,000 titles published in 1978 in 64 countries. Volume 32 comprises 54,449 entries in languages.

Statistical digest 1983

1983, 333 pp., ISBN 92-3-002159-8

Statistical digest 1984

1984, 331 pp., ISBN 92-3-002260-8
The digest provides a statistical summary of data on education, science and technology, culture and communication, by country.

A new Unesco publication, providing an indispensable ready reference in pocket-book format at a reasonable price. Selected data give an overview of the basic statistics available in the fields of education, science and technology, and culture and communication on a country-by-country basis for the 160 Member States of Unesco.

C. Books Concerning the message of Unesco

These publications provide background information about Unesco. They are intended to foster an awareness not only of the aims and activities of the Organization but also of its concern with some of the most challenging questions of our time.

Hope for the future

By Amadou-Mahtar M'Bow
1984, 292 pp., ISBN 92-3-102221-0

A companion volume to "Where the future begins", this collection of the addresses of Unesco's Director General to the General Conference at its 1982 and 1983 sessions indicates many ways by which the diversity of needs, aims and hopes of the international community many be forged into a new concerted effort.

Where the future begins

By Amadou-Mahtar M'Bow
1982, 118 pp., ISBN 92-3-102046-3

A penetrating analysis by the Director General of Unesco of the world problems that form the background to Unesco's 1984-1989 Medium-Term Plan including the arms race; hunger; human rights; the impact of certain human activities on the natural environment; the influence of scientific and technological progress on society; inequalities between individuals and between societies.

Building the future

By Amadou-Mahtar M'Bow
(Unesco and the solidarity of nations, 3)
1981, 258 pp., ISBN 92-3-101968-6

In the course of the 21st session of the General Conference, Belgrade, 1980, the Director General reviewed the problems facing the world and in this book he deals in depth with the possibilities offered by science and technology, particularly in communications, towards easing these problems. It also includes the preliminary report on the Medium-Term Plan for 1984-1989.

UNESCO 1984-1985

Introduction to the Draft Programme and Budget
By Amadou-Mahtar M'Bow

1983, 120 pp., ISBN 92-3-102149-4

Details on Unesco's draft programme for 1984-1985, covering the first biennial period of the Medium-Term Plan (1984-1989). Includes proposals on: education policies and training; communication; science, technology and the environment; development questions; the elimination of racial prejudice and apartheid; human rights; culture and the future; the status of women. A final chapter gives a breakdown of the budget proposed to fund these projects.

Consensus and peace

Edited by Beseat Kifle Selassie
1980, 231 pp., ISBN 92-3-101851-5

An examination of the concept of consensus as a way of establishing international peace. This collection by distinguished contributors, introduced by Amadou-Mahtar M'Bow, Director General of Unesco, investigates consensus through three main approaches.

The first, or institutional, approach shows the process, the result and also the practice of consensus in international organizations and international relations. The second, or interdisciplinary, approach throws light on the linguistic, cultural and philosophical and historical aspects, so circumscribing the concept of consensus. The final, or intercultural, approach analyses consensus with reference to present-day political, economic and religious situations in representative parts of the world, including developing countries, the Arab and Islamic world, Spain and Yugoslavia.

Questions of our time

Unesco Courier, August/September 1982
1982, 70 pp., ISBN 0041-5278

Examines certain aspects of a number of universally recognized world problems: the development crisis, the arms threat, the dangerous imbalances provoked by disparities in the conditions of life of different peoples, the disregard of human rights, the problems of the dissemination of knowledge.

A course for the future

Unesco Courier, January 1983
1983, 34 pp., ISBN 0041-5278

Presents in highly condensed form Unesco's Medium-Term Plan from 1984-1989, prepared on the basis of an analysis of current world problems.

D. Books providing General information about Unesco

A variety of booklets and pamphlets about Unesco and the Organization's programme activities are available free of charge from the Public Liaison Division of the Office of Public Information(OPI), Unesco, 7 place de Fontenoy. Information is contained in:

Unesco-what it is, what it does, how it works

An informative booklet giving an overview of the Organization, its structure and its main activities.

Backgrounder : Unesco

The first in a series of brochures outlining some of Unesco's principal activities.

E. InsightS Series

A series that focuses on the critical choices facing mankind.

The themes, reflecting the concerns of Unesco itself, are diverse and far-reaching: the rights of man, peace, development projects, population control, artistic and intellectual creativity, science cooperation broadening access to education and information, protection of the environment and improved knowledge of man's place in the biosphere.

In creating "Insights" Unesco hopes to acquaint a larger public as well as specialists with the contributions of many different disciplines to the resolution of the international problems of our time.

Suicide or survival?

The challenge of the year 2000
1978, 192 pp., ISBN 92-3-101534-6

Thirty eminent artists, politicians and thinkers from all over the world engage in a lively and informal debate on nuclear disarmament, the dwindling of natural resources, pollution, the manipulation of information, and the decline of ethical standards.

The participants at the Unesco-sponsored Round Table on "The Challenge of the Year 2000" including three Nobel Prize winners have expressed their feelings with candour, and often with eloquence and passion as well. They have raised all the vital questions of today, touching on such points as the growing gap between rich and poor, how energy needs for the year 2000 are to be met, the need to humanize the world's cities, and man's alienation from nature.

The subjects are grouped under four main headings:

Man-Puppet or Master of his own Achievements
Man Against the Powers That Be
A New Social Contract
The Continuing Battle of Culture.

Biology and ethics

Reflections inspired by a Unesco Symposium
By Bruno Ribes
1978, 202 pp., ISBN 92-3-101568-0

Thanks to our recently acquired knowledge on the chemical nature of genetic information, man now has the ability to induce mutation in organisms by manipulating their chemical building blocks. This new power to intervene in life and the questions it poses for scientists and other concerned with the ethical dimensions of biological research is the book's starting point.

Bruno Ribes has very neatly summarized the proceedings of a

Unesco conference on the relations between biology and ethics, while adroitly managing to suggest the ways in which genetic manipulations might be applied to the solution of vital world problems. There was a consensus at the conference that the problem is not so much to control science or limit experiments, as to draw up safety standards for research into genetic recombinations.

Ribes has indicated a direction in which research into ethics and the life sciences might be guided, and stresses why further exchanges on these vital questions must be encouraged.

Apartheid : power and historical falsification

By Marianne Cornevin
1980,144 pp., figs., tables, ISBN 92-3-101769-1

Among the great number of works published every year on South Africa, this volume stands foremost both for the originality of its subject and the way in which it is handled.

Marianne Cornevin, well known in French-speaking countries for the clarity and the objectivity of her historical works, sets out in the book a well-structured refutation of the major falsifications of South African history as officially presented. She bases her argument on the most recent research available, which is largely unknown to the general public. The author wishes, hereby, to be of help to South African Blacks who have a driving need to establish the historical truth of their past. But what she says is also intended for a much wider public.

So as to understand, and to make others understand, the role of historical falsification in the ideology of apartheid, the author studies the white settlement in South Africa before exposing the great myths of South African history, bringing out in a fascinating way the relationship between history and ideology. The South African pattern thus allows her to throw light on a problem that arises all over the work, namely, that of the relationship between history and power.

Violence and its causes

Methodological and theoretical aspects of recent research on violence.

1980, 269 pp., ISBN 92-3-101809-4

Since its inception, Unesco has undertaken studies on violence especially on the tensions which endanger international understanding, on human aggressiveness, and the impact of violence on the mass media. Violence in its various forms and manifestations clearly affects education, science, culture and communication. The Organization's activities have been concerned both with the consequences of violence in Unesco's fields of competence and with its underlying causes.

The first part of this work deals with transdisciplinarity and the manifold casualties of violence. The second part examines relations between individuals and societies and the third discusses economic and social violence.

The contributions are all by well-known authors and the fruits of their knowledge and reflection should add to our thinking on violence and our understanding of it, so that solutions can be found in a spirit of justice, equity and respect for the rights of individuals and peoples.

Domination or sharing?

Endogenous development and the transfer of knowledge.

1981, 292 pp., illus., ISBN 92-3-101842-X

Knowledge for understanding, understanding for action, this maxim of Auguste Comte applies to individuals as well as to social groups and peoples. This volume is the result of the recommendations of two meetings of international thinkers, one held in Paris in December 1975 and the other in Venice in 1978, and also contains the results of interdisciplinary studies undertaken by specialists. Following a general introduction, the authors deal with the problems of the transfer of knowledge, the sharing of technology and also with the capacity of societies to realize and benefit from their own creativity.

Harvesting ocean energy

1981, 192, pp., illus., ISBN 92-3-101873-6

During the last decade, the public concept of energy has shifted radically. Even 10 years ago the energy supply system was looked upon as a secure base for world industry and development. Today energy has become a critical element in the world economy for which there is a growing demand and an uncertain long-term supply.

F. Periodicals

1. *Copyright bulletin*

A quarterly to meet the needs not only of specialists in the field, but authors, librarians, publishers, editors, record producers, broadcasters, film makers, scientific researchers and lawyers. The magazine also furnishes ongoing coverage of international conventions, meetings, reports, texts of agreements and conventions as well as documents and books published in the field.

Published in English, French, Spanish and Russian.

2. *Educational documentation and information*

The quarterly bulletin of the international Bureau of Education (Geneva), indispensable for specialists and documentalists, presents selected annotated bibliographies on themes that highlight significant developments, current and future, in education; teaching and learning in adult education; health education; foreign students in comparative perspective.

Published in English, French and Spanish.

3. *Impact of science on society*

An interdisciplinary quarterly, it is devoted to the effect of science on our lives in an effort not only to document, but analyse and control the change stimulated by science and technology. Written by experts for laymen as well as scientists, each issue focuses on a single major theme.

Published in English, French, Spanish and Chinese, selections in Russian.

4. *International social science journal*

A quarterly interdisciplinary forum for the international spectrum of today's social scientists with a worldwide network of correspondents. Each issue concentrates on a major theme, the epistemology of social sciences; food systems; educational sciences; youth the world over. The journal also provides ongoing coverage of particular interest to social scientists, socio-economic data sources and professional and documentary services.

Published in English. French and Chinese.

5. *Museum*

The sole international journal that presents museological evolution and its multiple facets around the world, from security to cultural policies and curating; the museum as educator; museums and agriculture; practical innovations in museology; "ecomuseums"; show-cases, science and technology.

Published in English, French, Spanish and Russian.

6. *Nature and resources*

Provides international news and information about Unesco programmes concerning environmental activities, natural resources research and conservation; water resources and energy; environmental geology; land development in the tropics.

Published quarterly in English, French, Spanish, Russian and Chinese.

7. *Prospects*

Is a quarterly review of education which benefits from the direct collaboration of institutions and academics from more than 150 countries. Intended not only for specialists, it considers education in all its socio-economic and cultural contexts. Each issue contains four sections:

Viewpoints/Controversies in which internationally known specialists illuminate new problems and the most recent advances in educational research. This section also debates accepted theories, practices, approaches, methods, traditions and utopias as well.

Open File, in which seven to ten contributions focus on a subject of major importance, whether from a theoretical or case-study viewpoint; encouraging pupil achievement; early access to reading for young children; dependence and interdependence in education; the prospects of educational planning related to disarmament education.

Trends and Cases provides analyses of new methods of practical innovations introduced in various countries with possible transferability to others.

Reviews furnishes critiques of recently published works and also "Profiles" of educationists in which major theorists, past and present, are discussed in the light of current educational ideas.

Published in English, French, Spanish, Arabic and Chinese, selections in Russian.

8. *The Unesco Courier* A window on the world of yesterday, today and tomorrow, offers fascinating insights into every domain Unesco itself penetrates. Some of the forthcoming issues will focus on water and life; the treasures of the ocean; libraries and archives; youth throughout the world; Victor Hugo; migrant workers; the oral tradition; the Mediterranean; the city in the year 2000. This is a mere sampling of the magazine's breadth of vision.

It is published monthly in 31 language versions. In addition a selection in Braille appears quarterly in English, French, Spanish and Korean. Lavishly illustrated each month, several issues provide full-colour pages appropriate for framing or display in the classroom or elsewhere.

G. **Reports and papers on social sciences**

International Repertory of Institutions Conducting Population Studies (bilingual: English/French), 1959.

International Cooperation and Programmes of Economic and Social Development (bilingual: English/French), 1961.

International Directory of Sample Survey Centres (outside the United States of America) (bilingual: English/French) 1962.

The Social Science Activities of Some Eastern European Academics of Sciences, 1963.

Attitude Change ; A Review and Bibliography of Selected Research, 1964 (out of print in English, available in French).

International Repertory of Sociological Research Centres (outside the USA.) (bilingual: English/French), 1964.

Institutions Engaged in Economic and Social Planning in Africa (bilingual: English/French), 1966.

International Repertory of Institutions Specializing in Research on Peace and Disarmament, 1966.

Guide for the Establishment of National Social Sciences Documentation Centres in Developing Countries, 1969.

Ecological Data in Comparative Research: Report on First International Data Confrontation Seminar (bilingual): English/French), 1970.

Data Archives for the Social Sciences: Purposes, Operations and Problems, 1973.

Social Indicators: Problems of Definition and of Selection, 1974.

DARE-Information Management System, 1975.

Social Sciences in Asia: I, 1976

Social Sciences in Asia: II, 1977.
Selected Applications of the Unesco Educational Simulation Model, 1977.

Social Sciences in Asia: III, 1977.

Inter-regional Cooperation in the Social Sciences, 1977.

Indicators of Social and Economic Changes and their Applications, 1977.

Indicators of Environmental Quality and Quality of Life, 1978.

Social and Economic Consequences of the Arms Race and of Disarmament: Review of Research Trends and an Annotated Bibliography, 1978.

Threat of Modern Warfare of Man and his Environment: An Annotated Bibliography, 1978.

The Effects of Rural-Urban Migration on Women's Role and Status in Latin America, 1978.

Social Sciences in Asia: IV, 1980.

Peace Research. Trend Report and World Directory, 1979.

Employment-oriented National Youth Programmes in Africa: Situations, Problems and Prospects, 1982.

ARKISYST Feasibility Study, 1981

Selected Studies on the Dynamics, Patterns and Consequences of Migration. I. Mexico City, 1982.

Interconcept Report: A New Paradigm for Solving the Terminology Problems of the Social Sciences, 1981.

Social Sciences in Latin America and the Caribbean I, 1982.

World Directory of Peace Research Institutions. Fourth edition (revised), 1981.

Data-based Teaching in the Social Sciences, 1983.

Study on the Dynamics, Evolution and Consequences of Migrations, II. Three centuries of spatial mobility in France, 1982.

Selected Studies on the Dynamics, Patterns and Consequences of Migration III. Migration and Development: Major Features of Migratory Movement in India, 1982.

Selected Studies on the Dynamics, Patterns and Consequences of Migration, IV: Medium-sized Towns in Nigeria : Research and Policy Prospects, 1982.

Bibliography of Mono-and Multilingual Vocabularies. Thesauri, Subject Headings and Classification Schemes in the Social Sciences, 1982.

World Directory of Peace Research Institutions, 1984.

Directory of International Law Research and Training Institutes.

Help for Social Scientists : A New Kind of Reference Process, 1986.

PART VI

APPENDICES

A

UNIVERSAL DECLARATION OF HUMAN RIGHTS (1948)

Universal Declaration was adopted by UN General Assembly in 1948 without a dissenting vote.

Article 1
All human beings are born free and equal in dignity and rights. They are endowed with reason and conscience and should act towards one another in a spirit of brotherhood.

Article 2
Everyone is entitled to all the rights and freedoms set forth in this Declaration, without distinction of any kind, such as race, colour, sex, language, religion, political or other opinion, national or social origin, property, birth or other status.

Furthermore, no distinction shall be made on the basis of the political, jurisdictional or international status of the country or territory to which a person belongs, whether it be undependent trust, non-self, governing or under any other limitation of sovereignty.

Article 3
Everyone has the right to life, liberty and security of person.

Article 4
No one shall be held in slavery or servitude; slavery and the slave trade shall be prohibited in all their forms.

Article 5
No one shall be subjected to torture or to cruel, inhuman or degrading treatment or punishment.

Article 6
Everyone has the right to recognition everywhere as a person before the law.

Article 7
All are equal before the law and are entitled without any discrimination to equal protection of the law. All are entitled to equal protection against any discrimination in valuation of this Declaration and against any incitement to such discrimination.

Article 8
Everyone has the right to an effective remedy by the competent national tribunals for acts violating the fundamental rights granted him by the constitution or by law.

Article 9
No one shall be subjected to arbitrary arrest, detention or exile.

Article 10
Everyone is entitled in full equality to a fair and public hearing by an independent and impartial tribunal, in the determination of his rights and obligations and of any criminal charge against him.

Article 11
1. Everyone charged with a penal offence has the right to be presumed innocent until proved guilty according to law in a public trial at which he has had all the guarantees necessary for his defence.

2. No one shall be held guilty of any penal offence not account of any act or omission which did no constitute a penal offence, under national or international law, at the time when it was committed. Nor shall a heavier penalty be imposed than the one that was applicable at the time the penal offence was committed.

Article 12
No one shall be subjected to arbitrary interference with his privacy, family, home or correspondence, nor to attacks upon his honour and reputation. Everyone has the right to the protection of the law against such interference or attacks.

Article 13

(1) Everyone has the right to freedom of movement and residence within the borders of each State.

(2) Everyone has the right to leave any country, including has own, and to return to his country.

Article 14

(1) Everyone has the right to seek and to enjoy in other countries asylum from persecution.

(2) This right may not be invoked in the case of prosecutions genuinely arising from non-political crimes or from acts contrary to the purposes and principles of the United Nations.

Article 15

(1) Everyone has the right to a nationality.

(2) No one shall be arbitrarily deprived of his nationality nor denied the right to change his nationality.

Article 16

(1) Men and women of full age, without any limitation due to race, nationality or religion, have the right to marry and to found a family. They are entitled to equal rights as to marriage, during marriage and at its dissolution.

(2) Marriage shall be entered into only with the free and full consent of the intending spouses.

(3) The family is the natural and fundamental group unit of society and is entitled to protection by society and the State.

Article 17

(1) Everyone has the right to own property alone as well as in association with others.

(2) No one shall be arbitrarily deprived of his property.

Article 18

Everyone has the right to freedom of thought, conscience and religion; this right includes freedom to change his religion or belief, and freedom, either alone or in community with others and in public or private, to manifest his religion or belief in teaching, practice, worship and observance.

Article 19

(1) Everyone has the right to freedom of peaceful assembly and association.

(2) No one may be compelled to belong to an association.

Article 20

(1) Everyone has the right to take part in the government of his country, directly or through freely chosen representatives.

(2) Everyone has the right of equal access to public service in his country.

(3) The will of the people shall be the basis of the authority of government; this shall be expressed in periodic and genuine elections which shall be by universal and equal suffrage and shall be held by secret vote or by equivalent free voting procedures.

Article 21

Everyone, as a member of society, has the right to social security and is entitled to realization, through national effort and international cooperation and in accordance with the organization and resources of each State, of the economic, social and cultural rights indispensable for his dignity and the free development of his personality.

Article 22

(1) Everyone has the right to work, to free choice of employment, to just and favourable conditions of work and to protection against unemployment.

(2) Everyone, without any discrimination, has the right to equal pay for equal work.

(3) Everyone who works has the right to just and favourable remuneration, ensuring for himself and his family an existence worthy of human dignity, and supplemented, if necessary, by other means of social protection.

(4) Everyone has the right to form and to join trade unions for the protection of his interests.

Article 23

Everyone has the right to rest and leisure, including reasonable limitation of working hours and periodic holidays with pay

Article 24

(1) Everyone has the right to a standard of living adequate for the health and wellbeing of himself and of his family, including food, clothing, housing and medical care and necessary social services, and the right to security in the event of unemployment, sickness, disability, widowhood, old age or other lack of livelihood in circumstances beyond his control.

(2) Motherhood and childhood are entitled to special care and assistance. All children, whether born in or out of wedlock, shall enjoy the same social protection.

Article 25

(1) Everyone has the right to education. Education shall be free, at least in the elementary and fundamental stages. Elementary education shall be made generally available and higher education shall be equally accessible to all on the basis of merit.

(2) Education shall be directed to the full development of the human personality and to the strengthening of respect of human rights and fundamental freedoms. It shall promote understanding, tolerance and friendship among all nations for the maintenance of peace.

(3) Parents have a prior right to choose the kind of education that shall be given to their children.

Article 26

(1) Everyone has the right freely to participate in the cultural life of the community, to enjoy the arts and to share in scientific advancement and its benefits.

(2) Everyone has the right to the protection of the moral and material interests resulting from any scientific, literary or artistic production of which he is the author.

Article 27

Everyone is entitled to a social and international order in which the rights and freedoms set forth in this Declaration can be fully realized.

Article 28

(1) Everyone has duties to the community in which alone the free and full development of his personality is possible.

(2) In the exercise of his rights and freedoms, everyone shall be subject only to such limitations as are determined by law solely for the purpose of securing due recognition and respect for the rights and freedom of others and of meeting the just requirements of morality, public order and the general welfare in a democratic society.

(3) These rights and freedoms may in no case be exercised contrary to the purposes and principles of the United Nations.

Article 29

Nothing in this Declaration may be interpreted as implying for any State, group or person any right to engage in any activity or to perform any act aimed at the destruction of any of the rights and freedoms set forth herein.

B

DIRECTORS GENERAL OF UNESCO

1. *Julian Huxley* (1946 to 1948)

A British biologist, who had earlier headed the preparatory Commission which had launched Unesco, became the first Director General of Unesco in 1946 and served till 1948 when the Organization set up its headquarters in Paris using the temporary premises in the Hotel Majestic on the Avenue Kleher. Stated that Unesco activities can best be expressed in five words, "The Advance of World Civilization".

2. *Jamine Torres Bodet* (1949 to 1952)

A Mexican who knew well what development and under-development meant. His major development programme was the creation of two fundamental education centres-one for Latin America and the other for Arab States. Torres Bodet instinctively and whole-heartedly backed the early efforts on Unesco's participation in the United Nations Technical Assistance Programme.

3. *Luther H. Evans* (1953 to 1958)

Laid the firm foundation for the spectacular growth of the Organization in the development field. Unesco, he wrote, "is a living presence in the sense that it is a voice heard by many, a guide followed in a good few places, more and more a searchlight thrown on dark places, to point the road to advance in all the countless cases where advance is sought. But all this stimulus is preparatory to action-action in the schools and laboratories, action in the libraries and museums, in the fields and villages, in a word, action in the Member States".

4. *Vittorino Veronese* (1958 to 1961)

Became the Director General at the moment of Africans' liberation. He often referred to the golden rule, "primum vivere deinde philosophare" which means "live first then philosophize about".

5. *Rane Maheu* (1962 to 1974)

Observed, "education, science, culture and communication are not ends in themselves for Unesco, but simply ways and means of a spiritual undertaking and moral effort that constitutes its true mission".

On his election to the position of Director General of Unesco, in a message to Prospects, he observed, "It is education which enables the concept of justice, fraternity and progress to take root in the minds of men by linking them closely to the acquisition of knowledge and the expansion of the intellectual, creative and moral faculties in the children and young people who will be the adults of tomorrow. The first task which its constitution calls on Unesco to perform is to "contribute to peace and security by promoting collaboration among the nations through education, science and culture in order to further universal respect of justice, and I believe that, for more than a quarter of a century, the organization has shown itself worthy of this noble and difficult mission".

6. *Amadow-Mahtar M'Bow* (1974 to 1987)

On his election to the position of Director General of Unesco, in a message to Prospects, he observed, "It is education which enables the concept of justice, fraternity and progress to take root in the minds of men by linking them closely to the acquisition of knowledge and the expansion of the intellectual, creative and moral faculties in the children and young people who will be the adults of tomorrow. The first task which its constitution calls on Unesco to perform is to "contribute to peace and security by promoting collaboration among the nations through education, science and culture in order to further universal respect of justice, and I believe that, for more than a quarter of a century, the organization has shown itself worthy of this noble and difficult mission".

7. *Federico Mayor Zaragoza* (1987 -)

The Twenty-Third Session of the UNESCO's General Conference (Oct.-Nov. 1987) elected through secret ballot Professor Federico Mayor Zaragoza as the new Director-General of the Organization. He assumed his office on November 16, 1987 for a six-year period.

Professor Mayor (b. 27 January 1934), Spanish by nationality, is a well-known Biochemist with wide-ranging academic interests. Besides being Professor of Biochemistry at the University of Madrid, Professor Mayor has been a member of the Spanish Parliament and later Minister of Education and Science (1981-82) in his country. During 1978-81, Professor Mayor served as UNESCO's Deputy Director-General, and later as Special Adviser to the Director-General. In 1987, he became a member of the European Parliament.

A scholar of distinction, author of several books and scientific articles, poet and politician, Professor Mayor is a member of several academies and scientific societies, including the Club of Rome. He is recipient of several awards and decorations.

Besides his original contributions on cerebral metabolism and molecular pathology of the new born, Professor Mayor has extensively written and spoken on issues such as : science policy, role of the university, science and development, role of science and technology in the society of the future, regional cultures, scientific community and peace, and implications of development on the environment.

Professor Mayor continues to be an ardent supporter of the Human Rights and of international intellectual cooperation.

C

UNESCO AGREEMENTS AND CONVENTIONS

A. *Agreements and Conventions of a Normative Character*

(1) Agreement for facilitating the international circulation of visual and auditory materials of an educational, scientific and cultural character, with Protocol of Signature and Process-verbal of deposit of the model form of certificate provided for in Article IV of the above-mentioned Agreement. 10 December, 1948.

(2) Agreement on the Importation of Educational, Scientific and Cultural Materials, with Annexes A,B,C, D and E, and Protocol annexed. 17 June, 1950.

(3) Universal Copyright Convention, with Appendix Declaration relating to Article XVII and resolution concerning Article XI. 6 September, 1982.

(4) Protocol 1 annexed to the Universal Copyright Convention concerning the application of that Convention to the works of stateless persons and refugees. 6 September, 1952.

(5) Protocol 2 annexed to the Universal Copyright Convention con-

cerning the application of that Convention to the works of certain international organizations. 6 September, 1952.

(6) Protocol 3 annexed to the Universal Copyright Convention concerning the effective date of instruments of ratification or acceptance of, or accession to, that Convention. 6 September, 1952.

(7) Convention for the Protection of Cultural Property in the Event of Armed Conflict, with Regulations for the Execution of the Convention. 14 May, 1954.

(8) Protocol for the Protection of Cultural Property in the Event of Armed Conflict. 14 May, 1954.

(9) Convention concerning the International Exchange of Publications. 3 December, 1958.

(10) Convention concerning the Exchange of Official Publications and Government Documents between States. 3 December, 1958.

(11) Convention against Discrimination in Education. 14 December, 1960.

(12) International Convention for the Protection of Performers, Procedure of Phonograms and Broadcasting Organizations. 26 October, 1961.

(13) Protocol instituting a Conciliation and Good Offices Commission to be responsible for seeking the settlement of any disputes which may arise between States Parties to the Convention against Discrimination in Education. 10 December, 1962.

(14) Convention on the Means of Prohibiting and Preventing the illicit Import, Export and Transfer of Ownership of Cultural Property. 14 November, 1970.

(15) Universal Copyright Convention as revised at Paris on 24 July, 1971.

(16) Protocol 1 annexed to the Universal Copyright Convention as revised at Paris on 24 July, 1971, concerning the application of that Convention to works of stateless persons and refugees. 24 July, 1971.

(17) Protocol 2 annexed to the Universal Copyright Convention as revised at Paris on 24 July, 1971, concerning the application of that Convention to the works of certain international organizations. 24 July, 1971.

(18) Convention for the Protection of Producers of Phonograms against Unauthorized Duplication of their Phonograms. 29 October 1971.

(19) Convention concerning the protection of the World Cultural and Natural Heritage. 16 November, 1972.

(20) Convention relating to the Distribution of Programme-carrying Signals Transmitted by Satellite. 21 May, 1974.

(21) Regional Convention on the Recognition of Studies, Diplomas and Degrees in Higher Education in Latin America and the Caribbean. 19 July, 1974.

(22) Protocol to the Agreement on the Importation of Educational, Scientific and Cultural Materials. 26 November, 1976.

(23) International Convention on the Recognition of Studies, Diplomas and Degrees in Higher Education in the Arab States and European States bordering on the Mediterranean. 17 December, 1976.

(24) Convention on the Recognition of Studies, Diplomas and Degrees in Higher Education in the Arab States. 22 December, 1978.

(25) Multilateral Convention for the Avoidance of Double Taxation of Copyright Royalties and Additional Protocol. 13 December, 1978.

(26) Convention on the Recognition of Studies, Diplomas and Degrees in Higher Education in the States belonging to the Europe Region. 21 December, 1979.

(27) Regional Convention on the Recognition of Studies, Certificates, Diplomas, Degrees and other Academic Qualifications in Higher Education in the African States. 5 December, 1981.

(28) Regional Convention on the Recognition of Studies, Diplomas and Degrees in Higher Education in Asia and the Pacific. 16 December, 1983.

B. *Other Agreements*

Convention on Wetlands of International Importance especially as Waterfowl Habitat. 2 February, 1971.

Protocol to amend the Convention on Wetlands of International Importance especially as Waterfowl Habitat. 3 December, 1982.

C. *Recommendations*

Recommendation on International Principles Applicable to Archaeological Excavations. 5 December, 1956.

Recommendation concerning International Competitions in Architecture and Town Planning. 5 December, 1956.

Recommendation concerning the International Standardization of Educational Statistics. 3 December, 1958.

Recommendation concerning the Most Effective Means of Rendering Museums Accessible to Everyone. 14 December, 1958.

Recommendation Against Discrimination in Education. 14 December, 1960.

Recommendation concerning the Safeguarding of the Beauty and Character of Landscapes and Sites. 11 December, 1962.

Recommendation concerning Technical and Vocational Education. 11 December, 1962.

Recommendation concerning the International Standardization of Statistics Relating to Book Production and Periodicals. 19 November, 1964.

Recommendation concerning the Status of Teachers. 5 October, 1966.

Recommendation concerning the Preservation of Cultural Property Endangered by Public or Private Works. 19 November, 1968.

Recommendation concerning the International Standardization of Library Statistics. 13 November, 1970.

Recommendation concerning the Protection, at National Level, of the Cultural and Natural Heritage. 16 November, 1972.

Recommendation concerning Education for International Understanding, cooperation and Peace and Education relating to Human Rights and Fundamental Freedoms. 19 November, 1974.

Revised Recommendation concerning Technical and Vocational Education. 19 November, 1974.

Recommendation on the Legal Protection of Translators and Translations and the Practical Means to Improve the Status of Translators. 22 November, 1976.

Recommendation concerning the International Standardization of Statistics on Radio and Television. 22 November, 1976.

Recommendations on the Development of Adult Education. 26 November, 1976.

Recommendation on Participation by the People at Large in Cultural Life and their Contribution to it. 26 November, 1976.

Recommendation concerning the International Exchange of Cultural Property. 26 November, 1976.

Recommendation concerning the Safeguarding and Contemporary Role of Historic Areas. 26 November, 1976.

Revised Recommendation concerning International Competitions in Architecture and Town Planning. 27 November, 1978.

Recommendation concerning the International Standardization of Statistics on Science and Technology. 27 November, 1978.

Recommendation for the Protection of Movable Cultural Property. 28 November, 1978.

Recommendation concerning the Status of the Artist. 27 October, 1980.

Recommendation concerning the International Standardization of Statistics on the Public Financing of Cultural Activities. 27 October, 1980.

Declarations Adopted by the General Conference

Declaration of the Principles of International Cultural Cooperation. 4 November, 1966.

Declaration of Guiding Principles on the Use of Satellite Broadcasting for the Free Flow of Information, the Spread of Education and Greater Cultural Exchange. 15 November, 1972.

International Charter of Physical Education and Sport. 21 November, 1978.

Declaration on Race and Racial Prejudice. 27 November, 1978.

Declaration of Fundamental Principles concerning the contribution of the Mass Media to Strengthening Peace and International Understanding, to the Promotion of Human Rights and to countering Racialism, Apartheid and Incitement to War. 28 November, 1978.

D

IMPORTANT CONFERENCES AND MEETINGS CONVENED BY UNESCO ON ASPECTS RELATING TO SOCIAL SCIENCES

International Symposium on Islam, Philosophy and Science, Paris (France) July 8-11, 1981.

Meeting of Experts on Historical Seismic Records, London (Canada), July 27-30, 1981.

Sub-regional workshop to consider the Socio-Cultural Bases for Developing Innovative Policies and Programmes Relevant to Food Production and Marketing by Small Farmers, Bridgetown (Barbados), August 10-18, 1981.

Symposium on the Application of Indicators of Socio-economic Change to Development Planning, Seoul (Republic of Korea) September 1-4, 1981.

Meeting of Experts on Ecology in Practice : Establishing a Scientific Basis for Land Management, Paris, September 22-29, 1981.

Workshop for Students and Youth Leaders, Paris, September 28-October 9, 1981.

Regional Training Seminar for University Teachers in the Field of Disarmament, Caracas (Venezuela), October 13-17, 1981.

Meeting of Experts on the Tasks and the Challenges of the Social Science in the 1980s, November 30-December 3, 1981.

Meeting of Experts on the Elaboration and Utilization of Social Indicators of Disabled Persons, Brussels (Belgium), December 7-10, 1981.

Meeting of Experts on the Role of Women in the Education of Young People for Peace, Mutual Understanding and Respect for Human Rights, New Delhi (India), December 7-11, 1981.

Regional Meeting of Experts on Youth in the Arab States, Tunis

(Tunisia), December 14-19, 1981.

International Centenary Symposium Ataturk, Founder of a Modern State, December Paris (France), 16-18, 1981

Sub-regional Seminar on Social Communication Techniques in support of programme for the Advancement of Women and the Participation of Women in Development, Libreville (Gabon) February 22-26, 1982.

Meeting of Experts on Multi-disciplinary Research on Women in the Arab World, Tunis (Tunisia) May, 18-21, 1982.

Conference of Ministers of Education and those Responsible for Economic Planning in African Member States Harare (Zimbabwe), June 28 to July 3, 1982.

Meeting of the Jury-UNESCO Prize for Peace Education, Paris (France) July 5-8, 1982.

Meeting on Information Systems Dealing with Research Linked with Human Needs, Paris (France), July 19-23, 1982.

Meeting of Experts on the Teaching of Human Rights/Strasbourg (France), July 26-30, 1982.

Workshop on Social Communication for Women Professionals in Population Programmes, Shanghai (People's Republic of China), August 28 to September 3, 1983.

Asian Regional Training Seminar on Disarmament Education, Jakarta (Indonesia), August, 30 - September, 3, 1983.

Meeting of Experts on the Methods of Reducing Economic and Associated Socio-Cultural Inequalities, Stockholm (Sweden), August 30 - September 3, 1983.

Training Course for Students and/or Youth Leaders, Paris (France), September 13-24, 1983.

Symposium on the Organization of a Caribbean Peasants and

Agricultural Workers Association (CAPAWA), St. Philip (Barbados), September 20-24, 1983.

Symposium on the Creation and Functioning of a Caribbean Network of Social Scientists and Social Science Institutions for Rural Development (CANSIRD), Castries (St. Lucia), September 27- October 7, 1983.

Collective Consultation of Youth NGOS, Budya Montenegro (Yogoslavia), October 11-14, 1983.

Symposium on the Elaboration and Utilization of Social Indicators of Ethnic and Cultural Minorities, Ottawa (Canada), 25-28, October, 1983.

Regional Symposium on Evaluation Techniques in Social Action Projects in Latin America, Caracas (Venezuela) November 22-26, 1983

A Course in Population Education for Researchers and Producers of Radio and Television Programme from 15 countries in the Asia and Pacific Region, Kuala Lumpur (Malaysia), May 15-18, 1984.

Meeting of 2,200 Geographers from 86 countries, Paris (France), August 27-31 1984.

International Seminar on the Roles of Women in Decision making, Deebrounik (Yugoslavia), December 10-14, 1984.

Latin American Youth Seminar on "Economic Development and Protection of Environment", Caraces (Venizuela) November 12-18, 1984

Population Training Seminar for African States, Maputo (People's Republic of Mozambique), November 12-December 6, 1984.

Photo Exhibition on the International Youth Year (IYY) 1985, Paris (France), January 24-February 6, 1985.

Seminar on the Library, Centre for Promoting International Understanding, Salamance (Spain), June 9-14, 1985.

World Congress on Youth, Barcelona (Spain), July 8-15, 1985.

International Conference on the Environmental Training for Economists, Vienna (Switzerland), September 6-10, 1985.

Unesco Consultant with Youth Movements, Rhodes (SA), September 11-14, 1985.

Symposium on Environmental Management of Small Mediterranean Islands, Formentera (Spain), October 8-12, 1985.

Seminar on Population Education, Dakar (Senegal), July 7-August, 1986.

Anniversary: 40th Celebration of Unesco, Paris (France), November 3-4, 1986.

Conference on the Mobilization of Rural Youth, Accra (Ghana), November 6-12, 1986.

E

UNESCO REPRESENTATIVES AND LIAISON OFFICERS

I. *Full-Time Representatives*

1. *BRAZIL*

Unesco Representative in Brazil
Sector Commercial Norte
Quadra CN2, Lote B
Caixa Postal 04 0063, D.F.
70710 BRASILIA

2. *CAMEROON* (covers also the Central African Empire, Chad, People's Republic of the Congo, Gabon and OCAM)

Bureau due Representant de l'Unesco en Afrique centrale
et aupres de l'OCAM
B.P. 1168
YAOUNDE

3. *CARIBBEAN* (covers Bahamas, Barbados, Belize, British Eastern Caribbean Group, British Virgin Islands, Dominica, Grenada, Guyana, Jamaica, Surinam, St. Lucia, St Vincent and the Grenatdines, St Christopher/Nevis, Netherlands, Antilles, Trinidad and Tobago)

Unesco Representative to the Caribbean
First Floor
30 Grenada Crescent
Post Office Box 8203 C.S.O.
KINGSTON 5

4. *EGYPT* (covers also Sudan)

Unesco Representative in the Arab Republic of Egypt
8 Abdel Rahman Fahmy Street
Garden City
CAIRO
Arab Republic of Egypt

5. *ETHIOPIA*

Unesco Representative to Ethiopia and
Liaison Officer with ECA and OAU
Rooms 427, 429 and 433
4th Floor -- Old Building UN -- ECA
Menelik Avenue
P.O. Box 1177
ADDIS ABABA

6. *MEXICO*

Representante de la Unesco
Brasil, 31, 2 piso,

Despacho 329
Apartado 45-611
MEXICO, D.F.

7. *NIGERIA* (covers also People's Republic of Benin, Ghana and Togo)

Unesco Representative a.i. in Nigeria
C/o Federal Ministry of Education
P.O. Box 2823
LAGOS

Via Lagos Pouch

8. *QATAR* (covers also Saudi Arabia, Bahrain, United Arab Emirates, Iraq, Kuwait and Oman)

Unesco Regional Representative Office
P.O. Box 3945
DOHA

Via Doha Pouch

9. *TUNISIA* (covers also Algeria, Libya, Morocco, Arab League and Agencies)

Representant de l'Unesco aupres des pays
du Maghreb et de la Ligue arabe
C/o UNDP
B.P. 863
TUNIS

10. *UPPER VOLTA* (covers also Mali, Niger, CEAO and CILSS)

Representant de l'Unesco pour les Affaires saheliennes
s/c Representant resident PNUD
B.P. 575
OUAGADOUGOU

11. *ZAIRE* (covers also Burundi and Rwanda)

Unesco Representative Office
C/o Resident Representative of the UNDP
P.O. Box 7248
KINSHASA

12. *ZAMBIA* (covers also Botswana, Lesotho, Namibia and Swaziland)

Unesco Representative to Southern African Countries
P.O. Box 50591
LUSAKA

II. *PART-TIME UNESCO REPRESENTATIVES*

1. *CHILE* (covers also Bolivia and Peru)

Director de la Oficina Regional de
Education para America Latina Yel Caribe
Representante de la Unesco en Chile
Calle Enrique Delpiano 2058
Casilla Postal 3187
SANTIAGO DE CHILE

Via Santiago Pouch

2. *COSTA RICA* (covers also El Salvador, Guatemala, Honduras, Nicaragua and Panama)

Representante de la Unesco en Costa Rica
C/o Resident Representative UNDP
Apartado postal 4540
SAN JOSE

3. *CUBA* (covers also Dominican Republic)

Jafe de la Oficina Regional de Cultura
para America Latina yel Caribe,

Representante de la Unesco en Cuba
Calzada n 551 Esq. a D. Vedado
LA HABANA, 4

Via Havana Pouch

4. *ECUADOR* (covers also Colombia)

Representante de Unesco
C/o Resident Representative UNDP
P.O. Box 4731
QUITO

5. *HAITI*

Conseiller sous-regional d'education
Representant de l'Unesco en Haiti
C/o PNUD
B.P. 557
PORT-AU-PRINCE

6. *INDIA*

Director a.i., Regional Office for Science and Technology for South & Central Asia
Unesco Representative a.i.
Unesco House
17 Jor Bagh (Lodi Road)
NEW DELHI 110003

7. *INDONESIA* (covers also Malaysia, Philippines and Singapore)

Director, Regional Office for Science and Technology for Southeast Asia
Unesco Representative
United Nations Building (2nd Floor)
Jalan Thamrin 14
273/JKT Tromolpos
JAKARTA

Via Jakarta Pouch

8. *KENYA* (covers also Mauritius, Somalia, Tanzania and Uganda)

Director of the Unesco Regional Office
for Science and Technology for Africa
Unesco Representative
P.O. Box 30592
NAIROBI

Via Nairobi Pouch

9. *LEBANON* (covers also Jordan and the Syrian Arab Republic)

Representant de l'Unesco
transferee temporairement et jusqu'a nouvel
ordre a Paris 7 Place de Fontenoy
75700 PARIS

10. *PAKISTAN*

Director, Regional Office for Culture and
Book Development in Asia,
Unesco Representative in Pakistan
39 Delhi Housing Society
P.O. Box 8950
Bahadur Shah Zafar Road
KARACHI 29

11. *SENEGAL* (covers also the Gambia, Guinea, Liberia, Mauritania and Sierra Leone and Cap Verd)

Directeur, Bureau Regional de l'Unesco
Pour l'Education en Afrique
Representant de l'Unesco
B.P. 3311
DAKAR

Via Dakar Pouch

12. *THAILAND* (covers also Burma, Democratic Kampuchea, Laos People's Democratic Republic and Socialist Republic of Viet Nam)

Assistant Director-General, Regional Office
for Education in Asia and Oceania
Unesco Representative
P.O. Box 1425
BANGKOK 10500

Via Bangkok Pouch

13. *URUGUAY* (covers also Argentine and Paraguay)

Director de la Oficina de Ciencia
Technologia Para America Latina y el Caribe
Representative de la Unesco en Uruguay
1320-24 Blv. Artigas
P.O. Box 859
MONTEVIDEO

Via Montevideo Pouch

14. *VENEZUELA*

Representat de l'Unesco au Venezuela
Apartado de Correos 68394
Altamira
CARACAS 1062 A

15. *ZIMBABWE* (covers also Angola, Malawi, Mozambique, Sao Tome and Principe)

Unesco Representative
C/o Resident Representative of the UNDP, P.O. Box 4775

HARARE

III.*Liaison Officers*

1. *GENEVA*

Charge de Laison Pincipal
Unesco Liaison Office
Villa des Feuillantines
Palais des Nations
CH-1211 GENEVE 10

2. *NEW YORK*

Director
United Nations
9th Floor, DC-II Building
2 UN Plaza, Office No 900
NEW YORK, N.Y. 10017

3. *WASHINGTON*

Director, Liaison Office
918 16th Street N.W.
Suite 301
WASHINGTON D.C.
D.C. 20006

F

UNESCO RESEARCH CENTRE FOR SOUTH ASIA, DELHI

In 1954, Unesco's General Cnference at its 8th session took the decision to establish a Unesco Research Centre in India to carry out, on a continuing basis, research on the "Social Implications of Industrialization in South Asia". This Centre started functioning in Calcutta from February 1956. In 1961, it was moved to Delhi with a change in its nomenclature : it became Unesco Research Centre on Social and Economic Development in Southern Asia. The Centre was an integral part of the Unesco Scretariat and served 13 countries

: Afghanistan, Burma, Cambodia (now Kampuchea), Ceylon (now Sri Lanka), India, Indonesia, Laos, Malaysia, Nepal, Pakistan, the Philippines, Thailand and Vietnam.

The Centre was created to:

(a) Conduct social science research into problems of social and economic development in the participating countries;

(b) Provide expert advice and assistance to the participating countries on problems of social and economic development;

(c) Provide library and documentation services and act as a clearing house of information and literature on the subject; and

(d) Provide opportunities for training social scientists in the region in research methods and techniques.

The Centre undertook the following research projects:

i. Social aspects of industrialization : role of small-scale industries in the country's economy and social changes accompanying their growth;

ii. Changing social structures : groups within the social structure which operate as carriers and promoters of development;

iii. Leadership in rural areas : the role of rural leaders in introducing social and economic development at community level;

iv. Education and society : impact of education on economic development;

v. Subjective assessment of social status : social status as distinct from the picture provided by statistics;

iv. Social aspects of the distribution of income : study of the relevance of income distribution in a rapidly changing society to the problems of social and economic development.

The Centre also organized or sponsored seminars and conferences on development problems which included :

i. Regional seminar on techniques of social research (1958);

ii. Regional seminar on the public administration problems of new and rapidly developing towns in Asia (1960);

iii. Conference on social research on small industries in India (1962); and

iv. A round-table conference on the emerging patterns of rural leadership in Southern Asia (1964).

Under the auspices of the Centre, 10 young social scientists received individual training lasting about nine months. Five of them came from Asia and the other five from outside the region. In 1966, the Centre organized the first regional training course on the sociology of development which was attended by 20 participants from nine countries of the region.

The Centre developed library and documentation services and sent librarians to several countries to advise on the organization of such services in social science research institutes.

Although the Centre served a useful purpose it ceased to be a Unesco Centre when it got merged, in January 1967, with the Institute of Economic Growth, Delhi (India) upon the completion of 10 years during which Unesco subvention was provided. Unesco, however, continued to provide support to the Institute of Economic Growth for the organization of regional training seminars on "Development" until 1975.

G

REGIONAL UNIT FOR SOCIAL AND HUMAN SCIENCES IN ASIA AND THE PACIFIC (RUSHSAP), BANGKOK

The General Conference, at its 17th session (1972), authorized the

Director General to establish the post of a Regional Adviser for the Asia-Pacific region. The post was created in 1974 and the office of the Regional Adviser started functioning in Jakarta, Indonesia, from February 1975. In 1977, the office was relocated in Bangkok, Thailand, to become an integral part of the Unesco Regional Office for Education in Asia and the Pacific.

With the relocation of the Regional Adviser in Bangkok its activities also got enlarged. Initially, the post of the Regional Adviser was created within the Division for the International Development of Social Sciences (IDS), now renamed Division for Social and Economic Sciences (SES) ; his office was later made a separate unit to function under the direct supervision of the Assistant Director General of the Sector, with the responsibility of coordinating and implementing decentralized activities of the entire Sector that are planned for this region. The Regional Unit is a small office manned by a Regional Adviser (RASHSAP), a Programme Assistant, and two Associate Experts.

The Regional Unit for Social and Human Sciences in Asia and the Pacific (RUSHSAP) is entrusted with the following tasks:

i. Coordinate and execute Unesco's programme for the development of social and human sciences in Asia and the Pacific region;

ii. Help in planning Unesco's medium-term programme for the development of social and human sciences in the region;

iii. Maintain close working relationships with other United Nations agencies, in particular with Resident Representatives of the United Nations Development Programme, with Economic and Social Commission for Asia and the Pacific (ESCAP), and with UN institutes;

iv. Act as social science adviser to other regional offices especially in regard to programmes in science policy, environmental studies and educational programmes with special reference to integrated rural development;

v. Contribute actively to the planning and carrying out of the activities of the Sector in Asia and the Pacific and take appropriate steps to stimulate and facilitate the effective participation of all Member States concerned therein;

vi. Promote social science contribution to the Man and the Biosphere Programme (MAB);

vii. Develop documentation services;

viii. Carry out such other functions in the field of social and Human sciences as may be assigned by the Assistant Director General for Social and human Sciences.

The activities of the RUSHSAP cover the following 31 countries of the Asia-Pacific region.

Afghanistan
Australia
Bangladesh
Burma
Bhutan
People's Republic of China
Democratic Kampuchea
Democratic People's Republic of Korea
Fiji
India
Indonesia
Islamic Republic of Iran
Japan
Laos People's Democratic Republic
Malaysia
Maldives
Mongolia
Nepal
New Zealand
Pakistan
Papua New Guinea
Philippines
Republic of Korea
Singapore
Socialist Republic of Viet Nam

Sri Lanka
Thailand
Tonga
Turkey
Union of Soviet Socialist Republics
Samoa

The Unit has actively engaged itself in promoting regional cooperation and strengthening social science infrastructures in the member countries. Unesco's activities in the social and human science field include support for regional networks, organization of regional and national training seminars to develop indigenous capabilities, conduct of cross-cultural comparative researches on problems of contemporary relevance, review of the social and human science situation in the Member States, and convening of expert meetings, seminars and symposia. Several publications resulting from these activities have been brought out and distributed within the region and abroad.

H

ASSOCIATION OF ASIAN SOCIAL SCIENCE RESEARCH COUNCILS (AASSREC)

The Association of Asian Social Science Research Council (AASSREC) is an organization of national social science research councils or academies or their equivalents in the Asia-Pacific region. It is committed to working for the advancement of the social sciences in the region. It came into being at a Unesco conference on Teaching and Research in Social Sciences in Asia, held in Simla, India, in 1973. The Conference was organized at the initiative of the Indian National Commission for Unesco in cooperation with the Indian Council of Social Science Research (ICSSR), New Delhi, and the Indian Institute of Advanced Study, Simla. It was attended by leading social scientists from the following 14 countries : Afghanistan, Bangladesh, Cambodia (Khmer), India, Indonesia, Iran, Japan, Republic of Korea, Laos, Nepal, the Philippines, Singapore, Sri Lanka and Thailand.

The proceedings of the Conference brought out in a volume

titled Social Sciences in Asia (1974) appeared as the first publication of AASSREC.

Objectives

The main objectives of the Association are:

i. Exchange of information among Asian social scientists;

ii. Exchange of scholars;

iii. Promotion of research opportunities for the young social scientists;

iv. Promotion of joint research projects

The Association realizes these objectives through the following activities:

i. Publication of reports of its biennial conferences;

ii. Organization of problem-oriented seminars;

iii. Collaborative research programmes on specific problems.

Its long-term programmes include the following:

i. Publication of an Asian social science journal;

ii. Setting up of disciplinary and inter-disciplinary teams to carry out researches on specific problems of common interest to some or all of Asian countries;

iii. Periodic assessment of trends of research in Asian social sciences;

iv. Asian abstracting services; and

v. Ppromotion of translation of research material generated in

Asian countries.

Members

Presently AASSREC has membership from 12 countries of the region as shown below:

* Academy of the Social Sciences in Australia (ASSA). University House, G.P.O. Box 1956, CANBERRA ACT 2601, Australia.

* Social Science Research Council (SSRC), Bangladesh, Planning Commission, Sher-e-Bangla Nagar, Dhaka-7.

* Indian Council of Social Science Research (ICSSR), 35, Ferozeshah Road, New Delhi-110001.

* Lembaga llmu Pengetauhan Indonesia (Indonesian Institute of Sciences) (LIPI). Widya Graha Jalan Gatot, Subrato 10, Jakarta.

* Korean Social Science Research Council (KOSSREC) 304-28, Sachcick-Dang, Chongru-Ku, Seoul.

  Nepal Social Science Research Council (NESSREC) C/o Geography Department, Kirritpur Campus, Tribhuvan University, Kathmandu.

* Social Science Research Fund Committee (SSRFC), New Zealand, P.O. Box 1092, Wellington, New Zealand.

* Centre of Social Sciences and Humanities (COSH), Pakistan. C/o University Grants Commission, Park Road Chowk Shahzad, Islamabad.

* Philippines Social Science Council (PSSC), Don Mariano Marcos Avenue, U.P. Dilliman, Quezon City, Metro Manila.

* Natural Resources, Energy and Science Authority of Sri Lanka (NARESA) 47/5 Maitland Place, Colombo-7.

* National Research Council (NRC), Thailand 196 Phanolyothin Road,Bangkhen, Bangkok-10900.

* Vietnam Social Science Committee of the Academy of Sciences (VSSC), 27 Tran Suan Soan, Hanoi.

The Constitution of AASSREC also provides for Associate Membership to national organizations whose functions are akin to those of the national social sciences organizations, and national, regional or international funding agencies with substantial interest in providing financial support for social science research can become Associate Members of AASSREC.

Biennial General Conference

The representatives of the member councils meet once in two years to report on their activities, future programmes and trends of thinking and research. The occasion is utilized for developing collaborative research projects, and for discussing emerging issues of contemporary relevance.

The First General Conference of AASSREC was held in Teheran, Iran, in January 1976 when the Constitution of the Association was adopted and election of office-bearers held.

At the Second General Conference held in Seoul in October 1977, the Member Councils agreed to encourage collaborative research in two important areas. The first one on Bureaucracy and National Development has been carried out in India, Indonesia and Thailand; the second on the Role of Social Sciences in Plan Implementation and in the Evaluation of Development Plans has been undertaken in Bangladesh, Republic of Korea, and the Philippines.

The Third General Conference held in Manila in September 1979 dealt with the problems of social sciences in individual countries and indigenization of the social sciences. The papers presented at this symposium have been published by IFSSO as a special monograph for worldwide circulation.

The Fourth General Conference held in Bangkok in October

1981 focussed on (1) the problems of Urbanization in Asia and (ii) Tasks and Challenges for the Social Sciences in Asia in 1980s. Following discussion on Urbanization in Asia, it was agreed to encourage a collaborative research project on Metropolitan Primate Cities of Asia in the Regional and International Setting. India, Republic of Korea, the Philippines, Thailand and Vietnam are collaborating in this research project. The proceedings of the Conference have been published in three volumes. The research design of the project on Metropolitan Primate Cities has also been published under the title *Gateway Cities of Asia*. The project acronym is GACIT.

At the Fifth General Conference held in Sydney, Australia, in December 1983, a Symposium on National Perspectives on Social Science Development in Asia was held. The Conference also organized a panel discussion on the Economic Future of the Asian Region and the Role of the Social Sciences. The proceedings have been published in three volumes.

The focus of the Sixth General Conference held in Denpasar, Bali, Indonesia, from September 2 to 7, 1985, was on (i) Social Sciences and the Government and (ii) Youth and Society: Viewpoints for the future.

Research Projects

Currently AASSREC is engaged in two projects. One is a cross-cultural research project on the Gateway Cities of Asia (Project GACIT). This is being coordinated by Professor Moonis Raza of India.

The other is a project for the preparation of social scientific profiles of Asian societies. Coordinated by Professor W. Geddes of Australia, and financially assisted by Unesco, five country profiles are being prepared under this project covering Bangladesh, India, Indonesia, Republic of Korea and Thailand. These will be Portrayals of the societies based on published social science research monographs and papers.

Publications

AASSREC has brought out several publications:

(1) Asian Social Scientist (AASSREC Newsletter), Nos. 1 to 5.

(2) Social Sciences in Asia edited by Yogesh Atal.

(3) Social Sciences in Asia in 1980s: Tasks and Challenges.
(4) Urbanization in Asia : The Future of the City.

(5) Gateway Cities of Asia : Research Design.

(6) Asian Perspectives in Social Sciences.

(7) Economic Future of the Asian Region and the Role of the Social Sciences.

Publications 3 to 5 are priced at US $ 2 each and can be obtained from the Secretariat located at the Indian Council of Social Science Research and publication 7 can be obtained from Seoul National University Press, Seoul.

AASSREC Panorama

The first issue of this newsletter was brought out by the Association of Asian Social Science Research Councils (AASSREC) in January, 1987.

I

INTERNATIONAL FEDERATION OF SOCIAL SCIENCE ORGANIZATIONS (IFSSO)

7, Holmans Kanal DK-1060 Copenhagen K., Denmark

IFSSO was formally created as an autonomous organization in 1979, although in an embryonic form, it came into being as the Standing Committee of the International Social Science Councils and analogous bodies (CNSSC) in 1975. It consists of about 40 member organizations (both national and regional). The majority of the members are the national social science research councils. The principal objectives of IFSSO are:

* To continue the development of the social sciences at the national and international levels, particularly in developing countries;

* To further the exchange of information, experience and ideas amongst its members, to encourage international cooperation in the social sciences for the benefit of Mankind;

* To facilitate coordination of the international scientific activities of its Members;

* To foster concern about contemporary social problems and to encourage the application of the social sciences in the search for solutions;

* To foster cooperative ventures and mutual assistance in the planning and implementation of programmes of major importance to Members;

* To promote the free international movement of social scientists in the conduct of their research and other professional activities.

For fulfilment of these objectives IFSSO has established a Programme of Activities which include international meetings, seminars, symposia, colloqia, workshops and conferences. IFSSO also publishes a Newsletter which brings out the activities, programmes, problems and achievements of the respective national and regional social organizations.

Another programme instituted by IFSSO is the Administrative Visitors Fellowships Programme which enables social science research administrators to share experience and fostering cooperation among member organizations.

IFSSO has an NGO status with Unesco and has close relationship with the International Social Science Council (ISSC).

J

Asia-Pacific Information Network in Social Sciences (APINESS)

APINESS was launched in Bangkok at an experts' meeting convened by Unesco and the Association of Asian Social Science Research Councils (AASSREC) from May 12-16 1986, for the following objectives:-

1. To help in the development of infrastructure at the national level;

2. To promote an inter-institutional arrangement rather than act as a supra-national centre and thus National Contact Point (NCP) of each participating country should have its own pattern of interactions guided by the commonalty of interests and pattern of priorities;

3. To promote a system of linkages national, regional and international;

4. To enable each country decide its own priorities for development of information infrastructures; and

5. To promote a system of the financial resources which should be raised from Member Countries as well as from those agencies and organizations-national, regional international which are interested in net-working-programmes.

Action Programme (1986-1989)

1. Development of resources and capabilities.

2. Adoption and development of norms and standards information handling.

3. Development of linkages and cooperative activities.

4. Training of social scientists users of social science information.

5. Publication of state-of-the art reports on social science subjects

6. Processing and repackaging of social science information

research data for policy makers.

7. Inclusion of APINESS related activities in bilateral agreements.

8. Development/integration of specialized sub-networks like AMIC into APINESS.

9. Publication of *APINESS Newsletter* and publicity for APINESS in similar bulletins to keep members informed of development and on going projects/activities in the region.

The first issue of *APINESS Newsletter* was published in November 1986 on the occasion of the Unesco's 40th Anniversary.

K

MEMBER STATES OF UNESCO AT JANUARY 1986

Afghanistan	4 May 1948
Albania	16 October 1958
Algeria	15 October 1962
Angola	11 March 1977
Antigua and Barbuda	15 July 1982
Argentina	15 September 1948
Australia	4 November
Austria	13 August 1948
Bahamas	23 April 1981
Bahrain	18 January 1972
Bangladesh	27 October 1972
Barbados	24 October 1968
Belgium	29 November 1946
Belize	10 May 1982
Benin	18 October 1960
Bhutan	13 April 1982
Bolivia	13 November 1946
Botswana	16 January 1980
Brazil	4 November 1946
Bulgaria	17 May 1956
Burkina Faso	14 November 1960
Burma	27 June 1949

Burundi	16 November 1962
Byelorussian Soviet Socialist Republic	12 May 1954
Canada	4 November 1946
Cameroon	11 November 1960
Cape Verde	15 February 1978
Central African Republic	11 November 1960
Chad	19 December 1960
Chile	7 July 1953
China	4 November 1946
Colombia	31 October 1947
Comoros	22 March 1977
Congo	24 October 1960
Costa Rica	19 May 1950
Cote d'Ivoire	27 October 1960
Cuba	29 August 1947
Cyprus	6 February 1961
Czechoslovakia	4 November 1946
Democratic Kampuchea	3 July 1951
Democratic People's Republic of Korea	18 October 1974
Democratic Yemen	15 October 1968
Denmark	4 November 1946
Dominica	9 January 1979
Dominican Republic	4 November 1946
Ecuador	22 January 1947
Egypt	4 November
El Salvador	28 April 1948
Equatorial Guinea	29 November 1979
Ethiopia	1 July 1955
Fiji	14 July 1983
Finland	10 October 1956
France	4 November 1946
Gabon	16 November 1960
Gambia	1 August 1973
German Democratic Republic	24 November 1972
Germany, Federal Republic of	11 July 1951
Ghana	11 April 1958
Greece	4 November 1946
Grenada	17 February 1975
Guatemala	2 January 1950
Guinea	2 February 1960

Guinea-Bissau	1 November 1974
Guyana	21 March 1967
Haiti	18 November 1946
Honduras	16 December 1947
Hungary	14 September 1948
Iceland	8 June 1964
India	4 November 1946
Indonesia	27 May 1950
Iran, Islamic Republic of	6 September 1948
Iraq	21 October 1948
Ireland	3 October 1961
Israel	16 September 1949
Italy	27 January 1948
Jamaica	7 November 1962
Japan	2 July 1951
Jordan	14 June 1950
Kenya	7 April 1964
Kuwait	18 November 1960
Lao People's Democratic Republic	9 July 1951
Lebanon	4 November 1946
Lesotho	29 September 1967
Liberia	6 March 1947
Libyan Arab Jamahiriya	27 June 1953
Luxembourg	27 October 1947
Madagascar	10 November 1960
Malawi	27 October 1964
Malaysia	16 June 1958
Maldives	18 July 1980
Mali	7 November 1960
Malta	10 February 1965
Mauritania	10 January 1962
Mauritius	25 October 1968
Mexico	4 November 1946
Monaco	6 July 1949
Mongolia	1 November 1962
Morocco	7 November 1956
Mozambique	11 October 1976
Namibia	2 November 1978
Nepal	1 May 1953
Netherlands	1 January 1947

New Zealand	4 November 1946
Nicaragua	22 February 1952
Niger	10 November 1960
Nigeria	14 November 1960
Norway	4 November 1946
Oman	10 Februray 1972
Pakistan	14 September 1949
Panama	10 January 1950
Papua New Guinea	4 October 1976
Paraguay	20 June 1955
Peru	21 November 1946
Philippines	21 November 1946
Poland	6 November 1946
Portugal	12 March 1965
Qatar	27 January 1972
Republic of Korea	14 June 1950
Romania	27 July 1956
Rwanda	7 November 1962
Saint Christopher and Nevis	26 October 1983
Saint Lucia	6 March 1980
Saint Vincent and the Grenadines	15 February 1983
Samoa	3 April 1981
San Marino	12 November 1974
Sao Tome and Principe	22 January 1980
Saudi Arabia	4 November 1946
Senegal	10 November 1960
Seychelles	18 October 1976
Sierra Leone	28 March 1962
Somalia	15 November 1960
Spain	30 January 1953
Sri Lanka	14 November 1949
Sudan	26 November 1956
Suriname	16 July 1976
Swaziland	25 January 1978
Sweden	23 January 1950
Switzerland	28 January 1949
Syrian Arab Republic	16 November 1946
Thailand	1 January 1949
Togo	17 November 1960
Tonga	29 September 1980

Trinidad and Tobago	2 November 1962
Tunisia	8 November 1956
Turkey	4 November 1946
Uganda	9 November 1962
Ukrainian Soviet Socialist Republic	12 May 1954
Union of Soviet Socialist Republics	21 April 1954
United Arab Emirates	20 April 1972
United Republic of Tanzania	6 March 1962
Uruguay	8 November 1947
Venezuela	25 November 1946
Viet Nam	6 July 1951
Yeman	2 April 1962
Yugoslavia	31 March 1950
Zaire	25 November 1960
Zambia	9 November 1964
Zimbabwe	22 September 1980

Associate Members

British Virgin Islands	26 October 1983
Netherlands Antilles	24 November 1983

Index